BEN-GURION

Robert St. John

BEN-GURION

the biography of
an extraordinary man

Doubleday & Company, Inc.
Garden City, N.Y.

The article by David Ben-Gurion from which an excerpt appears on page 272 was originally published in the Times Magazine in March 1954, and is reprinted by permission of the author and the New York *Times*.

To

PAULA,

whose devotion made it possible
for him to become the great man
she always knew he was,
this book is humbly dedicated

EDITOR'S NOTE

Because the Hebrew language has its own alphabet, there is no standard English-language spelling for Hebrew words. Common nouns are spelled herein as they are most usually reproduced in English transliterations. Proper names are spelled as their owners spell them. This results in such inconsistencies as Yigael Yadin and Yigal Allon, and Chaim Weizmann and Haim Zohar, which are not typographical errors. Israel is used as an adjective, rather than Israeli, because Israel philologists insist that this is correct. Exact dates, such as that of Ben-Gurion's birthday, are often avoided because they change from year to year by the Gregorian calendar.

APPRECIATION

These are the people on three continents who supplied the stories, checked the facts, decided the spellings, gave of their time, and deserve thanks:

ISRAEL

David Ben-Gurion, Prime Minister
Paula Ben-Gurion, the Prime Minister's wife
Yigael Yadin, former Chief of Staff
Zeev Sharef, director of Inland Revenue
Yaacov Dori, president of Technion
Yigal Allon, former Palmach commander
Moshe Sharett, former Prime Minister
Yitzhak Navon, private secretary to the P.M.
Teddy Kollek, director general of the P.M.'s office
Moshe Pearlman, adviser on public affairs to the P.M.
Yehuda Levin, head, information dept., Foreign Office
Reuven Shiloah, political adviser, Foreign Office
Moshe Rosetti, secretary general, Knesset
David Hacohen, former Minister to Burma
Baruch Tal, executive of Mapai
Aryeh Paytan, deputy director, Press Office, Tel Aviv
Moshe Feldenkrais, Tel Aviv
David Landor, director, Press Office
Zipora Rubens, Tel Aviv
Misha Louvish, editor of publications, Press Office
T. R. Lurie, managing editor, Jerusalem *Post*
Haim Zohar, in charge Jerusalem office, Press Office
Shimon Fried, Sde Boker
Ruth Steinhardt, Sde Boker
Colonel Chaim Ben-David, military secretary to the P.M.
Dr. Arkady Frenkel, head, research section, Press Office
Lucien Harris, information services, Hadassah
Braha Habas, author of *David Ben-Gurion Ve Doro*
Zalman Shazar, former Minister of Education

Lea Ben-Dor, columnist, Jerusalem *Post*
Reuven Hecht, managing director, Dagon, Haifa
Moshe Brilliant, N. Y. *Times,* Jerusalem
Deborah Kaplan, research section, Press Office
Dr. Alexander Zak, Press Office, Tel Aviv
Arthur Saul Super, author and translator
David Anderman, director, photographic dept., Press Office

U.S.A. AND CANADA

Yaakov Herzog, Israel Minister, Washington
Michael Arnon, Counselor, Israel Embassy, Washington
Arthur Lourie, Israel Ambassador, Ottawa
Moshe Erell, First Secretary, Embassy, Ottawa
Mrs. Franklin D. Roosevelt
Sam Hamburg, Los Banos, California
Yitzhak Unna, Chargé de l'Information, Chicago
Dr. Judd Teller, political secretary, World Zionist Organization
Colonel Aron Yariv, Israel military attaché, Washington
Ruth Gruber, author
Nachman Karni, Israel Mission to the U.N.
Ephraim Evron, former secretary to the P.M.
Dr. Eliahu Casp, Shrewsbury, Massachusetts
Ruth Siegel, former member of the P.M.'s staff
Will Maslow, American Jewish Congress

ELSEWHERE

Eliahu Elath, Ambassador to the Court of St. James's
Abraham Kidron, First Secretary, Embassy, London
Lillian Alizi, press attaché's office, London
Dr. Sneier Levenberg, head, Zionist Information Office, London
Marcus Sieff, former adviser to the State of Israel
Jon Kimche, editor, the *Jewish Observer*
Mrs. Judith Giaquinto
David Walker, London *News-Chronicle*
Mrs. Florence Davidson, Paris

BEN-GURION

CHAPTER ONE

THE MAN with the wispy halo of white hair turned painfully in bed until his back was to those in the hospital room.

Someone said later that the silence was broken once by a single word:

"Nehemiah!"

Others said he spoke not at all.

After a few moments a low sobbing began to fill the room. They looked from one to another, embarrassed. Most of them had never seen him display such emotion before, although one or two remembered that he had cried also the day the Teacher was buried, years ago.

Quietly they made their way, one by one, to the door.

At last he was entirely alone with his heavy grief.

The wounds in his arm and leg, from which surgeons had dug small pieces of steel, suddenly began to pain again. But the hurt in his heart was the greater, for he knew that there was probably no man in the world to take Nehemiah's place. Everyone else knew it. Nehemiah had known it, too. That was why it was difficult to understand what Nehemiah had done.

They had been together for ten years. Nehemiah all that time had been his shadow, his constant companion, his faithful friend; always ready to listen; always full of eagerness to serve. It seemed incredible that he was now beyond call. Only yesterday—no, it was several days before yesterday—he was here, in this room, commenting on the letter to the parents of the man who had tried so diligently to become an assassin. Now he was gone. Why had he removed himself from life, or removed life from himself, at a time when he was still so greatly needed?

There had been some strenuous days during these ten years they had lived through together. There might be hard days ahead, too.

Nehemiah had not actually helped solve any of the problems of the past, and of course the problems of the future could be solved without him. But not having him always around . . . Not being able to . . .

The man with the wispy halo of white hair closed his eyes and let the memories of his seventy years flow through his mind.

It had all begun in Plonsk.

Plonsk, in the days of the Czars, was a small factory city astride a river by the same name thirty-eight miles northwest of Warsaw on the railroad leading in the direction of the Baltic. Plonsk once had been Polish and someday would be Polish again.

Pinsk was two hundred miles east of Plonsk, on the other side of Warsaw.

In Plonsk one stormy day late in 1886 Sheindal Green, a gentle woman in her late twenties, presented her young husband Avigdor with their sixth child.

In Pinsk at this time a gangling twelve-year-old boy named Chaim, from an outlying village, was enrolled in one of the local schools.

The sixth child of Sheindal and Avigdor Green became David Ben-Gurion, first Prime Minister of Israel.

The boy named Chaim was Chaim Weizmann, who became the first President of Israel.

History has seldom entangled the life threads of two men so oddly contrasted, yet they sprang from the same background, were born in the same half century, devoted their lives with equal zeal to the same altruistic cause, each in his own different way, and when it was all over the bones of the two would rest in the soil of the land called Israel, which, except for their joint labors, would certainly not have been revived when and as it was. Perhaps never at all.

David had a small frame, but his head was so extraordinarily large for the size of his body that his mother one day took him to a doctor and nervously asked if there might be something wrong with him.

"Calm your fears," the physician said after completing a careful examination. "Your child is quite all right. But I can tell you this, he will someday be a great man. That is very clear from the shape and size of the skull."

Perhaps the measurements of David's head had something to

do with it, but so did Avigdor Green, the father, who gave his son a good preliminary training for the task that destiny had chosen for him.

Avigdor Green, an unlicensed lawyer, was known as one of the wise men of Plonsk, and many of the five thousand Jews of the town came to him for advice. But he was at the same time a rebel, with enemies among those who considered unconventionality a sin. He put aside the caftan, or long tunic, and the fur hat popular with the tradition-bound Jews of Plonsk. Instead he wore a frock coat and striped trousers, and even, on occasion, a high silk hat. He smoked cigarettes now and then. His beard and mustache were not trimmed in exactly the customary manner. He had Gentile clients. His library contained books the local rabbis considered much too unorthodox. He insisted that David and the rest of the children become as proficient in spoken Hebrew as in Russian. This was sacrilege to the holy men of Plonsk, who held with religious fanaticism that Hebrew was for worship alone. You spoke Hebrew when you spoke to God; you spoke Yiddish when you ordered groceries. David was also required to make a diligent study of Biblical history and Middle Eastern geography. He went to a religious school and was a moderately good pupil, taking himself and his studies with no small degree of seriousness. Once he startled his classmates by solemnly announcing:

"One day I will be the leader of Israel."

Avigdor Green did not have such a monomania as his son would someday develop, but it was he who made the boy a Zionist. Avigdor Green's attachment for the land of his ancestors was firmly rooted and fundamental. It was largely his work that established Plonsk as the fountainhead of Zionism for that entire region of Russia. Committee meetings were held in the Green home just off the main street of Plonsk at all hours of the day and night. Always there were speeches, bitter argument, and endless talk. Sometimes David would listen from a distance. Sometimes, instead, he would try to concentrate on his books or on a problem of chess, a game that gave him the secret of fixing his mind on a single subject to the exclusion of everything else.

When David was ten years old, something happened in far-off Austria that deeply affected the Greens, and Jews all over the world. A paper in Vienna had sent one of its reporters, Budapest-born Theodor Herzl, to Paris to cover a spy case involving a Jewish army officer named Dreyfus. Herzl, although a Jew himself, had not until then taken much interest in Zionist matters, but the anti-Semitism he uncovered as he dug into the Dreyfus case led him to write a political pamphlet, *The Jewish State*, in which he suggested that the end of Jewish persecution in Europe would come only with the moving of great masses of European Jews to a place where they could set up a sovereign country of their own. The pamphlet gave Zionism a pulsating new dynamism. Also, a motto:

"If you will it, it is no dream."

After the Herzl booklet was published, meetings in the Green home became more frequent. The talk was louder and lasted longer than ever. Now there were articles for the press to be written, new cells of Zionism to be established, conferences to be held. Besides Zionists, the Green house in those days was full of children and domestic problems. Six of the ten babies Sheindal had born were still alive. And now she was pregnant again.

During David's twelfth year two things happened that greatly affected him. His mother died in childbirth, and Herzl called a world-wide meeting of Jews at Basle, Switzerland, to discuss how to bring the Zionist dream to quick realization.

Until the time of his mother's death David had been delicate and had had few friends. He had liked to walk alone. Some called him introspective and morose. He had been his mother's son, greatly influenced by her gentleness. Now he had to turn to his father, but his father was a busy man, with several small children to worry about, the intensified duties of a militant Zionist, and his legal work. So the boy David gradually developed a protective shell, and the gentleness he had inherited became less and less evident to those around him. But the mother worship was still deep in the fiber of his being. David himself may never have been consciously aware of what the death of his mother meant to him, but during the next sixty years his associates frequently saw in his writings, in his speeches, and in his relationship with women indications of the intensity of his feeling of loss. He often seemed to be reaching out for a mother substitute, and motherhood always remained for him a symbol of great importance.

The gathering at Basle generated much excitement, even among the young people of Plonsk. For the first time in almost two thousand years a Jewish parliament had been set up. For the first time in all these centuries Jews spoke about the return as if they really meant to go back someday soon instead of just talking about it. At Basle they discussed the erection of a Hebrew University in Jerusalem, the creation of a Jewish national fund, the setting up of a Jewish world bank in London to finance colonization. A design was adopted for a national flag of blue and white, the colors of the traditional prayer shawl. A song written in Hebrew was accepted as the national anthem of a country which did not exist and would not for another half century. But, most important of all, this body of world Jewry dared to state openly, for everyone to hear, that its aim was to bring into existence "a publicly recognized and legally secured Jewish home in Palestine." Any Jew in the world could take part in the great movement merely by stating that he agreed with this aim, and by paying one shekel, one mark, one shilling, or one American quarter.

When he was fourteen, David and other teen-agers of Plonsk founded a Zionist youth society, called after Ezra, the ancient priest and scribe. Members took a solemn oath that they would never speak any language but Hebrew to each other and that they would labor for "the dissemination of Hebrew culture among the working youth."

David quickly developed a reputation as an orator. He was especially effective in excoriating other teen-agers who refused to speak "the language of the Book." His fame spread, and before he was fifteen he had made the first major political address of his life, at a conference in the great city of Warsaw. No one today remembers the exact words, but there are still those alive who can recall the intensity of the boy, his shock of curly black hair which made his head seem even bigger than it was, his excellent Hebrew, his arresting gestures, the forensic evidence of his profound Zionism.

One of the celebrated rabbis of the day said:

"Ten more like him and Israel will be redeemed."

The year 1903 was one which few Russian Jews ever forgot, for the volcano of anti-Semitism erupted again, spewing destruction in all directions. In the Bessarabian city of Kishinev the Jewish dead were piled in the streets like cordwood. No one could foretell how far the destruction would spread. In Plonsk doors were barricaded and the timid went into hiding.

After long debate David and most of his friends agreed that Poalei Zion (Zionist Workers) was the answer. Under the banner of this socialist-Zionist organization they could work for co-operative justice and a return to the Promised Land simultaneously.

But that same year Zionism was split as it had never been before, or since. It was Herzl himself who did it. He had failed in a plan to buy Palestine from the Ottoman Empire. But he found an Englishman who had an idea. Colonial Secretary Joseph Chamberlain, having toured Africa during the Boer War, suggested that six thousand square miles of the highlands of Kenya be set aside for the Jews. There Herzl could establish his Jewish state under British protection. The spot was not in Uganda, but the scheme somehow came to be known as the Uganda Plan. Herzl himself put it before the sixth Zionist Congress at Basle in 1903, with a recommendation that the offer be accepted.

Seldom in the 1,833 years of the Jews' dispersal had any proposal precipitated such a violent schism. The pro-Ugandas, in the hope of winning over the anti-Ugandas, went so far as to argue that down in Africa they would be able to build a military machine which could someday sail to the Middle East and take the Holy Land back at the point of guns. But even the Jews already resident in Palestine were divided.

David and his friends were anti-Ugandas from the start. To them Zionism meant something more than merely fleeing from persecution. It was not enough just to seek safety anywhere outside of Europe. Zionism meant a return to the Land of the Book; to their own place; to the home from which they had so long ago been driven. Palestine was the scene of all the stories they had learned, all the folklore, all the accounts of early Jewish life as told in the Book.

For these reasons David and his friends were greatly relieved when the sixth Congress at Basle adjourned without approving Uganda.

When David was eighteen he went to Warsaw to study. He

lived there simply, on a small allowance from his father and on the money he gained from giving Hebrew lessons. These were exciting days for him. In Warsaw were important Jewish leaders whose speeches he could study.

One morning he was arrested. There was no valid reason. He had committed no crime. But he was Jewish, and he was a political agitator, and his mass of curly black hair, uncombed and unkempt, made him look as a policeman might have thought a dangerous political character would look.

After David had spent most of a day locked up, Lawyer Avigdor Green arrived from Plonsk by train, wearing top hat and frock coat. This was not the first young Jew he had tried to get out from behind bars. He presented his calling card to the police adjustant.

"Green?" the police officer said, studying the name on the card. "Green, that's very odd. My name is Green, too. Victor Green."

So, because of a coincidence, David was eventually freed, without having to stand trial.

There were three boys in Plonsk who were always together: Shlomo Zemach, whose parents were wealthy by local standards; Shmuel Fuchs, who hungered for adventure, and David. The youth organization had been their idea. Together they mourned the passing of Herzl. Together they planned the future.

The first to go was Shmuel, but instead of Palestine he chose America.

Then Shlomo one autumn night left without his parents' approval but with three hundred rubles of their money.

David had given up studying, even before his eighteenth birthday, much to his learned father's distress. He was busy now traveling around Poland making speeches, organizing workers, directing strikes; combining, always, his Zionism and his socialism. Then letters began to arrive from Shlomo. The second aliyah (wave of immigration) was on. Men, women, and children were pouring into Palestine from Europe. However, all was not yet milk and honey. Most of the work in Palestine, semi-skilled and unskilled, was being done by Arabs, even if the employers were Jewish. But young Zemach had found a job and was growing used to a diet of bread and dates. He was a pioneer.

Finally Shlomo Zemach came to Plonsk on a visit. He said he would soon be going back to Palestine. Life was hard there, but it made sense. The youth society members listened while he told them of the ancient land, of Bedouin marauders who stole in at night from the desert, of camels and mosques, of the hills surrounding Jerusalem, and of the piece of a wall which was all that remained of the Second Temple.

David announced one day to his father that when Shlomo left he was going with him, perhaps never to return. Lawyer Green entered strong objections. He said it was a disgrace that a boy should stop his studies before he had even an average education. He himself was full of the wisdom of books, and he had always hoped that his son someday would be, too. But going off now to become a common laborer on the desert sands of Palestine, what sense did that make?

Half a century later, speaking to a group of American editors and radio commentators who had come to call on him at his office in Tel Aviv, the man who once was David Green of Plonsk explained why he had left Europe. In retrospect he put it this way:

"I am not a refugee and I did not come here because I had been persecuted. . . . From my youth, from about five years of age, I did not ever think that I was at home where I was, in Poland. I thought that this was going to be my home, Israel. Israel has a long history of four thousand years, and it is something that lives in the hearts of its people. I think it is not only a matter of persecution, but also of spiritual need."

Then he looked at the American editors and commentators and smiled slightly.

"I am not sure that all the 102 people who came to your country on the *Mayflower* were refugees. They had an ideal of building a free country in a new land. In the same way many of us came here without persecution. We had a spiritual urge to live a free, full, Jewish life. This means a great deal to us."

CHAPTER TWO

Two travel-stained, voyage-weary boys stood at the rail of the Russian cargo ship that had brought them from the Black Sea port of Odessa, through the Dardanelles, and down the eastern coast of the Mediterranean.

They had made a wager as to who would be the first to see it, so they were staring hard at the line of the horizon.

The trip had taken weeks. Plonsk was far behind, part of another life.

"Look, David! There it is. Look hard! Just a little to the left of the bow. That's it. That's Jaffa!"

David stared and finally saw. It was just a small brown spot where sky met water, but this was the Promised Land. *His* land. He was the Wandering Jew finally come home to the place of his forefathers. The exile that had begun nearly two millennia ago was all over, for him anyway. Here he would live and die. Here he would help make the dream come true for others. He looked over his shoulder at the stern of the ship. There was only the vast green sea. But someday that sea would be black with a parade of ships bringing the displaced people home again.

Now they could see buildings and figures. This was a city famous in history. The Book told how it had originally been ascribed to the tribe of Dan. Of course, almost every place in this part of the world was famous in Jewish history. They were all in the Bible. He was glad his father had insisted he learn Middle Eastern history and geography. He knew that within sight of Jaffa, Jonah's ship had been wrecked by the wrath of God and he had been cast into the sea, to be swallowed by the whale. There had been terrible pogroms here again and again. About the time of the destruction of the Second Temple thousands of Jews had been lured into the waters of this very harbor by Greek fanatics and drowned.

But David, remembering all this, was nevertheless disappointed. Jaffa, as they came close enough to see it plainly, looked like any one of a dozen other seaport cities they had put in to already.

How many more disappointments were there waiting for him?

Was each part of the dream to lose its beauty immediately on contact with reality?

As soon as they were ashore, one Jew fell down and kissed the ground, clutching the sand with both hands, almost hysterically.

David was confused. This was a strange world, not at all as he had pictured it. The streets were full of Arabs in flowing white robes. The street smells were close to unbearable for a man with a sensitive European nose. The talk was nearly all in a language that slightly resembled Hebrew, yet David understood not a word of it. Occasionally two men talking Yiddish would pass.

At a ramshackle place called the Hotel Chaim Baruch, David had his first meal in this very old world with members of the local branch of the Zionist Workers who had heard of his coming.

"*Lehayim!*" they shouted in chorus as they raised their glasses of sweet Palestinian wine in the traditional Hebrew toast "to life."

They went that night to Petach Tikvah, the oldest colony in Palestine. It had been founded eight years before David's birth and was called "the mother of all Jewish settlements." It had been established by pious scholars from Jerusalem, most of them with a Hungarian background. These men had ignored the advice of a Greek physician brought in from Jaffa to examine the site they had chosen.

"Look!" he had said to them. "Even the birds do not descend in this place for worms or flies. Do you know why? Because the air is so polluted here."

It was a pleasant place of houses in neat rows, some of wood, some of mud. Eucalyptus trees lined the roadways, because of the generosity of Baron Edmond de Rothschild of Paris, and there were extensive groves of fruit trees. Most important of all, here were Jews who did not sit around cafés or follow the other parasitical pursuits of city people. Here were Jews who had become successful farmers.

From now on for the rest of his life David Green would have a fanatical belief that a return to Zion, a rebuilding of Israel, the emancipation of the Jews could come about only if they abandoned the ways of the Diaspora. Especially must they give up the occupations into which they had been forced so many centuries ago by their oppressors. Manual labor must be glorified. So must return to the land.

The boys from Plonsk were tired when they arrived. But David did not fall asleep easily that night. His mind was full of so many plans as he lay there listening to the muted noises of the desert, which was not far away in any direction.

"Who could sleep through his first night in the homeland?"

He asked the question rhetorically of his father in his first letter. Years later in recalling Petach Tikvah he said:

"The spirit of my childhood and my dreams had triumphed, and I was joyous. I was in the Land of Israel, in a Jewish village, and its name was the Gateway of Hope.

"I smelled the rich odor of corn. I heard the braying of donkeys and the rustle of leaves in the orchards. Above were clusters of stars, clear and bright against the deep color of the firmament. My heart overflowed with happiness, as if I had entered the land of a wonderful dream. Only now my dream was reality."

The next morning David and Shlomo went job-hunting. They trekked wearily from one Jewish farm to another, offering to do any kind of work, not quibbling about wages. But everywhere the answer was the same. These "gentlemen farmers," as David later sarcastically called them, used Arab labor. Arab labor was cheaper. Arab labor was experienced. These young Jewish visionaries were soft. Their hands bore no calluses. They would never be able to endure the desert sun. Arab labor could be controlled. These young Jewish zealots would soon be agitating instead of working.

The experiences at Petach Tikvah had a profound and lasting effect on the personality and political philosophy of David Green. He never lost his deep resentment of those he called "the rich Jewish squatters." He accused them of wanting to make the Holy Land into a middle-class heaven, a paradise for exploiters.

David and Shlomo eventually found work at eight piasters a day, a few cents. This was just enough to enable them to rent a bed and buy a meal in the evening when the day's work was done.

For a year David sweated in Judea. The work was new to him. The hunger he experienced caused him to lose a great deal of weight. Then he contracted malaria. Recalling it, he wrote:

"All three—work, hunger, and malaria—were new and full of interest. The fever would visit me every fortnight with mathematical precision, linger for five or six days, and then disappear.

"Hunger, too, was a frequent visitor. It would stay with me for weeks, sometimes months. During the day I could dismiss it, somehow, or at least stop thinking of it. But in the nights, the long racked vigils, the pangs would grow fierce, wringing the heart, darkening the mind, sucking the very marrow from my bones, demanding and torturing, and departing only with the dawn. Then, shattered and broken, I would drop off to sleep at last."

For a time during his first year David worked in the vineyards and the wine cellars that had been established at Rishon le Zion by Baron Rothschild, who was pouring millions of dollars into Palestine. Then to Kfar Saba, a new village.

"We are on a hill with mountains all around us," he wrote to his father. "The air is clearer and healthier. The land is mostly planted with almond trees, and was bought from the Arabs several years ago. As yet there are no houses. The Pasha of Nablus, who controls this area, will not permit foreigners to build houses except on payment of a heavy bribe. The price of land is increasing. We start work at six in the morning, and as the sun rises in the sky sweat pours from us like a river."

David expressed indignation with Jews who were too timid, too lacking in a spirit of adventure, too satisfied where they were, too unJewish in their feeling, or too tired to move to Palestine. This complaint he would be making to his dying day.

"Every ship brings tourists to behold the beauty of this country, but there are no Jews among them. Our people think praying three times a day for Israel is enough. In Rome there are Catholics, but in Zion there are no Zionists."

A year after David's arrival in Palestine a Zionist Workers conference was held. Some of the delegates showed their hardiness by walking the forty-five miles from Jerusalem to Jaffa. One of the presiding officers was a young man just two years David's senior, Itzhak Shimshelevitch, who had recently arrived in Palestine from the Russian Ukraine, a serious-looking youth, thin of face, almost gaunt. In Russia he had taken an interest in the Jewish self-defense movement and had hidden a large quantity of arms in his father's house. One day during his absence police made a search and arrested the whole family. Mother, father, and children were exiled to Siberia. Itzhak evaded the police and reached Palestine. When asked to register at a hotel in Jaffa, he signed the name "Ben-Zvi," which he eventually adopted as a surname.

David liked this young man from the Ukraine. He and Itzhak agreed on most political matters.

By now David, although not a natural-born linguist, had mastered Arabic through intensive concentration. Now he knew four languages, Russian, Yiddish, Hebrew, and Arabic, plus a smattering of Polish. During this first year he had also studied the geography of Judea. He knew every village, each crossroad, every dried-up watercourse. But he and Shlomo decided that they had had enough of farming in Judea.

David wrote later:

"The interminable hoeing and spading did not satisfy me fully. It was too mechanical and monotonous. The ceaseless thumping and thudding smacked of a factory. I yearned for the wide fields, for the waving stalks of corn, for the fragrance of grass, the plowman's song. And so I made up my mind to go north to Galilee."

David Green found his place of dreams at Sejera. He and ten others walked the entire distance, close to sixty miles, from Petach Tikvah straight north, across desert sands broken only occasionally by an Arab village, through the Judean hills, on north, and then east in the direction of Lake Tiberias.

There was beauty here in Sejera. It was enclosed by mountains. The settlement itself was on a hillside, with one line of houses a little above the other. There were thickets of eucalyptus trees, and pepper trees, too. Here there was land to be plowed, work to be done, and no one would deny a man the right to do it just because he was a Jew.

Here, David always said, he found the homeland for which he had so greatly longed. Here he felt that he was really in the place of his ancestors, where he belonged.

He wrote to his father:

"With the plow handle in my left hand and the oxgoad in my right, I follow the plow and see black clods of earth turning over and crumbling, while the oxen move slowly, gently and patiently, like helpful friends. Here there are opportunities to think and to plan and to dream."

In explaining why his days in Sejera were the happiest of all his life, David said:

"No shopkeepers or speculators, no non-Jewish hirelings, no idlers living on the labor of others.

"The men plowed and harrowed the fields and planted the seed; the women weeded the gardens and milked the cows; the children herded the geese and rode on horseback to meet their fathers in the fields. These were villagers, smelling wholesomely of midden and ripening wheat, and burned by the sun."

The conversion of the immigrants had begun. It must go on until all these desert wastes were covered with Jewish farmers working to make the Jewish homeland bloom again, as it had before the Great Dispersal.

"You are moved by urgings not of this world. In the silence you listen to the echoes of childhood. Legends of ancient times and visions of the last days take shape here quietly, flooding the soul and refreshing the anguished heart with the dew of hope and longing.

"And if you are exiled from this land and stray far from its soil and skies, to wander beyond distant waters and dwell in alien places beneath a strange firmament, you will take with you the lingering memory of these nights, the birthright of your land."

These were the words of a wandering Jew, home at last. He had made it clear to his father that he hoped to live out his life here, but if fate, the Turks, the Arabs, or someone else should drive him into exile again, as had happened to so many generations of his ancestors, he would at least have "the lingering memory of these nights" to take with him.

In other parts of Palestine the Arabs saw advantages for themselves in the influx of Jews. More jobs. Better pay. Medical treatment. But here in Galilee the Arabs thought they could force the Jews to quit the land if they harassed them enough: if they burned their buildings, stole their cattle, and attacked travelers on the roads. In the villages around Sejera there were Arab tribesmen skilled in the methods of terrorism, with little regard for human life. So Jewish property had to be guarded.

Although all the land here was worked by Jewish labor, the men who stood guard at night were Arab mercenaries, Circassians from the nearby Arab village of Kfar Kana, who had a monopoly on protecting Sejera—for exceedingly generous fees.

There were many explanations for this system. If the most dangerous Arabs, the Circassians, were employed as watchmen they would automatically be eliminated from the business of brigandage. Also, "It takes a thief to catch a thief." And, too, the bearing of arms for centuries had not been regarded as a Jewish profession. Jews might learn to till the soil, but in hundreds of years they had had little practice in defending themselves.

Almost as soon as David arrived in Sejera he became the leader of a campaign to change this. Jewish land everywhere must be guarded by Jewish watchmen. This was his goal, and he fought for it until he had it established as a fundamental part of what came to be known as "labor Zionism."

But the campaign was not easily won. The Sejera officials shook their heads. If the Jews went in for self-defense, it would cause resentment on the part of the Arabs. There was no telling where it might lead. If the Circassians were discharged, in their anger they might burn, pillage, and loot.

David and his friends spied for several nights and found that the watchmen did no "watching" at all. Instead they caroused in a nearby Arab village, relying upon their reputation to do their work for them. If anything was stolen, they would track down the missing property and return it to its owner—if a sufficient reward was forthcoming, which they shared with the thief.

One night, in an attempt to convince the farm manager, David and his colleagues stole his favorite mule and hid it. Then they informed him of the theft. He ran to the stables, found the mule gone, and shouted for the watchman, who was finally found asleep in the Arab village. He was discharged, and one of David's group was given the job.

This was the small start. It ultimately led to the 1948-49 victories of Israel's underground soldiers over the combined military might of six invading Arab armies. This was the beginning of Jewish self-defense in Palestine. It was also the start of David Green's concern with military matters. In another forty years he would be Minister of Defense in control of the first real Jewish army in centuries. But the road was to be strewn with graves. The first one had to be dug almost immediately.

The Circassians organized intimidation raids on Sejera. David argued that the colonists must be organized into a trained and disciplined defense force, and that arms must be procured. Arms? Where from? This was a problem that would never be satisfactorily solved. In 1907, David began to look for an adequate source of arms. In 1947 he was still looking. And in 1958.

The bailiff in charge of the farm at Sejera sent a wagon to Haifa. In some mysterious way the wagon came back loaded with antiquated double-barreled shotguns called *Jifts*. Years later David wrote about those shotguns:

"We played with them like children; we never let them down for a moment. Reluctantly we went to work next morning, for we had to say good-by to them for a whole day. As soon as we got home and unharnessed our horses and mules we dashed off to our beloved rifles, and they never left our hands until we fell asleep. Rifle in hand or on shoulder, we ate and washed, we moved and read or talked."

So they worked by day and stood guard by night, and they plowed the land with rifles slung across their backs.

On the last day of Passover a guard reported seeing two strange Arabs sitting on a hill inside the Sejera boundaries opposite the graveyard. One of the settlers, Israel Krongold, went to investigate. Half an hour later a volley of shots was heard.

The body of Israel Krongold was found on the edge of the settlement, a small hole through the chest. David helped carry him home. He died on the way.

This was the first time the boy from Plonsk, now almost twenty-two, had ever held death in his arms. It would not be the last.

That evening David was standing on the road leading to Nazareth with a group of colonists, looking toward the scene of the afternoon's killing. With him was his friend Shimon Melamed, a successful carpenter who had come to Sejera to be close to the soil. He earned only a third as much now as he had at carpentry, but David considered him the happiest man in the village. The dream he had carried in his heart had become a reality.

As they looked they saw three Arabs being pursued by two colonists. Three more colonists went to try to block the escape of the fugitives, Shimon Melamed, David, and one other. But then the entire Arab village entered the fray. The battle ended with

David helping to carry another dying man home. This time it was his close friend, Shimon Melamed.

They were traveling now the hard road of Zionism. There would be no turning back. They knew that. More Jewish blood would have to be spilled in defense of these fields, these hills before the fight for a reborn Israel would be won.

When David had come to Sejera he had been deeply appreciative of natural beauty. In his letters he had written of "drops of burning gold twinkling in the soft blue dome of the sky," and "the dim-lit purity of moonlit nights, the lucid crystal of the transparent mountain air."

In the future there would be less and less poetry in anything he wrote. Henceforth a sense of harsh reality would always be with him.

Shlomo Zemach, who had preceded David to Sejera, was against the idea of Jewish self-defense. He and David shared a room, and they argued long into every night. Shlomo contended that all of them had returned to the Land of the Book in order to lead a simple, peaceful life in the place where they belonged. If they stirred up the Arabs, there would be no *shalom*, no peace, ever.

David's answer was that they must face facts. They were in the Middle East now, not Europe. The law of the desert was the only law the Arabs understood. The law of the desert meant defending yourself. Survival was its own virtue in the eyes of the brigands. There was no national morality in Palestine that condemned the murder of strangers and the stealing of property. The authority of the Turkish Government had almost disappeared. Murderers were seldom punished, thieves were as free to conduct their business as were olive merchants.

David, even then, although hardly more than a boy, was already thinking in historical terms. The last time the Jews had fought for their honor, their rights, and their land had been at the end of the eleventh century, when the armies of Tancred and the Venetian Navy invaded Haifa. For the next eight hundred years there had been no Jewish armies. This had led the non-Jewish world to look upon Jews as cowards, unwilling to fight for their rights. They had relied on the forces of law and order in the Diaspora to protect them, but the forces of law and order had often joined the anti-Semitic mobs and shared in the sadistic pleasure of murder and in the rewards of looting.

All this must be changed if Jews ever wished to revive ancient Israel. This was a world in which force, and force alone, won respect. Until mankind organized civilization so that right instead of might decided issues, the Jews must make themselves strong in their own land.

David convinced others with these arguments, but not Shlomo Zemach, who went to Paris to study and did not return for years.

In the fight over self-defense David had the support of the Zionist Workers. Led by Ben-Zvi, they formed a secret society, Hashomer (The Watchmen), to train a corps of full-time Jewish guards.

It was Ben-Zvi who about this time sent David an urgent message to come to Jerusalem at once.

David did not have much liking for cities in general. He had seen a few of them: Warsaw, Odessa, Constantinople.

But Jerusalem was different. Jerusalem was "the City of David." David the Great had made it one of the illustrious capitals of the world. There Solomon had built the Temple with cedars from Lebanon and had adorned it with gold. For a time in Jerusalem there had been peace for the Jews, and general prosperity. But the shalom had not lasted long. Egyptians came, and Assyrians, Greeks, Arabians, Romans, Turks. Today Jerusalem belonged to the Ottoman Empire, but there were Jews there, and among them was Ben-Zvi, who had sent a message:

"Come at once!"

The Zionist Workers had held another conference and had authorized Ben-Zvi to start a weekly magazine in Hebrew to be called Ha'achdut (Unity). A young woman, Rachel Yanait, who had recently arrived from Europe (and who eventually would become Mrs. Ben-Zvi) would assist him, but she knew no Hebrew. They desperately needed David's help.

The young farmer from Galilee argued that he was already a reconverted Jew, that he belonged to the soil now. Ben-Zvi talked about duty.

At last they reached a compromise. After a brief trip to Russia to make a pretense of doing his military service (so the Russians in reprisal would not molest his father) David would go on a

tour of all the new Palestinian settlements. Then he would start
work as a journalist.

These things he did, and in 1910 he finally settled down in the
Holy City, a Zionist Workers official and one of the editors of
Unity. His first article was a statement of the aims of the paper.
He signed it "Ben-Gurion." This was the first time he used the
name by which the whole world would someday know him. He
chose it because it sounded like a name out of the Bible. Ben
is Hebrew for "son of." Gurion means "young lion." So he was
David, son of the young lion. This was the outward and visible
sign that he had severed the thread which bound him to the
Diaspora. From now on he was David Ben-Gurion, citizen of
Israel, a country which existed still only in the dreams of a handful of idealistic Jews.

He was almost twenty-four, a handsome young man with black
hair that looked as if it had been marceled, so regular and neat
were its waves. His black mustache was trimmed in the latest
Turkish style, with upturned points. He wore a suit with a high-
buttoned waistcoat, a white shirt, and a striped silk tie with an
exceedingly large knot. Fleet Street, London, or Park Row, New
York, might have taken him for one of their own.

The articles he wrote were trenchant. In them he argued for
greater Jewish unity, a wider use of Hebrew, and more support
for the socialistic policies of the Zionist Workers. Also, for more
subscriptions to *Unity*.

There were about a hundred thousand Jews in Palestine then.
Unity's circulation was two hundred and fifty copies within the
country, one hundred abroad. (The majority of Palestinian Jews
were still resisting Hebrew as an everyday language.) David Ben-
Gurion received, for helping to edit *Unity* and for his organizational work on behalf of the party, a salary of $2.25 a week.

He had found it easy to attach himself to the soil and become a
farmer. Now he discovered that it was even easier to acquire
an affection for the business of putting words on paper. For the
rest of his life, despite the fame he would achieve as politician,
statesman, soldier, military leader, head of government, he would
always refer to himself as a "journalist."

Once, after he had become Prime Minister, a reporter from
overseas asked him for some data for an article.

"I'm using that information in an article of my own," he growled. "Don't forget, I'm a journalist, too!"

CHAPTER THREE

IF THE young man who stepped ashore from a ship at Salonika one day in 1913 could have peered a year or two into the future, he might have decided he was making the greatest mistake of his life and should turn around and go back at once.

But David Ben-Gurion had no way of knowing that a world war would soon break out which would end with the collapse of the Ottoman Empire and with the liberation of the southeast corner of Europe and much of the Middle East, including Palestine, from the grip of the Turks.

This new move by the young farmer-watchman-editor-politician grew out of his sense of mission. He was not yet twenty-seven years old, but he was more certain than ever that he must prepare himself for leadership.

His several years in Jerusalem had given him an opportunity to study the political situation. The Jews of Palestine were a minority among strangers.

"We were entirely without roots in the civic, social, and political sense in this country which we were declaring we would turn into our homeland.

"So I made up my mind to go to Constantinople, to learn Turkish and study Ottoman law in order to become an advocate and, as such, to devote my life to the firm civil and political establishment of the Jewish population here in the Land of Israel."

He and Ben-Zvi had discussed it. Ben-Zvi wanted to go, too.

"Maybe someday we can sit as representatives of the Jewish people in the Turkish parliament."

They had agreed that Ben-Gurion would go first and that Ben-Zvi would follow soon afterwards. *Unity* now had a sizable staff. Others could carry on in their absence.

Ben-Gurion went first to the provincial city of Salonika because it had a large Jewish population and an active Jewish labor movement. Then to Constantinople, where he enrolled in the Ottoman University School of Law. By odd coincidence, one of his classmates was Abdullah Ibn Hussein, son of Hussein Ibn Ali, who in 1946 would become King of Jordan and several years later would be assassinated.

Ben-Gurion was soon joined in Constantinople by Ben-Zvi. They might easily have been mistaken by American tourists for young Turks. They wore red fezzes, black frock coats, and somber black ties. Their mustaches were identical and very Turkish. For a time they were referred to by their friends as "the Twins."

One by one others came, among them Moshe Shertok (later Sharett), a boy of nineteen, just out of a high school in the new, all-Jewish city of Tel Aviv, which had begun to develop on the seashore next to Jaffa. His career and Ben-Gurion's would be linked closely together for another forty years.

Also Joseph Trumpeldor, so tall that he made Ben-Gurion look like a pigmy. These two took an instant liking to each other. Trumpeldor was known from Siberia to the Black Sea for his military exploits. During the Russo-Japanese War he had been the only Jewish officer in the Czar's army. He had lost an arm almost to the shoulder during the seven-month siege of Port Arthur. Now he was a colonist in Palestine, at Degania. Even with one arm he could do more work than any of the other settlers. He had taught himself to dress, shave, eat, shoot a gun, and ride a horse, all with one arm. He was on his way back to Degania, after attending the eleventh Zionist Congress in Vienna.

When they first met, Ben-Gurion looked at the empty sleeve with what Trumpeldor must have known was envy. Here was a Jew brave enough to give an arm, a Jewish war hero.

Trumpeldor's favorite words in Hebrew were *ein davar* (never mind). Hearing the way Trumpeldor said "ein davar" inspired his friend Vladimir Jabotinsky to write this description of the phrase:

"There was a complete philosophy contained in this 'ein davar': do not exaggerate; do not see danger where none exists; do not regard a man who does his duty as a hero, for history is long, the Jewish people everlasting, and truth is sacred, but everything else—trouble and care and pain and death—ein davar."

Trumpeldor was a socialist, a vegetarian, and a pacifist at heart, despite all the fighting he did in his short life.

Together Ben-Gurion and Trumpeldor tramped the streets of Constantinople. They talked principally of war. Could the Sick Man of Europe survive? If a great war came, what of the Jews of Palestine?

Gradually Turkish became Ben-Gurion's sixth language, if one counted the little Polish he was already rapidly forgetting.

They all tried to apply themselves diligently to the study of law, though there was the smell of gunpowder in the air.

While the great powers were still exchanging angry notes, Ben-Gurion and his friend Ben-Zvi had time to write a slim little book, in Hebrew, on the manner in which the Ottoman Empire administered its provinces, a book which in another few years would be only of historical interest. Neither Ben-Gurion, Ben-Zvi, nor the others had any idea how soon and how thoroughly war would dispose of the Ottoman Empire. They made this clear by leaving most of their possessions behind in Constantinople when they went home to Jerusalem on a visit to see how things had been going in their absence.

In the Holy City they discovered that an aliyah in reverse was taking place. Money was not coming from abroad. Food shipments were no longer arriving. A feeling of panic was spreading. Turkey was about to go in on Germany's side, against Russia. The Turkish authorities had ordered that able-bodied men must either be drafted into the Army, locked up, or expelled.

Shertok went off to serve as an officer in the Turkish Army. Trumpeldor vanished, and in Degania it was said he had gone to help the opposite side; to shed his blood again, if necessary, for Russia.

In England, Chaim Weizmann was saying that Zionism ought to put all its resources behind the British. This brought about the first of many historic disagreements between Ben-Gurion and the undisputed successor to Herzl.

Great Britain and Russia were allies. If Great Britain won the war, so would Russia. But Ben-Gurion and most others who had experienced the whiplash of the Czarist regime and had a memory of pogroms held a secret hope that the war might somehow bring all this to an end. Weizmann's idea of making Zionism an ally of Great Britain meant making Zionism an ally of the Czars. The situation had all the elements of a Greek tragedy.

In his articles in *Unity*, Ben-Gurion wrote that Jews not drafted into the Turkish Army should enlist in a special Jewish battalion to defend Palestine from attack.

Trumpeldor popped up in Alexandria. So did Jabotinsky, a Russian journalist six years Ben-Gurion's senior, who had been a delegate to many Zionist Congresses.

Jabotinsky was not confused. His feelings against Russia were as strong as Ben-Gurion's, but his hatred of the Ottoman Empire was greater.

"Where the Turk rules, neither sun may shine nor grass grow."

He argued that the dismemberment of the Ottoman Empire was a prerequisite to a revival of the Jewish homeland.

He and Trumpeldor discussed the idea of a Jewish battalion. They agreed that one of the vital factors in deciding the fate of Palestine after the war might be what part the Jews had played, as Jews, in the conquest of the Holy Land. But the best they could get from British military authorities in Egypt was an agreement to allow them to form a labor battalion of mule drivers, "the Zion Mule Corps."

"Never!" Jabotinsky shouted. The very name "Mule Corps" offended him.

Trumpeldor was won over by a British general who promised "a Jewish Palestine after the war" if he and his followers would undertake the hazardous and inglorious job of driving mules loaded with ammunition into the front lines.

So the one-armed young Russian Jew went off to Gallipoli with six hundred Jewish mule drivers who helped him write a brilliant chapter in military history.

Meanwhile in Palestine the situation was chaotic. Already eighteen thousand Jews had fled to Egypt, and more were going every day. Turkish authorities were arresting Jews by the hundreds and sending them off in all directions: to prisons, to detention camps.

One day the *Unity* office was raided, files were seized, and both Ben-Gurion and Ben-Zvi were thrown into a Jerusalem jail.

A few days later they were ordered expelled from the country on the ground that they had been conspiring with others to form a Jewish state. From their cell they sent an appeal to Jamal Pasha, the Turkish Governor.

Their imprisonment had its amusing aspects. The jail was more like a third-rate hotel than a place of incarceration. The prisoners had at least as much freedom as boys in a boarding school. Ben-Gurion attended political meetings and kept business appointments.

One day on a Jerusalem street he came face to face with Jamal Pasha.

"I have rejected your petition," the Governor said sternly. "You are to be expelled."

When Ben-Zvi and Ben-Gurion reached Alexandria they were arrested again, this time by the British. The charge was that they were enemy aliens, loyal to Turkey, the country which had just expelled them. After intercessions by many people at many consulates and embassies they were given travel documents stamped with American visas.

"The Twins" reached New York early in the summer of 1915. They found rooms just east of Broadway in the Seventies. One of Ben-Gurion's first purchases was a book: a mammoth, unabridged English dictionary that he kept in the center of his room on a pedestal.

During his first few months in the country the young man from Plonsk developed a love of the United States. He had never seen Jews anywhere so free: free from persecution, from discrimination, from almost any form of "special treatment." But he was not happy about the mentality of many American Jews. From his socialist point of view too many had acquired a self-satisfied, bourgeois attitude. He risked the displeasure of new acquaintances by accusing them of having brought to the New World the worst instead of the best of their cultural background.

He found Hebrew an almost unknown language in America, outside the synagogues. These New World Jews seemed as reluctant to abandon Yiddish as a man might be to get rid of an old pair of shoes which were comfortable but worn out.

He found little unity among American Jews. They were split into a thousand fragments, and each fragment had its name, its officers, its committees, its arguments, and its own fund-raising campaign.

Ben-Gurion and Ben-Zvi, after they had been in America long enough to get the feel of the country, went on a two-man, nationwide campaign of recruiting settlers for Palestine. They wanted strong, healthy, idealistic young Zionists who would be willing to undergo many months of training in the United States to make themselves proficient in agricultural matters. During this period they must also learn Hebrew.

They went from state to state, arguing, pleading, explaining. They organized conferences, gave lectures, wrote for newspapers. Before long they knew the geography of America better than most Americans.

In those days Jewish speakers who actually lived in the Holy Land were a rarity in the New World, so the curious flocked to the meetings. Thousands of members were recruited for what they called Hechalutz (The Pioneer), an organization they hoped would help repopulate Palestine after the war.

They wrote two books, the first on the pioneer movement and self-defense, the other a definitive work on the history and geography of Palestine, *The Land of Israel*.

Late in 1915, Ben-Gurion met Paula. They were introduced to each other by Baruch Zuckerman, a New York labor Zionist, at a private social gathering in Manhattan.

Paula Munweis was twenty-three years old, six years Ben-Gurion's junior. She had been born in Minsk, the fourth of nine children. Her parents were prosperous and well known in that part of Russia.

In those days the Czarist government had a regulation limiting the number of Jewish children who would be educated in public schools to 10 per cent of the total. Father Munweis solved the problem by distributing his children among schools in various countries.

Paula was thirteen when she arrived in New York, with an ambition to be a doctor. It was the death of her father and the cutting off of funds from Russia that ended the hope. Instead she became a student in the Brooklyn Jewish Training School for Nurses, and later a student nurse in Beth Israel Hospital of Newark, New Jersey.

Paula, according to her own description, was "a plain, very serious-looking girl; a real Russian student type." She wore her hair waved back off her high forehead. The shape of her face reminded one of a Botticelli. Everything about her features indicated that she was a kind and generous person. She wore pince-nez glasses without rims, and simple dark clothes.

David Ben-Gurion was dressing in those days in the style of the times. On important occasions he wore an extremely high, stiff collar. His hair was still black and wavy. He had shaved off his Turkish mustache.

It was odd that these two should have fallen so quickly and so much in love. They came from the same part of Europe and they were both Jewish, but that was all.

Ten years in America had made Paula a typical New Yorker in many ways. She had not the slightest interest in the Holy Land and had never had any connection with Zionism. She was not a "bookish" person; her reading was confined to light novels. She was an extrovert, and was happiest when there were people about. She spoke her mind bluntly, never holding anything back. She boasted that she was "almost" an anarchist. Until Ben-Gurion came along, the person she admired more than any other in the world was Emma Goldman, who had already been in prison for inciting a riot.

By contrast, Ben-Gurion was basically an introvert. He liked solitude. The New York way of life frightened him. All his ambitions centered in the Holy Land. Zionism was more important to him than food, comfort, happiness. Books were all he ever wanted money for. He never read anything but "serious" books. He thought carefully before he spoke, and often decided that silence was the better part of wisdom.

Yet they did fall in love, almost at once.

Paula was fascinated by the stories of his adventures. He had traveled, had been in prison, had written a book or two. He talked brilliantly, sometimes in languages she did not know, and often on subjects she barely understood. But it was his earnestness that won her. He predicted to her that someday there would be a Jewish state and that he would be one of its leaders.

"He believes it so deeply he almost makes me believe it, too," she told a friend.

"I knew from the day I met him that he was a great man. I

could tell that he was like one of the prophets out of the Bible, a man of real vision."

It was an indication of the nature of the relationship that she always spoke of him as "Ben-Gurion." This is what he would be called for the rest of his life by those who knew him the best. Not "*Mr.* Ben-Gurion," nor "B.G.," as he would be called by many behind his back, but plain "Ben-Gurion."

The wedding was shrouded in secrecy. The only person they took into their confidence was Ben-Zvi. Paula's own sister, who had arrived a few years earlier from Russia and was living in Brooklyn, was not told until later. The ceremony was performed at City Hall, Manhattan, before a municipal official. There was no chance for a honeymoon. After the wedding he rushed off to a meeting and she went back to the hospital.

Thus began a relationship between a man and a woman unique in many respects. For the next forty years or more the girl from Minsk was to play an unimportant role in an important way in the life of the boy from Plonsk who, she had sensed upon meeting, was a "great man."

During most of this time she would grow accustomed to hearing people laugh at his dreams and call him crazy. But as each dream in its own good time became a reality she would have her chance to gloat and say:

"See, didn't I tell you so!"

Pinchas Rutenberg, a Russian revolutionary who was one of Kerensky's associates, arrived in the United States advocating a Jewish state in Palestine, with a Jewish army to protect it and a Jewish legislative body to run it. His ideas had a profound influence on Ben-Gurion.

In February the revolution broke out in Russia. In March the Czar abdicated. In April the United States declared war on Germany. These events cleared the atmosphere, and world Jewry ceased being divided, for the moment.

In London, after beating on many doors and suffering many rebuffs, Jabotinsky finally obtained permission to form a Jewish Legion.

In Russia, Trumpeldor was trying to raise a Jewish army of a hundred thousand men to force their way to Palestine through the Caucasus.

In America, Ben-Gurion and Ben-Zvi set to work to recruit
Jews for a Jewish Legion to serve with the British. It would help
liberate all Palestine from the grip of the Turks, and would
create a living link between workers in America and Palestine.
Ben-Gurion and Ben-Zvi hoped that many of the soldiers from
Canada and the United States would decide to settle in liberated
Palestine, after they had fought for it. The Jewish Legion had
to be attached to the British Army rather than the American because the United States had not declared war on Turkey.

Then came November and an announcement in London that
caused Zionists all over the world to rub their eyes in amazement
and then to celebrate wildly. The Balfour Declaration was actually nothing more than a letter from Foreign Secretary Balfour
to Lord Rothschild, but it had the approval of President Wilson,
and it would later be indorsed by both Italy and France. It
stated that His Majesty's government "view with favour the
establishment in Palestine of a national home for the Jewish
people."

Then in December, Jerusalem was captured from the Turks.
It began to look as if better days had arrived for the dispersed
people.

In April 1918, Ben-Gurion himself enlisted in the Jewish Legion, and several weeks later left with other volunteers for training in Canada. In the twilight of his life he would still vividly
remember how someone flagged down their troop train as it was
going through Bangor, Maine, so that the crowd lining the tracks
could see and embrace these Jewish soldiers going off to help
fight for their homeland.

Ben-Gurion's parting from Paula had been difficult. She was
expecting her first child in four months. Almost the last thing the
young husband did before he left was to make out a will which
asked that his first-born be named Amos, if a boy; Geula (the
Hebrew word for redemption) if a girl. He left his wife in the
care of her older sister in Brooklyn and made the promise that
every soldier makes when he leaves for a war—to write often.

Jabotinsky's battalion was called the 38th Royal Fusiliers. Ben-
Gurion and his North American recruits were formed into the
39th Royal Fusiliers. In August they landed in Egypt, where they
were joined by hundreds of volunteers from Palestine itself.

Ben-Gurion was made a full corporal, Ben-Zvi a lance corporal. They sewed the stripes on their uniforms with as much pride as if they had been decorations from the King.

Morale in the desert camp of the 39th Fusiliers went quickly to pieces. This was not the sort of adventure Ben-Gurion and Ben-Zvi had promised the volunteers when they signed up in America. Instead of taking part in a dangerous and exciting holy crusade to liberate the Land of the Jews from Turkish oppression, the disgusted fusiliers were doing nonsensical drills, engaging in make-work projects, and becoming more frustrated by the hour.

Soon after arrival in the desert Ben-Gurion was sent to a hospital with dysentery. He was there when news came from Brooklyn that Paula had given birth to Geula.

The Palestinians were shocked by their first sight of what had happened to the Promised Land. There were barely sixty thousand Jews left, against at least six hundred thousand Arabs and more British soldiers than anyone could count.

The suffering during the war had been great. Just looking into faces was enough to tell how little food there had been. There were not one tenth enough hospital beds for the ill and the diseased.

Then Dr. Chaim Weizmann arrived. He was by now the undisputed leader of world Jewry. He was given full credit for the Balfour Declaration. He had come to Jerusalem as head of a Zionist Commission, which many thought might be the nucleus of the government of the new Jewish state, as soon as the new Jewish state was organized.

Corporal Ben-Gurion decided that there were many matters which he, as one of the leaders of Jewish labor, should discuss with Dr. Weizmann. The problem was that Corporal Ben-Gurion was stationed near Tel Aviv, Dr. Weizmann was forty-five miles away in Jerusalem, and Corporal Ben-Gurion's superior officer had little appreciation of the importance of political matters.

So one day Corporal Ben-Gurion went A.W.O.L. He had no trouble getting to Jerusalem, and his talk with Dr. Weizmann was pleasant and satisfactory. At the conclusion he mentioned the small matter of his absence without permission.

"I shall arrange with army headquarters here in Jerusalem for an official, twenty-four-hour leave for you," Dr. Weizmann reassured him.

At the end of the twenty-four hours Corporal Ben-Gurion was back in Tel Aviv. As he entered his tent, two stalwart British M.P.s appeared and placed him under military arrest.

"But I was granted a twenty-four-hour leave by Jerusalem headquarters," he protested.

"Yes, we know all about that," one of the M.P.s snapped back. "But your leave began the moment it was granted in Jerusalem. What we're charging you with is being A.W.O.L. from the time you left here until you reached Jerusalem."

A court-martial deprived him of his stripes, sentenced him to thirty days' C.B. (confinement to barracks) and ordered him transferred to another company.

David Ben-Gurion's days in the Jewish Legion of the British Army during World War I were not the happiest of his life.

CHAPTER FOUR

DURING his entire life David Ben-Gurion had but three real friends with whom he had a deep spiritual and intellectual rapport. Perhaps only two. Some say one.

The intimate friendship with the one began soon after the war's end.

Palestine was a place of considerable confusion then. Some of the sixty thousand sat waiting for the victors to live up to their pledge, certain that the Promised Day was just around the corner. Others knew that they were ill prepared at this particular moment for independence. Much work had to be done before Israel would be ready to be reborn.

In the years that Ben-Gurion had been away, a few new leaders had arisen. One was Berl Katzenelson. Another was Eliahu Golomb.

Perhaps it was only a coincidence that these two men and Ben-Gurion were of an exact height, all three considerably shorter than the average man. They had much else in common.

Berl Katzenelson (young and old alike called him simply Berl)

had also come from Russia. There he had started his adult life as
a librarian and teacher. He would continue to be connected with
books in one way or another all his life. In his later years he
would be the author of many books himself. (Twelve volumes of
his writings were published after his death.) And he would always remain a teacher. Ben-Gurion and many others referred to
him for years as "the Teacher," implying that there was no other.

Katzenelson was a few months younger than Ben-Gurion. He
arrived in Palestine three years after the boy from Plonsk.

Like Ben-Gurion, he went almost immediately onto the land,
becoming one of the founders of the collective farm at Kinneret,
on the edge of the Sea of Galilee.

While Ben-Gurion was helping to recruit the Jewish Legion in
America, Katzenelson was helping to recruit a Jewish fighting
force inside Palestine. About the time Ben-Gurion joined up himself, Katzenelson did, too.

Berl Katzenelson in many ways resembled Albert Schweitzer
when the Alsatian doctor was a young man, both physically and
in character. His hair was bushy, his eyebrows shaggy and dark.
So was his full mustache. His eyes were those of a gentle man,
without vanity; a profound respecter of the importance of human
dignity. He was restless, resourceful, and imaginative. He was an
aristocrat in taste. Most of all, he was an inspiration to those
whose lives touched his. He had a passion for justice, and believed in both the quality and the equality of man.

His friends said that he never neglected anybody or anything,
except his own physical well-being. As a result he was often ill.

He was a modest man. He never sought or held high office in
the councils of his fellow Jews. He was content during the last
quarter century of his life to do the fundamental thinking for
others, such as Ben-Gurion, and let them hold the center of the
stage. He never measured up to Ben-Gurion as a leader of men,
and he had no ambition to do so, but he could inspire.

There were more facets to Katzenelson's intellect and to his
personality than there were in those days to Ben-Gurion's. Katzenelson knew the Bible well, but he also had a love of other
literature, and of poetry, a form of expression that did not
especially appeal to Ben-Gurion.

What the two men had most in common was that they saw the

world with Israel as the hub. Events, people, places, ideas interested them only if they were able somehow to relate them to their *idée fixe*. Every nerve of their bodies, every thought in their heads, every emotional impulse they had was connected with Israel.

They both had that singleness of purpose generally found in great men.

Without Katzenelson, Ben-Gurion might never have grown up to the task history had assigned him. For a quarter century he basked in the light of the Teacher's personality and drew strength from his wisdom. He clarified his own thinking when he listened to Katzenelson, or when he himself was doing the talking in Katzenelson's presence.

The Teacher was never hesitant about expressing a minority opinion, even if it meant splitting with his friend Ben-Gurion on an issue. Often they disagreed on matters of policy.

As a writer and newspaper editor Katzenelson sought to keep the Jews of Palestine in touch with the trends of current thought throughout the world. Like Ben-Gurion, he was a convinced socialist, but not a narrow-minded, class-war rabble-rouser. He was a practical idealist, always seeing problems in terms of people. He was an intense nationalist, yet he was free of narrow chauvinism.

He hated crowds, but he had an uncanny way of feeling out the temper of any large gathering by wandering around eavesdropping until he had his finger exactly on the pulse of the group.

Actually the two men perfectly complemented each other. Often after Katzenelson's death Ben-Gurion was heard to say:

"I wonder what Katzenelson's reaction to this would be."

Once he said:

"I think we decided right, but I wish I could drop in on Berl and talk it over."

During their early years in the country the two men never met. They became intimate only after the first world war. From then on their paths lay close together.

Katzenelson had deep respect for Ben-Gurion as a man of action, yet he knew that there was need for someone to control him. The trouble was that there was only one man in the world to whom Ben-Gurion would listen. That one man was Berl Katzenelson. So Katzenelson undertook to do the controlling.

He also had respect for Ben-Gurion's intellect, which he described in this manner:

"His mind is like a powerful searchlight. He knows how to pick out the most important issue of the moment and to focus all his light on that one spot."

Katzenelson's principal avenue of expression was the printed word. He wrote with great vigor. Ben-Gurion's own style was as much influenced by his friend's as it was by the Bible. From him Ben-Gurion took three words and made them favorites in his own lexicon: strength, dignity, destiny. Once he worked all three into a single sentence:

"A nation must discover in itself its strength and its dignity if it is to achieve its true destiny."

Despite his dislike of crowds Katzenelson was a gifted speaker. Brevity was not considered a forensic virtue either by him or by those who came to listen. At the end of a three-day youth congress held in 1934, Katzenelson was called upon to summarize the discussion. He did, speaking for six hours with hardly a pause. No one left the room. After Katzenelson's death Ben-Gurion delivered several six-hour speeches of his own and held his audiences as well as his mentor had done.

Eliahu Golomb did not belong to the group of men who, like Katzenelson and Ben-Gurion, began their Palestinian careers on the land. He was a few years younger than either of them and had gone to the Herzlia Gymnasium in Tel Aviv with Shertok, whose sister he married.

Golomb was one of the organizers of the Jewish volunteers who had offered their services to the British the moment Allenby's army set foot in Palestine. He saw in the Jewish Legion what he called "the most important deed in our time." He was critical of Weizmann, but a great admirer of Jabotinsky.

Golomb fought, along with Jabotinsky, to try to keep the Legion alive. He saw it dwindle from five thousand men at war's end to three or four hundred by the start of 1920. He knew that the anti-Jewish attitude of some of the British officers was largely responsible for the American and Canadian volunteers accepting discharges as soon as they were offered.

So Golomb talked to whoever would listen about the necessity of the Jews having their own secret military organization. Ben-Gurion was one of those who listened, impressed by this intent young man with the sharp Russian-Jewish features, the bright eyes, the incisive mind, and soon they became friends.

When Golomb began formation of the underground army called Haganah (Defense), Ben-Gurion, Katzenelson, and Ben-Zvi all supported him.

The affection which Ben-Gurion developed for Golomb had to do with the older man's sense of history. Eliahu Golomb personified a new phenomenon in this ancient part of the world: a young Jewish intellectual, a socialist, who could sit up with Katzenelson and Ben-Gurion all night discussing the most abstruse aspects of political theory, and who at the same time had set out to make himself a military expert, not because he had a love of killing, but because he was convinced that the Jews would someday have to fight for their Promised Land.

In another twenty-five years such a man would no longer be a phenomenon. The myth of the Jew as a coward would be annihilated for all time by the achievements of an all-Jewish army in 1948. But in 1920, Eliahu Golomb fascinated Ben-Gurion because he represented what Ben-Gurion dreamed might someday be normal in the Land of the Jews, and so Ben-Gurion encouraged him, made a confidant of him, furthered his political education, supported his military plans, and used him. Golomb was an ideal go-between for Ben-Gurion because he seldom took sides. Ben-Gurion could send him to Weizmann and Weizmann would listen. Then Golomb would come back and loyally report. He was a first-class negotiator.

Golomb died before he could see his work come to fruition, but it was he more than any other who laid the groundwork for 1948. He and Ben-Gurion together. Except that in this case it was Ben-Gurion who was the thinker, the planner, with Golomb as the man of action.

When Paula and her infant daughter finally were able to get passage from New York and arrived in Palestine, new problems (petty and personal, but almost as insurmountable as some of the political problems Ben-Gurion faced) insinuated themselves into his life.

Paula was neither timid nor afraid of work, but Palestine was a frightening place for a girl, especially a girl with a small baby, who had spent most of her life, at least her remembered years, in the relative serenity, luxury, and orderliness of New York. Here there were streets full of surly Arabs who frightened her. The Middle Eastern standard of living, the dirt, the lack of decent sanitation equipment, the flies, the beggars, the strange food people ate—all these things discouraged her. She spoke only what Russian she remembered from her childhood, some Yiddish and English. Most of these people spoke Hebrew or Arabic.

"I went through a very difficult readjustment," Paula told her friends, and that probably was no exaggeration.

Ben-Gurion found them a small apartment in Tel Aviv. During the short time they remained in it, Paula worked hard at trying to get accustomed to what was for her a primitive life, virtually on the edge of a desert.

This decade, the twenties, was a busy time in Ben-Gurion's career, a critical one for the people of Palestine, and a sad one, in some ways, for Paula. For all of them they were years of uncertainty, nervous tensions, occasional moments of accomplishment and joy, more frequent periods of sadness, sometimes even of frustration and despair.

In April 1920 at the seaside Italian resort city of San Remo the Allied powers met to hand out the spoils. No formal action had yet been taken on Palestine.

"What will happen?" Paula asked her husband.

Ben-Gurion shrugged his shoulders. Who knew? Who could possibly predict the outcome of any peace conference?

The Jews of Palestine were nervous while they waited. Then one day the announcement came. The Balfour Declaration had not been a scrap of paper. San Remo had honored it. Great Britain had been given a Class A mandate over Palestine.

"Class A? What does that mean?"

Ben-Gurion patiently explained. It meant that the men who had just carved up an empire were telling the world that in the case of this mandate the people involved were nearly ready for self-government and that the period of the mandate would accordingly be short.

The Jews of Palestine went through the streets singing. Toasts were drunk in red Palestinian wine. There was dancing, and a little crying, too.

Israel lives again!

After almost two thousand years!

But David Ben-Gurion did no celebrating that day. He studied the words of the mandate and wrinkled his brow.

Article Four. The Mandatory Power must recognize a Jewish Agency to represent the Jewish people as they work to establish their national home. How would it be picked? Who would be the chief? What powers would it have?

Article Six. Jewish immigration is to be permitted. Jews are to be encouraged to settle on the land. How? By whom? When? Where?

They danced in the streets, but Ben-Gurion did not join in the celebration. He would always be this way. When others celebrated, he would temper the joy with cautious thinking, just as in moments of public gloom he would be the one to point out that there was a slim possibility of success.

In July the military regime was succeeded by a civil government sent out from London. The first High Commissioner would be Sir Herbert Samuel.

Again there was shouting in the streets.

"Do you hear this?" one man would say to another. "A Jew! After two thousand years of waiting, at last a Jew will sit in Jerusalem again and run the country!"

On the first Sabbath after his arrival Sir Herbert went to a synagogue in the Old City of Jerusalem and demonstrated that he had retained the faith of his ancestors.

Ben-Gurion was cautious.

What sort of a Jew is he? Whose side will he be on? Can we trust him? Let's not celebrate yet.

When the Ottoman Empire's immigration restrictions were lifted, a new aliyah began, although Palestine was not yet ready to receive many more wandering Jews.

Again there was rejoicing.

"They will help build our new nation!"

But Ben-Gurion saw them crowding into Tel Aviv until the new little city's seams were ready to burst. Only a few were going onto the land. Many came with a little money and wanted to open shops or start small businesses, using cheap labor.

"This is not the way we planned it," Katzenelson and Ben-Gurion would say to each other.

About the time the peace conference opened in Paris, Ben-Gurion and Katzenelson succeeded in forming a new political party, Achdut Avoda (Unity of Labor). Unfortunately there was more unity in the name than there was in fact. Unity of Labor had only about two thousand of the three thousand organized Palestinian Jewish workers.

Then the great Trumpeldor arrived home from the wars. He had come by way of Yalta and Constantinople, recruiting new pioneers wherever he went.

He was not happy at the political disorder he found. The confusion. The lack of a program. He went back to the soil, having missed the soil for so long. He went back to Galilee and there found thousands of Bedouin bandits roaming the hills, terrorizing the population. He went to one of the settlements, Tel Hai, to help them with their defenses. While he was there, the Arabs attacked. It was a vicious fight. Ten to one. Perhaps a hundred to one. There were many dead. Trumpeldor was shot in the stomach. It was ironical that tall, stalwart, one-armed Joseph Trumpeldor, hero of two big wars, died in a petty Arab raid, defending a village of half a dozen wooden buildings surrounded by desert.

Soon after San Remo an important Zionist conference was called in London, and Unity of Labor decided to send Ben-Gurion as its spokesman. This was the first international gathering he had ever attended. It was held in Albert Hall, a frighteningly large place, big enough to have accommodated every member of Unity of Labor, plus all their wives and all their children, as well as quite a few of their neighbors.

On the platform were distinguished speakers, eminent personalities; men from New York, Boston, Paris, Warsaw, from all over the world. And he, David Ben-Guiron, age thirty-three, the head of a political party of two thousand members, was on the program.

At that conference Chaim Weizmann and David Ben-Gurion clashed head on for the first time. During the next thirty-two years these two men between them would control the destinies of millions of Jews in Israel and elsewhere in the world. Weizmann's friends called him "the architect of the Jewish state." If Weizmann was the architect, Ben-Gurion was the general contractor and builder. At times during the next third of a century they worked together as harmoniously as architect and builder should. But there were other periods, when they were so far apart in their thinking that it seemed impossible they would ever be reconciled.

They were both Jewish and both had been born in Russia, Weizmann not far from Paula's birthplace. They both devoted their lives to bringing about the creation of what today is the State of Israel. There the similarity ended.

Chaim Weizmann was tall, slim, and distinguished-looking. When he entered a room, people automatically got up, even without knowing who he was. He was bald during his later years, without a halo. His mustache was close-cropped and his black goatee was almost diabolical-looking. Ben-Gurion is exceedingly short, quite stocky, and looked in the early days of his career exactly like a labor organizer.

Chaim Weizmann was elegant in every way. Ben-Gurion prides himself on being a common man, "one of the people."

Weizmann was a good mixer. Ben-Gurion is uncomfortable at parties. His idea of the way to behave at a reception or cocktail party is to pick out the most interesting person present, take him off in a corner, or down the hall, or even into the basement, sit him down, and then encourage him to talk on a subject he is qualified to discuss.

Weizmann was a gourmet. He knew wines and enjoyed well-cooked food. Paula Ben-Gurion once said, "Our diet is made up mostly of fruit and vegetables. My husband likes grapefruit and polony best." (Polony is a Polish sausage made of partly cooked meat.)

Weizmann spoke French, the language of the courts and of diplomacy, like a true Parisian. Ben-Gurion knows a little French, but does not speak it well.

Weizmann, the cosmopolite, was as much at home in Mayfair as any English aristocrat. Ben-Gurion made many trips to London, but never discovered the West End. Charing Cross Road was his street, because that was where the bookshops were.

When Weizmann at last decided to settle in Palestine he built a European-type house with dining room and library each more than fifty feet long, separated by an open court and swimming pool; a home exquisitely furnished, its art objects including priceless Chinese porcelains and many valuable French paintings. As Prime Minister of Israel, Ben-Gurion has the use of a modest house in Jerusalem; his own home in Tel Aviv is little different, on the outside, from the hundreds of others around it.

Weizmann had studied in Berlin and Switzerland, had had a fine Continental education, and was the proud possessor of many degrees. Ben-Gurion is a self-educated man, with no degrees of any sort until he was given an honorary one by Hebrew University.

Weizmann was wealthy because of his patents and entertained like an English gentleman. Ben-Gurion often entertained, even after he became Prime Minister, around the kitchen table, and his guests sometimes even had to help wash the dishes.

Weizmann was host to such statesmen as Lord Balfour, General Smuts, Léon Blum, Lord Cecil; soldiers like T. E. Lawrence and Orde Wingate; distinguished Americans. He had known Winston Churchill when both were still young lads. He was on speaking terms with the King of Italy, the Pope, Lady Astor, and Ramsay MacDonald. Ben-Gurion, even after he became head of the government of Israel, preferred to entertain *kibbutzniks,* young pioneers, army officers, men of the underground.

Weizmann had intimate friends in every important city of the world. Ben-Gurion in all his life has had only a few.

Weizmann was a man of rapidly changing moods. He could be as gay and jolly as a carrousel one moment, and then quickly sink into a black mood of depression. Ben-Gurion is rarely what one can call "gay and jolly."

Weizmann was a skeptic. He approached all problems with his mind open, in the scientific manner. Ben-Gurion nearly always thinks with his heart.

Weizmann was the gentleman persuader, who pleaded eloquently in the chancelleries of Europe. He rarely lost his temper. He knew that a diplomat must have patience and he therefore was always willing to bide his time. Ben-Gurion often loses his temper, has little tolerance of stupidity, mediocrity, or obstructionism, and refuses to wait very long for anybody.

Weizmann had a keen sense of humor and could outdo almost anyone in telling a joke. Yiddish stories were his favorites. Ben-Gurion has almost no sense of humor. He is always in deadly earnest. He can smile at somebody else's story if it illustrates a pertinent point, but he hardly ever tells stories of his own. Yiddish humor has no appeal to him because he feels it reflects the mentality of the ghetto.

Weizmann was a master of the *bon mot*. He was credited with two classic remarks, one of which he denied originating, although he did at least popularize it:

"Miracles do happen, but you have to work hard for them."

And:

"You don't have to be crazy to be a Zionist, but it helps."

The older Ben-Gurion grows, the more his writings become masterpieces of fine literature, vigorous in style, colorful in expression, but he never tries to sprinkle them with bons mots.

Weizmann was once asked why the Egyptian Army had fared so badly in the war, to which he quickly replied:

"The men were too lean and the officers too fat."

During the controversy over the British proposal to give the Jews part of Uganda, Weizmann was trying to explain to Balfour why he was against the idea.

"Mr. Balfour, suppose I were to offer you Paris instead of London, would you take it?"

"But, Dr. Weizmann," Balfour quickly shot back, "we *have* London."

The tall Zionist smiled and suavely replied:

"True, but we had Jerusalem when London was a marsh."

In arguing the necessity for a Jewish homeland Weizmann said:

"You will always be well treated as a guest if you too can play the host. The only man who is invited to dinner is the man who can have dinner at home if he likes. Switzerland is a small country. There are more Swiss outside Switzerland than in. Yet there is no anti-Swiss sentiment because the Swiss has a home of his own to which he can retreat—to which he can invite others."

Ben-Gurion could never have used such an example as this. Dinner parties and entertaining are of no interest to him. Home, for him, is principally a place where a man has his books.

Weizmann once wrote, "I feel equally at home in Brussels or

Paris or San Francisco." Ben-Gurion constantly uses the expression "my own, my native land" about Israel.

Weizmann barely mentions his first sight of the Promised Land in his autobiography, whereas Ben-Gurion wrote hundreds of pages of ecstatic descriptions of how it looked to him and how he reacted to it. When Weizmann was forty-five years old he finally wrote, "One must be a participant on the spot" to "get the feel of the country and its institutions," and he thereupon went to Palestine, but a short time later he was off again, not to return for a long time. Only when the state was formed and he was elected its President did he move permanently to Israel, to spend the last several years of his life there. Until then all his sojourns had been of relatively brief duration. Ben-Gurion dug his roots deep into the soil of the homeland and developed a great affinity for it. Although he often went abroad on political missions, his home has always been where his heart is, in Israel.

During World War I, Weizmann made a major contribution to Allied victory by directing the British Admiralty laboratories and developing a method of synthetizing acetone for use in manufacturing smokeless powder. During World War I, Ben-Gurion and his Jewish Legion were frustrated from making any contribution at all to victory.

Weizmann was friendly toward the labor movement of Palestine but never took part in politics. Ben-Gurion's whole career has been founded on political action.

Weizmann was a liberal. Ben-Gurion is a socialist.

Weizmann was often academic. Ben-Gurion is generally empirical.

Weizmann felt that Ben-Gurion showed too little concern for world opinion. Ben-Gurion felt that Weizmann showed too much concern for what those outside the Middle East might think.

Weizmann often spoke of "the demagogic appeal of the politicians" as contrasted with "the honest intellectual process" of the scientific laboratory. Ben-Gurion has spent most of his life as a politician and labor leader.

Weizmann was a gradualist. He described himself as "a moderate man." Ben-Gurion is volatile, impatient, eager for quick results.

Weizmann was an ardent believer in *havlagah,* the art of self-restraint. Ben-Gurion feels there are often times when the situation calls for action rather than forbearance.

In writing his 482-page autobiography Weizmann barely mentioned Ben-Gurion. The only reference in the index reads:

Ben-Gurion: opposition to Weizmann, 442

Ben-Gurion was more generous. When the time came, he made a supreme gesture of generosity to the older man.

Weizmann during most of his life felt that there was no hope for a Jewish state except through the kind offices of the British. Ben-Gurion grew impatient with the British and finally bitterly antagonistic, especially after the behavior of Foreign Secretary Ernest Bevin and the broken promise of the Labour party.

Most of these contrasts between the two men were apparent to everyone, including the two principals. The comparison left Weizmann with a perhaps unconscious feeling of superiority in the presence of the short, stocky labor leader. This accentuated the differences. Ben-Gurion's attitude often seemed to be one of instinctive resentment of Weizmann, his way of life, his philosophy, and his policies, even though he appreciated Weizmann's great importance to the Zioinst cause.

After 1920, Ben-Gurion and Weizmann shared the dais and the spotlight on innumerable occasions. Ben-Gurion used every ruse to avoid having to walk onto the platform with Weizmann. He knew what the audience reaction would be to their great difference in height. And so, just as Weizmann would start to go onto the stage, Ben-Gurion would find it necessary to have some last whispered words with someone in the wings, or he would look for a place to get a drink of water. After the audience had thundered its applause of "the architect of Israel," Ben-Gurion the builder would quietly take his chair among the other speakers.

At Albert Hall in 1920, Ben-Gurion listened to speaker after speaker advocating caution, the slow approach, restricted immigration because funds were lacking. The more he listened, the angrier he grew. Dr. Weizmann seemed to be the apostle of this *laissez-faire* policy.

The first speech Ben-Gurion ever made at an international conference may not have been a masterpiece of diplomacy, nor even a gem of oratory, but it was the voice of the Jews of Palestine speaking.

He told the delegates about the reservoir of enthusiasm that was gradually being dissipated by all this equivocation. He demanded bold plans and aggressive leadership. He was not gentle with those he saw as the enemies of Jewish labor. He accused Dr. Weizmann's Zionist Commission of standing between the people of Palestine and the new rulers of the country.

"In the past we had direct access to Jamal Pasha," he shouted, "but now we have to do everything through an intermediary."

When Paula came to London with Geula, Ben-Gurion rented a modest flat for them in Maida Vale, only a few minutes by underground from the heart of the city. There Amos was born.

When Ben-Gurion had originally chosen this as his favorite name for a son, Paula had asked:

"Why Amos?"

Ben-Gurion, in a voice that even then sounded like that of a prophet to Paula, told her the story of the Biblical Amos, the herdsman who conceived the idea of a God not merely for Israel but for all mankind; Amos, who warned of the dreadful punishment awaiting those who oppressed the poor and crushed the needy.

"He sounds like a socialist," Paula said.

Ben-Gurion smiled.

Even more important than being a socialist, Amos had held out hope for a return of the people of Israel to their own land. He predicted an era of peace and prosperity for the wandering Jews, who would wander no more.

Ben-Gurion was disappointed that his son had not been born in Palestine. Geula had arrived in New York. Now Amos in London. Perhaps the third could be a *sabra*.

To the flat in Maida Vale came Moshe Shertok, now a student in the London School of Economics. With him on several occasions was a fellow student, David Hacohen, son of a distinguished Hebrew writer. The three often argued political matters while Ben-Gurion took care of Geula and Amos so Paula could go shopping on Edgware Road.

"Golomb is in Vienna," Hacohen announced one day, "trying to buy arms for his new underground army."

A little later Hacohen received a message from Golomb to come at once to Vienna. It turned out to be a historic occasion; the first all-Jewish army of modern times was establishing its first arsenal. In Vienna, Golomb had found a place to buy rifles. He and another labor party member, Levi Shkolnick, were packing the weapons in a suburban warehouse when Hacohen arrived.

"Get to work," he was told, "and help us."

Hacohen did—just in time to be caught when police raided the building. Golomb and Shkolnick were finally released. Hacohen was held as the ringleader. He spent a month in prison, which was good training, for this would not be the last time he would be imprisoned for political reasons.

Amos was still only a few months old when Ben-Gurion decided to take all his family with him on a tour he had to make of European cities. They went across the Channel by ship, an experience Paula never forgot. Most of the passengers were seasick. Paula thought longingly of Brooklyn and what life had been like before she fell in love with a Palestinian politician.

But Paris was exciting. So was Vienna, a city she remembered her parents telling her about.

It went on for weeks. It was enough to test the strength and devotion of any wife. Dirty trains. Third-rate accommodations. Days alone in a small hotel room with the children while Ben-Gurion was at meetings. Evenings alone while Ben-Gurion was off somewhere making speeches.

Occasionally she would get someone to come and stay with the children while she went and listened to her husband. He seemed to convince people with his sincerity and devotion to his ideals.

They ended their trans-European tour in Plonsk. Lawyer Green had married again. Several of the children were still living at home.

"It was the nicest house in Plonsk," Paula later said, impressed with the birthplace of the man she had always called "great."

CHAPTER FIVE

HISTADRUTH is the Hebrew word for the General Federation of Jewish Labor. Ben-Gurion was one of the founders, thirty-eight years ago, and has always dominated its policies.

Histadruth is probably the oddest labor organization in the world. Artists, bricklayers, writers, miners, teachers, truck drivers, scientists, even children belong—half Israel's population.

It is an employer as well as a protector of employees. It controls the country's principal insurance company, several banks, 96 per cent of transportation, a majority of the stock in the country's only oil well, and nearly half of all other industry, including a building construction company that enjoys a virtual monopoly. It even has its own theater.

In Israel today no one eats, sleeps, travels, or dies without some contact with Histadruth.

Ben-Gurion's theory was that Histadruth would take risks which private capital, especially in the early days, would never take.

Histadruth has for its headquarters a great, seven-story cement building in Tel Aviv that many tourists assume to be the nation's Capitol. For that reason, and because of Histadruth's influence on politics, it has been nicknamed "the Kremlin."

Ben-Gurion was elected secretary general of Histadruth in its early days and immediately started a campaign to enlist Arab members. This won him new enemies.

"Imagine," they said, "a Jew organizing Arab workers to demand more pay from Jewish employers!"

In the twenties Ben-Gurion went to Moscow to represent Histadruth at an agricultural exhibition. He was not much impressed with what he saw, and Soviet officials were not much impressed with the enthusiasm for Histadruth and labor Zionism which this little man without a necktie or hat tried to pass on to them. Many Jews had already been sent to Siberia for Zionist activities.

After several years world Jewry finally set up the Jewish Agency, which the mandate said should represent the Jewish people as they struggled toward their independence. It was a state within a state, with its own budget, its own cabinet, its own army, and its own intelligence service. Ben-Gurion became a member of the Cabinet (the Jewish Agency executive), but because he was already drawing a salary from Histadruth he served the agency without pay.

"I believe in practicing my principles," he explained bluntly.

The mandate made no provision for the Jewish Agency to have an army, but it had one anyway, Haganah, the underground force Golomb was building. Ben-Gurion was its champion from the start.

"We must make the Jews who come back home proud they are Jews."

To be proud they had to stop cringing. That meant losing their fear. But to lose their fear they had to have a way of striking back. Until Ben-Gurion's time few Jews had ever dreamed of going onto the offensive.

After a visit to England he said:

"The English are judged by what they are. We will always be judged by what we do."

He wanted to help create a place where Jews could relax and get rid of twenty centuries of tensions; tensions about the imminence of a pogrom, or the embarrassment of being refused admission to a country club.

Labor's position in Palestine began improving as soon as Ben-Gurion's friend Katzenelson became chief editor of a new daily newspaper called *Davar* (*The Word*). From now on Katzenelson would sit at his editorial chair plotting the course for Ben-Gurion and Jewish labor. He would develop the theories; Ben-Gurion would put them into action. It was a perfect combination.

One day in 1928, Mr. and Mrs. Ben-Gurion, Amos and Geula, Mr. and Mrs. Katzenelson, and a driver and his wife were on their way by automobile to a youth rally. Between Lydda and Ramle the driver engaged in an impromptu race with another car. After finally passing it he turned around to gloat. The car left the road, hit an olive tree, and overturned. The labor movement almost lost its two most valuable members.

Zeev Sharef (Secretary to the Cabinet after the creation of Israel) was following in his own car. He pulled the three families from the wreckage. Katzenelson had a broken leg and face injuries. The other seven were all badly cut and bruised.

Ben-Gurion's first thought was about Paula and the children.

Katzenelson, in great pain, called to Sharef. There was only one thing worrying him.

"See that no blame is attached to the driver. He must not be punished."

After taking all eight victims to a hospital Sharef went on to the rally and informed Shertok, the chairman, that he would have to make all the speeches himself.

That same year at a conference in Warsaw, Ben-Gurion one morning received a cable which caused him to display such exuberance that his colleagues tried all day to guess what good news he had received.

"Do you think England has issued a new White Paper favorable to us?"

"Is it possible that America has . . . ?"

In the evening he finally showed them the cable. It was from Paula announcing that Amos had passed his spring examinations at school.

In the late twenties Ben-Gurion's mass of wavy dark hair began to grow thin and streaked with white, although he was still a young man. Perhaps it was because of what was happening. Most of the joy, the anticipation that had swept Palestine during the early days of the decade had been vitiated by subsequent events.

Sir Herbert Samuel, in whom so many had had such faith, appointed an advisory council to help him run the country. Of the seventeen members only three were Jews. The rest were Arabs and Britishers.

"Is this the way they prepare us for self-government?" the people of Tel Aviv and Jerusalem asked each other.

"Is he really a Jew?"

"Why is he so unsympathetic to us?"

"And what about Article Six?"

Article Six enjoined Britain to "facilitate Jewish immigration," but no Jew could enter the Promised Land any more without a certificate and London was not giving out many certificates.

Many blamed Sir Herbert.

"Imagine a Jew, one of our own, doing this to us."

Weizmann went to see the British Colonial Secretary and got a dusty answer:

"There is no room to swing a cat in Palestine any more. It is full. Nobody can enter. What is the use asking me for immigration certificates?"

Weizmann waited seventeen years to reply to the Colonial Secretary. Then he said:

"Count up the number of cats that have been swung, the number of new industries that have been created, and judge whether the country has been impoverished."

But this was still 1929 and Britain was attempting to appease Arabs by restricting Jews. Whenever Weizmann, Ben-Gurion, or anyone else made a clamor, another commission was sent to the Middle East to conduct an investigation, take testimony, listen to witnesses, make a report.

Ben-Gurion went to Vienna for the next Zionist Congress and spoke for the angry Jews of Palestine. Standing before the two hundred delegates with his shirt open at the neck and his jaw raised defiantly, he made one of the bitterest speeches of his life. First he aimed at Sir Herbert.

"We regarded him with reverence when he came. What did he give us? Haj Amin Eff el Husseini [one of the most anti-Jewish of the Arab leaders] as Mufti of Jerusalem!"

Next he went after the British.

The chairman banged his gavel frequently. Delegates squirmed in their chairs with embarrassment.

These were the nervous, unhappy, frustrating years.

Ben-Gurion saw signs of discrimination against his people wherever he looked.

All British civil servants were armed. Except Jews. The rifle was even taken from an English Jew who had become Attorney General.

On the labor front all was not well either. Tel Aviv was growing like a bed of mushrooms after a summer rain.

"But within the rising walls of this Jewish city," Ben-Gurion reported, "you rarely hear a Hebrew phrase or melody. Arab labor is doing the work."

The farmers of Petach Tikvah had a scheme to import cheap Egyptian labor.

In Jerusalem a writers' home was being built as a memorial to Herzl, author of *The Jewish State*, but not a single Jewish laborer was working on it.

The twenties ended with a pogrom and bloodshed. Arab hotheads spent two hours in Jerusalem killing, destroying, looting. London appointed another commission, which in due course made an investigation. A report was finally issued saying that the Mufti had been largely to blame. The British Government reacted by issuing a White Paper that restricted Jewish immigration and the buying of land by Jews. What disturbed Ben-Gurion most was that this was done by a Labour government; that the Prime Minister was Ramsay MacDonald, who had professed sympathy for the Jewish cause. Ben-Gurion neither forgave nor forgot.

Now began a decade of assassination, a terrible foreshadowing in Europe; Arab rioting; British bungling; more commissions, reports, and White Papers; and finally war.

In Jerusalem, Paula gave birth to another girl, who was named Renana (Rejoicing). Ben-Gurion had a sabra at last.

In the thirties Ben-Gurion was away from home most of the time, on business somewhere, talking, traveling, conferring, being a politician as well as a labor leader.

In the next Zionist Congress, Jabotinsky and Weizmann were the star performers.

Jabotinsky was a polished orator, with eight or nine languages on the tip of his tongue; an idol of a large segment of Jewish youth in Poland and Palestine; poet and scholar, a critic of painting and sculpture; but above all, a fighting Zionist. He had attracted the attention of Maxim Gorky and Leo Tolstoy.

Jabotinsky and Weizmann were a match for each other. On this occasion Jabotinsky delivered one of the most inflammatory addresses of his career as he advocated a Jewish state on both sides of the Jordan as large as the original Palestine had been. When he finished, Weizmann arose, smiled, and said:

"The walls of Jericho fell to the sound of shouts and trumpets. I have never, however, heard of walls being raised by that means."

Several days later Weizmann was defeated for the first time for the presidency of the Zionist organization, and went into retirement.

By now Ben-Gurion was the head of a new, united, labor front, Mapai. Jabotinsky's followers called themselves the Revisionists. It was the left versus the right, with no quarter asked and none given; and it led to Palestine's first political assassination.

The Nazis had come to power, and the world was learning something from its newspapers about one of the ugliest of all expressions of human hate, anti-Semitism. This was the period when Hitler was letting it be known that German Jews would be spared if they would move quickly out of Germany, preferably out of Europe. To investigate the possibility of saving perhaps a million German Jews the head of the political department of the Jewish Agency, Chaim Arlosoroff, was sent to Berlin. He came back some weeks later with his report.

One warm summer evening Chaim Arlosoroff and his wife were promenading along the Tel Aviv waterfront. A stranger stopped them and asked for a match. Arlosoroff reached into his pocket. A shot rang out. Arlosoroff fell, dead. The assassin escaped into the shadows.

Abraham Stavsky, a young Revisionist, was arrested. Ben-Gurion publicly said he was convinced that Stavsky was the murderer.

The case was argued from Dan to Beersheba.

Until now Zionism had done all its fighting with words. This new departure frightened many people. With the greatest pogrom of all time beginning in Europe, were the Jews of the Promised Land going to start killing each other?

Stavsky eventually was released, but in another fifteen years he would be killed, not many yards from where Arlosoroff had fallen.

That was the background of the 1933 Zionist Congress, at which the poet-warrior Jabotinsky and the labor politician Ben-Gurion fought for power. When the votes were counted, Ben-Gurion's labor socialists had enough of the 320 seats to control the Congress. The man with the build of a diminutive giant now sat in the place of power.

One spring day in 1935 three men and three women set off from Jerusalem on a five-day motor trip. One of them was Eliahu

Epstein, who had come only ten years earlier from Russia and
had been practicing what Ben-Gurion had been preaching, first
as a laborer in a kibbutz, helping to drain swampland until he
almost died of malaria, and more recently working as a laborer
for a Haifa contractor who was building an R.A.F. base near the
frontiers of Transjordan and Saudi Arabia. He had become
friendly with the Bedouins, and had made a trip with some of
them to the northern tip of the Red Sea, where there was a fishing
village called Aqaba, in Transjordan, and opposite, in Palestine,
a place designated on maps by its Arabic name, Umm-Rashrash,
where there was nothing but a primitive hut belonging to an
Englishman who was prospecting for minerals. Down there young
Epstein had acquired a love of the desert, a knowledge of Arabic,
and a vision of what Umm-Rashrash might someday be if the
Jewish dream ever became cloaked with reality. Now he wanted
his wife and his friends (Mr. and Mrs. Ben-Gurion and Mr. and
Mrs. Katzenelson) to see this desert spot, too.

They drove from Jerusalem to the Jordanian city of Amman,
and then down the Jordanian side of the Dead Sea to Umm-Rashrash. It was the route of Moses in reverse.

They timed it to reach their destination on the eve of Passover,
so they could celebrate the traditional Feast of the Seder in this
place which had played so important a part in the history of the
ancient Jewish people.

It was the first time that the other five had ever been here, so
their guide showed them around. There was not much to see that
man had created.

"But look at the harbor!" Epstein exclaimed.

They all knew their Biblical history, and so there was no need
to tell each other that, in the days of Solomon, Umm-Rashrash
had been Elath, and near here the great Jewish king had made
"a navy of ships," and that from this gulf the wealth of ancient
Israel had been shipped to distant places, and that not far from
here once stood the industrial plants which had processed the
copper from the royal mines, and that in the story of the Queen
of Sheba told in the second Targum of Esther the ships she sent
to King Solomon in advance of her own visit, loaded with costly
woods, precious stones, and six thousand boys and girls all born
the same hour on the same day, all the same height and all

dressed in royal purple, may have anchored in these very waters.

They were all intrigued by the colors of Elath. Here the sand was not beige, like sand almost everywhere else, but blue and pink and delicate purple.

As the others talked of the past, the man with the hair that had already started to grow thin and white looked across the harbor, then half closed his eyes and seemed to be having a dream.

A few months later Ben-Gurion, in a letter to United States Supreme Court Justice Brandeis, set down his prophecy that a Jewish state before long would come into existence and that in it "Elath will play a greater economic and political role than she did in Biblical times."

Not long after the Elath trip Ben-Gurion became chairman of the Jewish Agency, which amounted to being made Prime Minister—except that it was a "shadow" government—the government of a country which did not even exist.

One of Ben-Gurion's most intimate Arab friends was Musa Alami, a man of culture and breeding, who had been educated in Europe, had family connections with the Mufti, and had once been Attorney General of Palestine. He lived in Jerusalem, and it was there one day in the spring of 1936 that Ben-Gurion, with the knowledge of Weizmann and the Mufti, began a series of negotiations with Musa Alami in the hope of bringing about an agreement which would permit the Arabs and the Jews each to have a state of their own.

It was a dangerous undertaking for both of them, especially for Musa Alami. Any Arab even suspected of dealings with Jews was likely to be dragged from his bed and killed by his own people.

While Ben-Gurion and Musa Alami were holding their second meeting, the Arab riots of 1936 began. First in Jaffa. Then wherever there were Arabs and Jews in the same place. The list of dead mounted every day. The Arabs went on strike. Soon the whole country was almost paralyzed.

The British Government sent in military units from Egypt. Then more military units from Malta. Then a whole division from England. And finally the inevitable investigating commission.

Often in those days when Ben-Gurion felt he was about to lose his temper he would stalk from the meeting room in Jerusalem with his head bent and would climb Mount Scopus to the Hebrew

University and there bury himself in books until he had regained his composure.

The investigators who came from England to look into the Arab riots were called the Peel Commission, after Lord Peel, their chairman. The report they issued ran to four hundred pages. Ben-Gurion read and absorbed every word, and then went to London and sat for days in the gallery of the House of Commons and then the House of Lords, listening to the debate.

When someone asked him later how Englishmen behave when they argue, he replied:

"I thought I was attending a Zionist Congress!"

What had he learned from listening to the debate?

"You can do many things with an Englishman but you cannot change him into a non-Englishman. The Englishman does not see things through Jewish eyes, he does not feel things with a Jewish heart, and he does not reason with a Jewish brain."

What the Peel report proposed was partition of Palestine into independent Jewish and Arab states. The difference between this plan and the one eventually passed by the United Nations was that Lord Peel's commission proposed that Britain continue to hold Jerusalem, Nazareth, Bethlehem, Haifa, and a corridor from Jerusalem to the sea; the Arabs would get about 75 per cent of what was left, including the Negev Desert; the Jews would have the remaining 25 per cent, principally Galilee and a narrow coastal strip.

Europe was about to blow up. Hitler was closing the doors of Germany. Franco and Fascism were winning in Spain. But in the summer of 1937 the leaders of world Jewry fought for most of a week in their Zionist Congress over partition.

For the first time in all the years of their friendship Ben-Gurion and Katzenelson opposed each other in public. The black-mustached editor was against partition. So were the two great rabbis from the United States, Stephen Wise and Hillel Silver. So were all the rest of the American delegates. So was Mrs. Golda Myerson (later Meir), whom Ben-Gurion would someday choose as his Foreign Minister in a moment of crisis. They all made brilliant speeches. Their logic was almost irrefutable.

"It may be necessary to make compromises," said Katzenelson, "but the one who makes concessions must see that he gets real possibilities."

Then finally the man with the hair that was now white and stood on end as if full of electricity went to the podium and began to speak. His entire body seemed charged with a contagious dynamism.

"The best mandatory government in the world is not to be compared with a government of our own."

Heads nodded. This was logic, too.

He became prophetic. He said he could foresee the possibility of a million and a half Jewish immigrants arriving during the first decade of a new Jewish state. (He was not far wrong. Almost a million immigrants did arrive in Israel during the first ten years.)

"This is the beginning of the redemption for which we have waited two thousand years."

Finally a resolution was passed that saved everyone's face but settled nothing. It instructed Congress leaders to get more details from the British about what they had in mind.

Ben-Gurion had had his dream of a Jewish state since childhood, but he put it definitely into the record that year:

"For the first time I now offer myself as a candidate for the Zionist executive in order to campaign for the establishment of the Jewish state. That will be the purpose of my life from now on."

Here was a new David facing a many-headed Goliath.

The British (although it was a British commission that proposed the idea of partition) would fight him.

So would the Arabs, who would turn out to be his greatest enemy.

The American Jewish leaders were unanimously against him.

So were Jabotinsky and the Revisionists.

His usual allies, his advisers, many within his own party, refused to accept his leadership on this issue.

And Berl Katzenelson, the man to whom he always went for advice, was also on the opposite side.

Ben-Gurion was now fifty years old.

The battle would go on for ten long years before another partition plan would be offered. And that would only be the start of the struggle for the right of Jews to live like other people, in a country of their own, on the site of their own ancient civilization.

In 1937, Ben-Gurion became more than ever a dedicated man.

CHAPTER SIX

ARAB murder and savagery had gone on for more than two years, and there still was no sign of the end.

Bands of armed guerrillas roamed the countryside killing Jews without reason or discrimination. Trains were derailed. Roads connecting Jewish colonies were planted with mines. Telephone wires were torn from their poles. The oil pipeline from Iraq was cut. Forests were set afire and crops destroyed. Fruit trees were ripped up by the roots. Travelers were ambushed and convoys were attacked.

Everyone knew that the Palestinian Arabs were being supported with money and arms from adjoining Arab countries.

These were nervous days, sleepless nights for most Palestinians.

Paula Ben-Gurion was one of the thousands who volunteered for guard duty.

"Night after night I would put the children to bed and go out and do the night watch. I would return during the early hours of the morning before the children woke up."

One day the newspapers told how Hitler had taken over Austria, and then from Berlin came a dispatch in which the madness of the Nazis was made apparent for all the world to see. Because a young Jew had shot a German diplomat in Paris, Heinrich Himmler had ordered his S.S. troopers into action. Hundreds of synagogues and Jewish apartment buildings had been set afire. Twenty thousand Jews were arrested in Germany, and another twenty thousand in Vienna. More than seven thousand Jewish shops were looted. There were many Jewish deaths, and the hospitals were full. Two days later a committee headed by Herman Goering imposed a fine of two hundred million dollars on the Jewish community. From now on all Jews must wear the yellow star of David. From now all Jews must . . .

Ben-Gurion applied to the Colonial Office in London for permission to bring in a hundred thousand Jews marked for death. The Colonial Office said a curt "No!" so the hundred thousand were left to their fate.

Ben-Gurion then asked for immigration certificates for twenty thousand Polish children and ten thousand young people from the Balkans. Again he was turned down. (Just so it would be on the record, he stated publicly a few years later that, to his definite knowledge, all thirty thousand of these young people who might have been saved were put to death.)

The Jews of Palestine were confused and bitter. The world seemed full of chaos. Death was everywhere. They wanted a leader, someone to show them the way.

Weizmann could not do it, for Weizmann was the one who had been telling them that they must trust always and only the British.

Jabotinsky had an answer. It was terrorism, against both the Arabs and the British. An eye for an eye and a tooth for a tooth. He called his underground army Irgun Zvei Leumi (Organization of the National Army). From inception to disbandment almost fourteen years later it operated without scruples. You try to terrorize us, and we'll terrorize you. If you humiliate the least of us, we'll humiliate the best of you. If you hang one of our men, we'll hang three of yours. We'll kill, torture, and terrorize until you behave yourselves. These were the principles of Jabotinsky's Irgun.

At this painful second in Jewish history there were many in Palestine, especially among the young, who were attracted by the idea of striking back, and so Jabotinsky began to win a good measure of support. But there were others who were disturbed and confused, and wanted to hear the quiet, clear voice of reason.

The quiet, clear voice spoke to them on August 3, 1938.

"We are fighting on three fronts at once. Our own ranks are divided. Our quarrel with the Arabs has taken a violent turn. The political conflict with the British is of the gravest."

He made no attempt to deceive them. He told them the worst. But then, as he would always do, he tried to act as the counterbalance. Just as he refused to dance in the streets when the news was good, so at a time like this he refused to become a disciple of doom and a preacher of desperation.

"This is no national uprising," he told them, speaking of the riots that had crippled Palestine. "The Arab people is not involved, not even the bulk of it; it lacks the will, the capacity, and the strength to revolt. A small minority is fighting to the death, using any and every means, perpetrating the foulest crimes."

Then he gave them a historical view.

"For us, looking back on a Land of Israel in existence two thousand years ago . . ."

He would be talking this way, always, from now, fitting the present into the mosaic of the whole, giving a third dimension of depth to the events of the day; reminding them that one of the profoundly wonderful things about being a Jew was having this historical perspective.

Then he became a moralist.

"We reject the infamy of assailing an Arab just because he is one. It means we reject revenge wreaked upon Arabs who had no hand in terrorism. We will not play the terrorists' beastly game."

He was talking to Jabotinsky now.

"It is a sin to spill innocent blood."

But then the moralist became a realist.

"Unhappily, the world in which we live is not moved by the voice of conscience. When we explain that the Bible commands us not to kill, nobody listens, not even the observant Jews."

So he gave them pragmatic reasons for not meeting lawlessness with more lawlessness. Terrorism would cause chaos. Chaos in Palestine would benefit the Arabs alone. In a state of chaos Jews would never be able to buy land, build settlements, or save fellow Jews in distress.

He called on them to have courage.

"Are we scared because Jews are murdered every day? Jews have been killed ever since resettlement began sixty years ago. Did this frighten us away?"

He answered the argument that killing is all right if done for patriotic purposes.

"What is wrong for Arabs is wrong for Jews. . . . The Arabs too have their patriotic excuses. They do not murder just for fun."

Then he gave them news to cheer.

"We have achieved something sensational. For the first time in nearly two thousand years a defense force has been established which is Jewish, for a Jewish reason, to protect the Jewish population."

Although Haganah was a secret body, the British had sworn in five thousand of its members to defend Jewish settlements, and had issued to each man a rifle. Jews were now authorized to guard railway depots. And along the northern and eastern frontiers . . .

Ben-Gurion's brown eyes sparkled as he told how the impossible had been achieved.

One thousand Jewish men and women had built a wall of barbed wire stretching for sixty miles along the border in order to hamper the organized movement of foreign Arabs who had been coming into Palestine to join in the murder and pillage.

"It can never be done," British officials had said.

The region was wild, and some of it was marshland, where a man might easily vanish from sight if he made a misstep. Besides, the workers would be easy prey for Arab guerrillas, who would pull down the wall as fast as it was erected.

Ben-Gurion went up to see for himself, and now he was reporting. One thousand men and girls, Jews, had done the job, while three hundred other Jews had guarded them. Arab snipers had killed only two of the thirteen hundred.

He wound up:

"Hitler may occupy Austria by brute force, destroy Jews, and threaten France and Czechoslovakia. We are a small folk, with no army, no state, no power to compel. We cannot overawe the world. Our strength lies in the one great asset we possess, the moral purity of our lives and works, our aspirations and our philosophy. Given courage, understanding, and clean hands, we shall win."

That night in Palestine a great many Jews who had been troubled and confused slept better.

Ben-Gurion may have slept better, too, for he had come to a crossroad and had decided which was the right way to go. There would be a dozen such crises in his life; a dozen times when he would have to make an irrevocable decision on a fundamental matter of importance.

The first was when he decided to leave Poland and settle in Palestine.

The second was when he came to the conclusion that Jews should have the right to defend themselves in their own settlements.

This was the third, his decision that Jews must never resort to terrorism, no matter how great the provocation.

There had been also the question of illegal immigration. This was another time he and Katzenelson had disagreed. The editor felt that the situation justified rescuing Jews in any way possible. Ben-Gurion argued, at first, that illegal immigration would handicap him in persuading the British to increase his allotment of certificates.

While the two men debated it, the Jewish pioneering movement in Poland chartered a two-thousand-ton Greek tramp, the *Vellos*, which had been engaged in the white slave traffic. They smuggled three hundred Polish Jews across one frontier after another until they reached the Greek seaport of Piraeus. There they packed the human cargo below decks on the *Vellos* and many days later landed them at night close to Tel Aviv.

But when the *Vellos* returned with a second load, the British were on the alert. An R.A.F. plane flew overhead. Police boats patrolled the shore line. The captain abandoned hope of landing his passengers and returned to Greece, but Greek authorities refused to permit the Jews ashore.

For ten weeks the *Vellos* steamed from one Mediterranean port to another, a phantom ship. It was permitted to refuel but never to put any of its human cargo ashore. The illegal immigrants finally had to return to Poland and to go into a detention camp.

There were other attempts. Jabotinsky and his Irgun went in for immigrant smuggling. So did a considerable number of private racketeers who chartered derelict ships and charged Jews exorbitant prices to run them through the British blockade.

Then Ben-Gurion slowly changed his mind. It was not a moral issue. It was not that Katzenelson convinced him. It was just that he lost hope of persuading the British. So he finally gave his approval to the creation by Haganah of a Committee for Illegal Immigration, which was soon called Mossad for short. Paris became its headquarters, and before long its agents were scattered all over Europe. Embarkations were at night. The ships were always in communication with Haganah headquarters in Palestine by radio. They were directed to lonely spots along the shore where Haganah men and girls helped the immigrants ashore and hid them before the British had a chance to sound an alarm.

About this same time Ben-Gurion crossed paths with the most storybook character he had ever met.

Orde Wingate, who already was being called the T. E. Lawrence of Judea, had had a short pro-Arab period in his youth when he decided he wanted to learn the language of the nomadic people of the desert. Instead of engaging a teacher or studying a book he went to the East End of London, located a boarding-house full of Arab seamen, rented a room, and for weeks lived like an Arab, ate like an Arab, looked like an Arab, and tried to think and talk like an Arab.

Some years later he was sent to Jerusalem by the British Army as an intelligence officer, but before long he found a way of combining duty and living in a kibbutz in order to learn Hebrew.

The men of Haganah were suspicious of him at first, but he eventually won their confidence. Wingate had a theory about how to discourage Arab attacks on Jewish settlements. At night he would lead Haganah squads deep into Arab territory, and they would overpower or kill the sentries, locate the Arab arsenal, steal the store of weapons, destroy any ammunition, and then return home loaded down with all the booty they could carry.

Wingate also devised the idea of patrolling the Haifa-Mosul oil pipeline by motorcycle to keep the Arabs from cutting it.

He was a legendary-looking figure who had developed a love of the Old Testament as a child and a love of Hebrew while he was teaching young kibbutzniks how to outwit their enemies.

Ben-Gurion was puzzled at first by Wingate, although he developed great respect for him, and once paid him high praise in a public address for his work in organizing the "night squads."

Early in February of 1939 the British with great solemnity and to the fanfare of many trumpets opened in St. James's Palace, London, a conference between themselves, the Arabs, and the Jews.

The first trouble was that the Arabs refused to enter the palace by the same door as the Jews. That was easily remedied. St. James's is a palace of many doors.

Then they refused to sit in the same room with the Jews. That was more troublesome. The British had been holding diplomatic conferences for hundreds of years, but a conference with half the conference in one room and half in another——

But that was just the way it was done; Arabs in one room; Jews in another room; the British delegates divided fifty-fifty; two simultaneous conferences.

This was not, of course, an auspicious start for an attempt to reconcile all the differences between the three peoples.

For this occasion Ben-Gurion dressed like a gentleman from Whitehall, with black morning coat, striped trousers, batwing collar, and gray silk tie. But he spoke his mind just as bluntly as if he had been deshabille in Tel Aviv.

"The suspension of Jewish immigration will prove impossible without the aid of British bayonets."

The Arabs demanded that not a single additional Jew be permitted to set foot on Palestinian soil, that the mandate be replaced by an all-Arab state, and that the British leave.

Ben-Gurion and Weizmann asked for nothing more than development of the national home in accordance with the mandate and enough immigration certificates to accommodate the needs of European Jews.

British patience and diplomacy finally brought the delegates all together in the same room, but not until the Arabs had been assured that this did not imply recognition of the Jewish Agency.

The talks went on for a month and a half with no sign of anyone weakening.

In March, Czechoslovakia was dissolved. But the talking continued in St. James's Palace.

Then one day the British Colonial Office made a slight error. An envelope was delivered to Dr. Weizmann, large, thick, and very official-looking. He took it to his hotel suite and opened it. It was a preliminary draft of a White Paper the British Government was planning to issue. This copy was apparently intended for the head of the Arab, not the Jewish, delegation. (It was never explained how the error was made.) The British Government wanted the Arabs' advance approval.

Weizmann read on and on with incredulity. Then he showed the document to Ben-Gurion and the rest of the Jewish delegation.

They soon found out that it was no practical joke. Two months after the St. James's conference adjourned in stalemate, the British Government published a White Paper technically called Command 6019. It provided that fifteen thousand Jewish immigrants could come into Palestine each year for five years. After that not a single Jew would ever be admitted unless the Arabs gave their full approval. Thus the Jews would always be forced to remain a minority; a third, perhaps someday only a fourth, of the total. Jews would not be permitted to acquire land except in limited areas of Palestine. And the British Government would do all in its power to enable an independent Arab state to come into being within ten years.

Command 6019 violated almost every article of the League of Nations mandate. Instead of helping Jews to settle on the land, as the League had directed, Britain would keep them off the land. Instead of facilitating Jewish immigration Britain would close it off entirely. Instead of a Jewish homeland Palestine would become an Arab state.

Command 6019 killed the hopes of millions of Jews in Europe, who now had no place to go except to the gas chambers and the crematoria.

Seldom had any British government ever taken a step that was so widely condemned. Neville Chamberlain was Prime Minister. The man who before long would succeed him, Winston Churchill, talked about "moral and physical bankruptcy," and called it "a mortal blow to the Jewish people."

Another Englishman, whom Churchill would make one of his cabinet members, said:

"The watchword is 'Appease the Arabs; appease the Mufti.' Appease them by sacrificing all the prestige we might have gained from either Arabs or Jews by consistency, by firmness, by justice to both sides."

In Tel Aviv and Jerusalem there were demonstrations that quickly turned into riots.

Three months later the twenty-first Zionist Congress met in Geneva, Switzerland, in an atmosphere of black dejection. Lights were going out all over the world. The doors of Europe were being slammed shut, one after another. The gates of Palestine

were barely ajar. Britain had gone back on her word. Where was
hope to be found?

Weizmann, the lifelong champion of Great Britain as the Jews'
friend, had little to say.

Ben-Gurion talked about illegal immigration as the one bright
hope.

Rabbi Silver from America tried to argue him down, pleading
for moderation.

Then Berl Katzenelson, whom many called the father of illegal
immigration, stepped up to deliver the last major public address
of his life.

In almost Biblical language he described the heroism of the
young Jews who were defying the British Army, Navy, and Air
Force to smuggle European Jews who had been marked for
death through the blockade. He talked of the significance of the
sea to Jews, and pictured a day when the Mediterranean would
abound with ships coming from all parts of the world to con-
verge on the Holy Land.

"Behold, I believe that the time is not far off when songs will
be sung in honor of our own seafaring people, and maybe even
prayers will be composed for their welfare. Who knows, there
may even come a time when such prayers will be said in the
temples of American Jewry. [This was directed at Rabbi Silver.]

"At this moment I recall a wonderful prayer, the sea prayer of
Rabbi Nachman, who seven hundred years ago began an immigration to Israel which was not legal in its time either. In this
prayer evil spirits and the dangers of the sea are mentioned, but
he had no knowledge then of the British Navy and its motor-
boats, or of Anglo-Arab patrols along the coast.

"Is there in our days no Jew to sing a song of the sea for us,
no one to pray for the safety of our Jewish seafarers?"

Those who heard were spellbound, Ben-Gurion perhaps even
more than the others. This speech by the Teacher inspired him
to turn his own eyes toward the sea. A few years later he would
make a sea speech of his own and sing the praises of Jewish
nautical heroes.

While the Zionist Congress was still in session, Germany and
the Soviet Union announced their ten-year non-aggression pact.

Everyone knew that war was now inevitable, so the Congress quickly adjourned.

Weizmann went back to his hotel suite and wrote a letter to Prime Minister Chamberlain which wound up:

"The Jewish Agency has recently had differences in the political field with the Mandatory Power. We would like these differences to give way before the greater and more pressing necessities of the times."

Ben-Gurion issued a statement of his own, which contained one sentence that for years would serve as a motto and guide for his people:

"We shall fight the White Paper as if there were no war, and the war as if there were no White Paper."

CHAPTER SEVEN

AT A secret meeting place eight days after the war started, Ben-Gurion violated British regulations by meeting with officers of the Haganah underground army. Most of them were confused and in need of guidance. The white-haired man told them bluntly that they had a two-front fight on their hands. He cautioned them against "enmity for Britain or the British people," but—

"In defiance of all restrictions, immigration will continue and increase; pioneering will go on despite all obstacles."

He was a prophet that day, for he told them:

"We now stand on the threshold of a tremendous world upheaval, and we must be clear in our minds about the road the nation should take and the goals it should seek. The first world war brought the Balfour Declaration. The second world war should bring the Jewish state."

There was hardly a Jewish family in Palestine that had not been emotionally involved in the war from the start. Warsaw was being bombed out of existence. Almost everyone had friends, relatives, next of kin in Poland. Ben-Gurion's brother Abraham had a daughter living there with her husband and children. As the days went on and the aerial attacks on Warsaw grew more

and more savage, it seemed doubtful that anyone at all could
still be living there.

Ben-Gurion and his associates in the Jewish Agency suggested
that a voluntary registration be held for those who wanted to
help the British war effort. In a short time eighty-five thousand
Jewish men and fifty thousand Jewish women had signed up.

In that first month of war forty-three young Jews were placed
on trial in Jerusalem, charged only with having engaged in secret
military training. All forty-three were members of Haganah. The
defense pointed out that Haganah had been armed by the British
for military service during the Arab riots, that the "illegal" military training had been given under the supervision of British
officers, Orde Wingate among them, and that the forty-three
were charged with no overt act or even aggressive intentions.

These arguments had no effect. One of the forty-three was
given a life sentence; the others, ten years.

Ben-Gurion called on every Jew in Palestine to join in a two-
hour work stoppage the next day as a gesture of protest.

When regulations prohibiting Jews from buying land in 95 per
cent of the country were put into effect, Ben-Gurion signed a
"manifesto" that called it "an intolerable humiliation" and told a
meeting of Zionist leaders in Jerusalem:

"The Land Law was passed because they wished to placate
the Mufti and his gunmen, as they once tried to placate Hitler."

(The Mufti, whom Ben-Gurion had once called Sir Herbert
Samuel's gift to the Jewish people, was now shuttling back and
forth between Rome and Berlin, an unblushing tool of the two
dictators.)

Eight months after the war's start Ben-Gurion packed a single
bag, took some of his favorite books under his arm, and set off
for England.

"I must help Weizmann get a Jewish army for us," he told his
wife. "I'll be back as soon as I can."

By this time Paula Ben-Gurion was well accustomed to the
long absences. She had had to work hard to reconcile herself to
his almost fanatical interest in a Jewish state. At times it put
dark rings under his eyes, forced him to go for long periods
without sleep, destroyed what little home life he had.

When he was in Palestine, she could see that he ate nourishing

food and could keep people from disturbing him when he ought
to be sleeping. But when he went abroad she knew what happened, because once she had gone along on a trip. Other men
with some degree of his fanaticism would keep him awake half
the night talking. He would never think of food unless someone
reminded him.

Now he was off to London, and London was under attack
almost every day, every night by German planes.

But all she said were those words that women have used to
the men they love in every age in every language:

"Take care of yourself, won't you?"

Then he was gone.

Ben-Gurion reached London just as the British were suffering
one of the worst defeats in their entire military history. France
had collapsed, Belgium had surrendered. Nine hundred boats of
all descriptions were bringing a third of a million British and
French soldiers across the Channel so that they might fight another day.

In years to come Ben-Gurion would often retell the story of
Dunkirk when his own people were discouraged by defeat.

"I happened to be there . . . the small remnant of the British
Army of the Continent . . . did not wait for the luxury of the
Queen Mary and the *Queen Elizabeth*, nor did they care about
the seaworthiness of the ramshackle, filthy little boats which
assembled from all parts of England to save that valiant remnant.
All the British people were proud of Dunkirk, and rightly so."

Ben-Gurion found a small room in a modest boardinghouse
near the underground station called Swiss Cottage, not far beyond Madame Tussaud's Waxworks on the edge of Regent's Park.

It was several miles by bus, subway, or brisk walk to a three-
story, yellow brick building with an odd little iron balcony on
Great Russell Street which housed the Jewish Agency and was
the headquarters for various Zionist organizations. There they
gave Ben-Gurion a small, bare office on the second floor, just off
the conference room. From the window he could see the rooftops
of Bloomsbury and two flowering trees in Montague Street.

In London during 1940 a new and strange period in Ben-
Gurion's life began. It may have been because death was so
close at hand and destruction was in every street. It may have

been partly because he had reached the age when a man often looks back on the ground already covered. He was almost fifty-four now. His hair was whiter than ever, and very thin in front. A few wrinkles had started to line his face. He grew tired more easily.

Often he would sit in his small office on Great Russell Street with his eyes closed, just thinking. He kept to himself more than ever before. He seemed to be growing introspective. He would be silent for long periods.

Once when there was an air raid and everyone else had gone to a shelter, someone asked:

"Where's B.G.?"

An hour after the raid was over, he walked casually into the building. When they asked him where he had been, he quietly explained that he had been to a cinema.

"That one at the top of Tottenham Court Road."

What was the film?

He didn't know. He had had his eyes closed.

Why did he sit in a cinema with his eyes closed?

Because the seats were comfortable, the admission charge was not great, and it was such a good place to think.

It was in London in 1940 that Ben-Gurion began to add new facets to his character. It was here that he first started to make a scholar of himself.

The Jewish headquarters building was only a city block down Great Russell Street from the British Museum, which would normally have contained one copy of every book ever published in England, as well as a great store of archaeological wonders, sculpture, manuscripts, and other literary and artistic treasures. But unfortunately for Ben-Gurion the doors were locked and sandbagged. Most of the contents had been trucked off to the countryside to be hidden against bombing destruction in underground caverns or camouflaged caves.

But the side streets of Bloomsbury were sprinkled with small establishments specializing in particular literary subjects, and the bookshops along Charing Cross Road, only a few blocks away, were still open.

Ben-Gurion plunged first into a study of British colonial history, going back to the start of the empire. After some months, with characteristic sharpness of decision, he dropped this interest.

"I have discovered from my investigation," he told one of his Jewish Agency acquaintances, "that unless you fight for your freedom you do not get it."

The booksellers of Bloomsbury would smile when they saw his white-fringed head coming through the door.

He never talked much to them, but he knew exactly what he wanted. Sometimes a bookseller would search months to fill his order for some out-of-print work.

In 1958, eighteen years after his wartime sojourn in London, a letter came to the Jewish Agency office on Great Russell Street addressed:

Mr. Ben-Gurion

It was opened and found to contain a report on a book which the man from Palestine had asked a Bloomsbury bookseller back in 1940 to find for him. The book at last had been located. Would Mr. Ben-Gurion please drop in and pick it up? Apparently the bookseller was too deeply buried in his dusty volumes to be aware that the man who had placed the order was now a Prime Minister and a world figure, living a considerable distance from Great Russell Street.

Several months after Ben-Gurion arrived in London, the blitz began. Once a bomb landed on a wing of the nearby British Museum.

One day when he had been forced to spend several hours in a shelter he turned to the person beside him and said:

"If I have to do this I'm going to use the time to study ancient Greek."

"Why Greek?"

"After reading British colonial history I have decided that the future of Israel may depend upon our knowing something about military matters."

"And what does this have to do with Greek?"

"I want to read Thucydides on military strategy."

Later Ben-Gurion gave another reason for his new interest. He wanted to know more about Plato, who had always been his favorite philosopher.

The sky was often black with German planes, and there was

death in the next street, but David Ben-Gurion taught himself ancient Greek in the air raid shelters of London in 1940. His quick, incisive mind helped. Also his strict self-discipline. And, too, his passionate desire for knowledge.

Here was a phenomenon, a man who grew younger in mental facility and intellectual interests as he grew older in years.

He was impressed by Plato's theory that evil will not pass from states or from the human race until philosophers become rulers or rulers become philosophers, even though Plato's ideas about the superior man were in conflict with the teachings of Israel's prophets, who contended that the ideals of goodness, justice, and mercy would be realized by *people* rather than through the role of superior leaders.

During this period Ben-Gurion began to attain intellectual stature. Until now he had been principally a clever politician, adept at swinging delegates into line, haranguing party lieutenants, directing campaigns. From now on the screen of his vision would rapidly enlarge until he became a man of wide interests, able to discuss Greek philosophy with either a Greek or a philosopher and metaphysical problems with men who had no interest in politics.

While Ben-Gurion that year in London was thinking more than ever before about life, God, eternity, cause and effect, good and evil, he fell under the influence of Britain's great war leader.

There was little in common between David Ben-Gurion, self-educated socialist, lacking in many of the social graces, and Winston Churchill, Tory, born of the Marlboroughs, Harrow and Sandhurst, a gentleman of distinction.

Winston Churchill stood for political principles that were anathema to Ben-Gurion. But in this hour Churchill was a leader of men and Ben-Gurion absorbed from him qualities that he would need in another eight years when he himself would have to inspire people whose backs would be to the sea and who would be armed only with "broomsticks."

The one Churchillian attribute Ben-Gurion unfortunately did not acquire was the British Prime Minister's sense of humor. Perhaps this was understandable. Churchill was faced with a tragedy of the moment. Ben-Gurion's mind and soul were saturated with the essence of a tragedy that had been going on for two thousand years.

It was a mark of the new Ben-Gurion that he stopped smoking in 1940 and never returned to it again. He had been chain-smoking sixty to eighty cigarettes a day. It was not a matter of health, or economics. It was entirely an exercise in self-discipline.

"I decided I would no longer be a slave to a habit."

At his desk in Bloomsbury, Ben-Gurion worked on a program that had four objectives: to help the British beat their enemies, to raise Jewish prestige, to save as many Jewish victims of war as possible, and to pave the way for the creation of a Jewish state after hostilities came to an end.

He assumed that because Churchill had replaced Chamberlain the White Paper was dead. He hoped to convince Churchill that Haganah should no longer be harassed, that the British police in Palestine should be instructed to behave, that the Jews should be permitted to drain the swamps of Galilee and develop Tel Aviv as a port and, most urgently, that two Jewish divisions should be created, one for Palestinians, the other for Jews who lived in the Diaspora.

Ben-Gurion and Weizmann took the plan together to the Colonial Office, where it was treated with frigidity.

Lord Lloyd testily asked:

"If you are really interested in a British victory why don't your people just enlist in the British Army?"

Ben-Gurion snapped back:

"Why don't you ask this of the French or the Czechs or the Poles?"

Lord Lloyd suggested that a Jewish Legion would "just increase our troubles out there."

"I guess the real trouble is that we exist," Ben-Gurion replied.

The war news was bad that day. Colonial Secretary Lord Lloyd probably had his mind on graver matters. He only half listened. When he said his guests should realize what a crucial hour this was for Britain, Ben-Gurion replied:

"For you to be faced with the threat of destruction is a novel experience. We have been facing such an ordeal for almost two thousand years."

Failing all else, Ben-Gurion asked one small favor. Would the

British please release the forty-three Haganah men who were held on such a foolish charge?

Lord Lloyd shook his head even to this. Then he suggested that if Weizmann and Ben-Gurion really wanted to assist Britain in this time of her distress one or both of them should go at once to the United States to persuade the Jews of New York to put pressure on Washington to end America's neutrality.

Weizmann was engaged in some war-important chemical research for the British Government, so Ben-Gurion faithfully packed his bag, put Plato in one overcoat pocket and a Greek dictionary in the other, and headed for New York.

CHAPTER EIGHT

THERE was not much time for Plato in New York.

Ben-Gurion checked into a modest hotel on East Seventieth Street and started to work.

Paula's sister and her children wanted to entertain him at family dinner parties. Other people insisted that when in New York one really ought to go to the theater. He was too busy.

It was the start of 1941, and Americans in general and American Jews in particular were hungry for "inside news." What was really happening in England? Was the bombing on London as bad as they said? Could Britain hold out? And the Jews—what about the Jews of Europe? Would there be any left by the time it was over?

Ben-Gurion met James A. Farley, who had played an important role in making Franklin D. Roosevelt President, and Wendell Willkie, who had just failed to defeat Roosevelt for a third term, and Senator Robert Wagner, the political idol of New York Jews. He had long talks with Rabbi Stephen Wise and Supreme Court Justice Louis D. Brandeis.

He even borrowed a dinner jacket and black tie in order to take his place at the speakers' table at a dinner for Brandeis. He looked very smart and not nearly as unhappy as he had in striped trousers at St. James's Palace.

He addressed a mass meeting in Carnegie Hall, denouncing

the White Paper, and he spoke to leaders of Hadassah, the organization of American Jewish women, telling them:

"We must help Britain. We must recruit a Jewish army, partly right here in the United States. . . . There is no more sacred task at the moment than the defeat of Hitler and Nazism, and they cannot be defeated by mere words."

He was following his own motto—making war on both fronts, trying to help Britain and fight her at the same time. It was a juggler's trick, and not an easy one. It confused many Americans.

After three months he was off again. They wanted him back in Palestine, urgently, but German submarine warfare had been stepped up, and space on planes was at a premium, so he went east by going west, stopping off in New Zealand to have a friendly talk with Peter Fraser, the Prime Minister.

"Have you really been all the way around the world?" Renana asked when she greeted him.

His only son, Amos, had grown by now to man's estate and had joined the British Army, in which he would rise to the rank of major and see action on many fronts.

Geula, after graduating from the Herzlia Gymnasium, continued her studies in a teachers' seminary. One day she arrived some hours late to class and without a word of explanation went to her seat.

"Geula, the least you could do is to apologize and explain why you are late," said the annoyed teacher.

"I have perfect reasons to be late," Geula replied. "I just got married and I am coming straight from the rabbinical office."

Paula was glad to see her husband back. She had been worrying about submarines, and—

"Did you see my sister in New York? What are the children like? Did you go out to Brooklyn?"

Jabotinsky had died.

Katzenelson was not in good health.

Abraham Stern, one of the founders of Irgun, had broken the truce with the British by organizing a new terrorist band called the Stern Gang. The Sternists did not stop at harassing the British and attacking Arabs. One day, to provide themselves with funds, they robbed a Tel Aviv bank of twenty thousand dollars. The bank was Jewish-owned and everyone knew it.

Palestine was an anthill of activity. There were Allied troops everywhere. Britain had asked the Jewish Agency to try to supply twelve hundred specialists for service outside the country. Fifteen hundred had volunteered. Two thousand Jewish industrial plants were working overtime to turn out war material for the British, everything from hospital equipment to concrete ships. Jewish scientists were producing scarce drugs.

Less than five months after coming home he set off again, this time for Cairo, London, New York.

The Biltmore means different things to different people.

To New Yorkers it is a hotel on Madison Avenue at Forty-third Street.

To the people of Palestine it was a challenge to the British.

To Ben-Gurion it was another major crisis.

At the Biltmore Hotel in May of 1942 an emergency conference was held by the American Emergency Committee for Zionist Affairs. The six hundred delegates were from all parts of the United States and represented all shades of political thinking. There were among them many European Jewish leaders who had only recently sought asylum in the United States.

There had been no international Zionist Congress in 1941, war would probably prevent one from being held in 1943, and this Biltmore conference had no authority to bind anyone. Anything done here would have to be approved by the organizations which the delegates represented.

But Ben-Gurion had some prophetic ideas.

Even if the Allies won the war, he foresaw that Great Britain was on the decline as a major power and that the United States would probably be catapulted into world leadership.

The war was also changing something else. A few years ago there had been twice as many Jews in Europe as in the United States. If the stories seeping out of Germany and Poland were correct, there might soon be more Jews in the New World than the Old. This made America and American Jewry more important than ever before.

Ben-Gurion's critics often called him an opportunist. He was, if they meant patterning the key to fit the lock.

Five months ago all of America had been stunned by what had happened at Pearl Harbor.

American Zionists were still angry about the White Paper.

The awful truth about the gas chambers and crematoria was beginning to leak out.

So Ben-Gurion decided that this was the perfect moment to put "the hesitaters and the minimizers" to rout and get a united Zionist policy. This was the time to demand all that the Balfour Declaration, the League of Nations, and the mandate had promised.

Of course he would have opposition.

Dr. Weizmann, the gentle, warmhearted liberal who placed his faith in moderation, reason, and the assumption of human decency in his opponents, was against this bold new plan.

So were many members of Ben-Gurion's own political party.

So was Dr. Judah Magnes, American-born president of Hebrew University, who advocated a bi-national state, Arabs and Jews.

So was Henrietta Szold, the American-born Florence Nightingale of the Jews, who had started Hadassah, which had founded a great hospital in Jerusalem, and had a large following even among non-Zionists and non-Jews.

That was the atmosphere of the emergency Biltmore conference, at which Ben-Gurion decided to "proclaim the Jewish state."

Some called him mad.

If he failed to win the six hundred delegates to his plan he might be finished as a leader and, much more important, realization of the dream would probably be set back for years. But he was spurred by what Lord Moyne had told him just a few months ago. Lord Lloyd had died, and Lord Moyne was now Colonial Secretary. In London, Ben-Gurion had seen him to plead again for a Jewish army. During the conversation the new Colonial Secretary had let drop *his* idea for the solution of "the Jewish problem." He had in mind a small place in Europe (he never mentioned just where) which he thought would be ideal as a small self-governing ghetto for the few Jews who would be left at war's end.

When Ben-Gurion said "For three million?" Lord Moyne had changed the subject.

So the determined little man with the fringe of white hair stepped to the rostrum to try to convince the six hundred. Instead of appealing to emotions he set out to educate, enlighten, and inspire. He spoke in a scholarly style, as if addressing men with minds as well as hearts.

He cleared the air at the start by saying that the plight of Europe's Jews had killed the old argument about whether Zionism is something spiritual or political.

Then, slowly, patiently, almost like a schoolmaster, he told them the story of modern Israel. The number of *dunam* of land that had been irrigated. The swamps that had been drained. The number of dunam of empty land there was for new immigrants. He talked of the Negev, of Galilee, the sands of Rishon, the rocks of Motza, the stony hills of Hanita, the Huleh basin.

He was in no hurry. He had waited a long time to make this speech, and he had come a long way. For almost two thousand years history had been building up to this particular moment.

He mentioned Benjamin of Tiberias, the Persians, the tyrants of Byzantium. He swung easily from 1942 to the seventh century, back to the present, then to the age of the prophets.

Ben-Gurion's one real friend, Berl Katzenelson, lay ill in Jerusalem. But he paid indirect tribute to him.

"The youngest Jewish adventure in Palestine," he told his audience, "is the sea. Jews as seafaring people may seem fantastic to those who know only the Jews of Europe and America.

"Forty years ago the idea of Jews becoming farmers seemed strange and unbelievable. But it happened.

"Six years ago there was not a single Jewish sailor on the seas of Palestine, although the main sea trade was Jewish. . . . Now ships manned by Jewish skippers and seamen traverse the seven seas.

"It was a Hebrew-speaking tribe that gave the world maritime trade and navigation, the people of Tyre and Sidon, who founded the great empire of Carthage.

"Then Jewish privateers fought the Romans in a bloody sea battle off Jaffa before the fall of Jerusalem.

"Tyre and Sidon perished and disappeared. But the descendants of the Jews who fought the Romans at Jaffa are very much alive today. Many are back in Palestine and more are still to come. They went first to the soil. Now they are going back to the sea.

"Palestine is a small country. But the two seas of Israel, the Mediterranean and the Red Sea, are big, and Jewish sailors and fishermen will make it possible for us to take our place among the maritime nations of the world."

This was the Teacher's sea speech, brought up to date and embellished a little.

Ben-Gurion's plan, which came to be known as the Biltmore Program, was simplicity itself.

1. Unlimited Jewish immigration under Jewish Agency control.
2. The creation of a Jewish army.
3. All Palestine to become a Jewish commonwealth.

Weizmann was nervous as the program was outlined. This was not the cautious approach. It would surely annoy and antagonize Whitehall, Downing Street, and Buckingham Palace.

There were speeches in opposition, and talk in the hallways and anterooms against Ben-Gurion for being impatient of compromise and intolerant of opposition. Some called him obstinate. Some called him worse.

There was one small evidence of his genius. He insisted that the resolution mention a Jewish *commonwealth*.

"But the British will think this means 'commonwealth' the way *they* use it; perhaps we ought to say 'state,' " declared the critics.

Ben-Gurion smiled.

"If we say 'state,' the Americans will misunderstand. 'State' to them means one unit in a federation. That is not what *we* mean at all."

So Ben-Gurion had his way, which indicated not just that he was persuasive, or that he had at last climbed into the position of authority, but that a new era had arrived.

America was now important. If Britain misunderstood—too bad.

He had named the goal for all the world to hear. He might have to settle someday for less, but the Jewish state had been proclaimed.

He had routed the forces of moderation. Dr. Weizmann would continue for a few years more to testify before committees and be the elder statesman of the movement, but a younger man had moved into control. Ben-Gurion was almost fifty-six. His real career was now about to start.

When the Biltmore conference adjourned, the delegates went home to explain it all to their various organizations and take a vote. Ben-Gurion had to obtain the approval of the Jews of Palestine. It would be embarrassing if *they* turned it down.

In Jerusalem he paused long enough to leave his bag, give Paula and the children several small gifts he had brought for them, hear the news, and then rush off to the hustings, to barnstorm from village to village, pleading for support of his new child. He seemed to be electrified, as if with the energy of a newly recharged battery.

Meanwhile, in America, one organization after another was sending in its vote. The victory was overwhelming. Not all American Jews were Zionists, and not all who wanted a Jewish state approved of Ben-Gurion's ideas, but most American Jews in 1942 were thinking with their hearts, and they were unified in wanting to help the victims of Hitler and war. This seemed one way of doing it.

Ben-Gurion had not been home long before the heads of state in Washington, London, and Moscow made a joint announcement:

From all the occupied countries Jews are being transported in conditions of appalling horror and brutality to Eastern Europe. . . . None of those taken are ever heard of again. . . . They are worked to death . . . left to die of exposure and starvation . . . mass executions . . . bloody cruelties . . . hundreds of thousands . . . innocent men, women and children. . . .

When Ben-Gurion recovered enough from the laceration of it he cried out in anguish:

"What have you done to us, you freedom-loving peoples, guardians of justice, defenders of the high principles of democracy and the brotherhood of man?

"What have you allowed to be perpetrated against a defenseless people, while you stood aside and let it bleed to death, without offering help or succor, without calling on the fiends to stop, in the language of retribution, which alone they would understand?

"Why do you profane our pain and wrath with empty expressions of sympathy which ring like a mockery in the ears of millions of the damned in the charnel house of Nazi Europe?

"Why have you not even supplied arms to our ghetto rebels, as you have done for the partisans and underground fighters of other nations?

"Would you have kept silent if every day thousands of your infants and children had had their skulls cracked against stone pavements and walls?"

Ben-Gurion was not accusing just for the sake of unbottling his emotions. He had a purpose. It came out in the next sentence.

"If it is not in your power to put a stop to the slaughter, why do you not let us avenge the blood of millions of our brethren and allow us to take up arms against the Nazis as a nation, as Jews in a Jewish army, under a Jewish flag?"

Three months after Allied troops stormed across the Channel to take the war back to Europe, Churchill told the House of Commons:

"The government has decided to accede to the request of the Jewish Agency for Palestine that a Jewish Brigade group should be formed to take part in active operations. . . . It seemed to me indeed appropriate that a special Jewish unit, of that race which has suffered indescribable torments from the Nazis, should be represented as a distinct formation among the forces gathered for their final overthrow."

Ben-Gurion had won another battle in his long personal war. It had taken him five years and thousands of miles of travel. Around the world and more.

But at last the thousands of Jews in active military service from Palestine and the million or more from other parts of the world could go into a Jewish unit if they wished and wear on their shoulders a patch bearing the star of David, that emblem which Hitler forced the Jews of Germany to wear as a mark of their ignominy.

One August day in 1943 two British soldiers were caught in the act of stealing weapons from a British arsenal. Their trial lasted more than a month. Whereas reporters were normally never admitted to such proceedings, on this occasion British authorities issued special invitations to representatives of all papers, magazines, and radio stations to cover the trial. American correspondents were flown from Cairo, although planes were scarce.

Privates Stoner and Harris were not the real defendants. This was a trial of the Jews of Palestine. The reporters had been assembled to hear and then broadcast the story of the defense. Privates Harris and Stoner were pictured as two poor boys who had become victims of a wealthy organization of Jews with "tentacles" spreading all over the Middle East. Its purpose was to buy war materials.

It was no secret by 1943 that there was a brisk trade in arms. Vast stocks of weapons, abandoned by both Axis and Allied forces in the western desert of Egypt, were being sold on the black market at a high profit. Also, whatever guns and ammunition could be stolen from Allied camps and munitions dumps. The principal thieves were Arabs. The principal purchasers were Jews. Haganah had to equip itself. If Haganah did not buy the weapons, Arabs would, and then they would probably be used someday against Jews.

The British knew Haganah was armed, and on many occasions had been very happy about it.

Before Lebanon's liberation the British asked for Jewish volunteers to blow up the oil refineries at the Lebanese city of Tripoli. Twenty-three Jews volunteered. The British said no arms were available for them, so would they please bring their own. The twenty-three went off armed with "illegal" weapons. Not a man of them ever came back.

The use of Haganah personnel in commando operations armed with their own weapons did not prevent the British from prosecuting them, when the occasion arose, for the illegal possession of arms.

During the Harris-Stoner trial the fact was read into the record that after the two soldiers had been arrested they were given eighteen photographs and asked to pick out the man they said they had once seen in a Haifa café in company with "the chief of the Jewish arms-smuggling ring."

Thoughtfully the police had included a photograph of Ben-Gurion. One of the soldiers pointed to it and said:

"That's the man!"

Neither the prosecution nor the defense seemed surprised.

The court finally accused the Jewish Agency of operating "a vast and dangerous arms ring," and referred to Histadruth as a "Nazi-like" organization that was depriving Allied soldiers of weapons.

Ben-Gurion accused his accusers of trying to slander the Zionist movement in order to justify the White Paper policy.

Berl Katzenelson died one summer Sabbath in 1944, a blood clot in the brain.

They said that Ben-Gurion fainted when he heard the news, and was unconscious for several hours.

He spoke to no one that entire day.

It was as if part of his heart had been torn out.

The next day the funeral procession went from Jerusalem to Tel Aviv, forty-five miles, and then another one hundred to Kinneret, where Katzenelson had worked on the land when he first came.

The Friday before it happened Zeev Sharef and Teddy Kollek, one of his youthful admirers from Kinneret, had called on the editor and during the conversation crowds had been mentioned.

"I have never been able to get over my aversion for masses of people," Katzenelson had said.

Forty-eight hours later crowds such as Palestine had rarely seen before lined the country roads and the streets of the cities to pay their respects.

It took most of the day for the pilgrimage to reach the agricultural settlement on the shore of the Sea of Galilee.

Ben-Gurion rode in the front car after the family.

His friend was gone. Perhaps the only friend he had had or ever would have.

He spoke not a single word the entire day.

The Teacher was gone.

Two years later the hurt was still acute. Addressing a convention of Mapai, the party he and Katzenelson together had founded, Ben-Gurion said:

"I cannot keep from you the personal sorrow, the agony, the sense of painful loss that has haunted me since David Hacohen brought me the tidings, one blackest night, that Berl Katzenelson is with us no more. The burden of this grief will bear me down until my dying day. . . ."

CHAPTER NINE

EVERYONE remembers something about 1945. The events of that year changed the life of almost everyone on earth.

In 1945, Franklin D. Roosevelt died. Hitler and Goebbels committed suicide. Mussolini was captured and killed. The first, second, and third atom bombs were exploded. The war in Europe ended. The United Nations was formed. Japan surrendered unconditionally. Winston Churchill was forced into retirement by British voters.

For Ben-Gurion, 1945 was a year to remember for other reasons.

In March, with the help, encouragement, and blessing of Great Britain (some added the word "pressure") seven Arab states with a total population of forty million formed the Arab League. They had only one matter in common, their desire to drive both the French and the Jews out of the Middle East.

While the Arabs were planning how to spend two million dollars during the next year on propaganda, Ben-Gurion was in liberated Paris in secret conference with leaders of the Committee for Illegal Immigration (Mossad), which had reached a crisis in its existence.

Mossad agents who were scattered through seven European countries had applications in hand from a hundred and fifty thousand European Jews who wanted to get to Palestine as quickly as possible. But the agents knew that this was just the start. Each day that Allied troops liberated a little more of Europe the total number of Jews who wanted to leave the Continent rose again.

"What is it you need most?" Ben-Gurion asked the Mossad high command.

"Ships," someone replied.

"Money," said another.

Ben-Gurion smiled at the young men clustered in front of him. These were Jews of a new type. He knew the parents of many of them. Some of these boys had been born in the kibbutzim and settlements of Palestine. Sabras. As tough and prickly as the fruit of the cactus. They had received their training in Haganah. During most of the war they had been risking their lives in Europe, sneaking across frontiers that were carefully guarded, directing the movements of an underground railroad that smuggled human beings to the edge of the Mediterranean, where ships would be waiting, if nothing had gone wrong.

"You can see, Comrade Ben-Gurion, that when the British and Americans finally liberate Belsen and Buchenwald——"

"I know," said the Old Man, which was what some of them called him behind his back. "I know, and I think I will be able to help you."

May was the month Germany formally surrendered.

There was dancing in the streets of every city in Palestine, and in the kibbutzim and villages.

Ben-Gurion, as usual, tried to act as a balance wheel.

"Europe is liberated, but . . .

"Now we are being told that new order will arise, an order of peace, of justice, of freedom . . .

"But who can guarantee that what happened once cannot happen again . . . ?

"Hitler was not the beginning. How can we be sure he will be the end?"

In June, Ben-Gurion went to Europe to see for himself. First, Bulgaria. He found the Jewish community literally decimated. He saw faces that he would never forget. Especially the faces of children who still did not understand what had happened. They flocked around him as if he had popped out of a fairy tale. He tried to make friends with them. They understood some of the Slavic words he said, but they were timid and afraid. They just stood there staring, eyes deep-sunk in their thin faces.

For months afterward Ben-Gurion talked about the eyes of the small Jewish children of Bulgaria.

Then to Germany.

General Dwight Eisenhower was also making a tour, and he

met the man who had commanded the liberation forces. They got along well together.

"Nazi Germany is in ruins," Ben-Gurion wrote back home. "Once more the Jewish people stand by the grave of one of their oppressors."

He also said:

"I looked on the survivors of the Nazi charnel houses. I was in Dachau and Belsen. I saw chambers where hundreds of Jews were throttled every day. They were brought naked, as if to bathe, and the Nazis would peer through peepholes and watch them writhing in their death agonies.

"I saw crematoria in which millions of Jews were burnt alive. I saw the gallows in Belsen where Jews were hanged each Jewish holy day, while the rest were paraded to witness the ghastly punishments of men who had perhaps come a few minutes late to their daily grind. I saw kennels where ferocious dogs were bred and trained to attack any straggler as the Jews were driven to work or led to their graves. I saw racks whereon Jewish men and women were stretched out naked to be shot at by warders.

"I saw the pitiful relic of European Jewry, what is left of six million, butchered before the gaze of a world frigid, aloof, and indifferent to the fate of a people that had been hounded and tormented for two thousand years of exile."

Then to London.

Weizmann and Shertok were at headquarters on Great Russell Street. Those who had known Ben-Gurion for years said they had never seen him like this before. He had new fire, a new militancy. By comparison with him his associates seemed hesitant and despairing.

"You should all go to Germany and see what I have seen," he told them.

Then New York.

He took a sizable staff to New York because he had a vital job to do: Reuven Shiloah, his political secretary, who would one day become Minister to Washington; Chaim Slavin, an engineer, and Eliezer Kaplan, treasurer of the Jewish Agency, who would be Minister of Finance in the first Cabinet.

They went to a hotel in mid-Manhattan, and there the next day among Ben-Gurion's visitors was Rudolf G. Sonneborn, wealthy

New York businessman, tall, handsome, with angular features and an intensity about everything he did or said, who had for many years been a Zionist leader. Ben-Gurion knew and liked him, and invited him to stay on "for a little supper."

"We American Jews," Sonneborn said, "are hopeful that the British Labour party will win next month's election. If they do they will of course live up to their promises, won't they?"

Ben-Gurion raised his eyebrows, shrugged his shoulders slightly, and said:

"I am afraid we have little to gain by a change in government."

"You mean the British Socialists would go back on their word?"

"It could happen."

"Then how do you see the future?" Sonneborn asked.

"There is a possibility the British will withdraw from Palestine. I think they have had about enough. If they do, then a local war is inevitable."

Everything Ben-Gurion was saying was contrary to the forecast of other people. Sonneborn was skeptical, but asked:

"If that should happen, are the Jews of Palestine in any shape to defend themselves?"

Ben-Gurion frowned.

"No, and that is why I am here."

The next day Sonneborn made nineteen telephone calls, several of them to California, one to Maine, one to Florida.

"There is a distinguished Palestinian visiting here in New York," he told his friends. "He will meet with us at my home on Fifty-seventh Street on Sunday morning at ten. Do everything in your power to come. It's quite important. And please keep it an absolute secret!"

Sunday, July 1, 1945, was a blistering-hot day in New York. But there was only one absentee. Albert Schiff was there, and Henry Montor, Julius Fligelman, Charles Gutwirth, Joel Gross, Harold Goldenberg, Abraham Berkowitz, Shepherd Broad, Samuel Cherr, William S. Cohen, Barney Rappaport, Max Livingston, Charles Rosenblum, Ezra Z. Shapiro, Dr. Jacob Shahan, William H. Sylk, Philip W. Lown, and Samuel J. Zachs.

They gathered in the large Sonneborn salon. Ben-Gurion stood beside a grand piano as he talked. He told them a little of what he had just seen in Europe. Then to Palestine itself.

A buffet luncheon had been laid out at the far end of the room, but it was ignored. Some of the men who sat listening sipped cool drinks, but Ben-Gurion himself, his shirt open at the neck and perspiration streaming down his ruddy face, went on and on as if he were talking to a Mapai labor conference back in Palestine.

His sincerity slowly won over these hardheaded, tough-minded bankers, industrialists, lawyers, merchants, businessmen. They listened to him for three hours, then began bombarding him with questions.

Ben-Gurion argued that statehood was the only solution. But the fight for statehood would probably mean a war.

"I am imposing nothing on you," he told them. "But what we may have to do is going to affect you, as Jews, and I have a duty to warn you. Great burdens may be placed upon your shoulders."

Kaplan told what a war might cost. Shiloah spoke of the political consequences of war.

Twilight came and they were still talking. Night came and only a few had left.

Before they finally adjourned, four points were agreed upon. All eighteen Americans would help to the limit of their ability. Every man pledged himself to absolute secrecy. The code name of the operation would be "the Sonneborn Institute." Ben-Gurion would find some way to communicate with them when he could give them definite information as to what was needed and when the time was ripe.

In this manner the Sonneborn Institute became an informal, nationwide, secret organization to aid Haganah.

Then back to Palestine.

Ben-Gurion was at home when, in July, Great Britain held its first general election since the war and Labour won.

No political party in any country at any time had ever taken a more unequivocal position on any issue than the British Labour party had on Palestine. A Labour convention had passed a resolution in favor of extending Palestine's frontiers, moving out Arabs, permitting free Jewish immigration into the entire area, and eventually setting it all up as a Jewish state. This was more than Ben-Gurion, Weizmann, or anyone else had even asked for.

On the night of July 26, 1945, the Jews of Palestine went wild as they listened by radio to the election returns. They celebrated in Jerusalem, Haifa, and Tel Aviv, in the university on the top of Mount Scopus, and in remote kibbutzim down in the Negev. They celebrated as if the promises had already been fulfilled.

While they celebrated, Ben-Gurion quietly went to his study and wrote a long paper entitled "The Only Solution of the Jewish Problem." There were many passages directed at the men who had just moved into No. 10 Downing Street and the offices at Whitehall.

"The war is over now, and nobody can expect us any longer to tolerate the White Paper. . . .

"The parting of the ways, either the White Paper or a Jewish state."

It hurt Ben-Gurion that he and his people had to be so dependent, always, on the whims of others. Once to a youth conference he said:

"In our littleness is it strange that the great ones of the earth should dazzle us with the blinding radiance of their overpowering strength and numbers? It demands superhuman effort to have faith in ourselves."

In August, President Truman received a report from Europe: a hundred thousand stateless European Jews, many still behind barbed wire in unsanitary, crowded camps, living in idleness, with morale low, the death rate high. So he recommended to Prime Minister Atlee that all one hundred thousand be evacuated to Palestine as quickly as possible.

Shortly after the Labour party victory the first post-war Zionist conference was held in London. There were more than a hundred delegates from seventeen countries, but most of the old familiar faces were missing. No policy pronouncement had yet come from Ernest Bevin, the new Foreign Secretary, still most of the delegates, including Weizmann, were hopeful.

Ben-Gurion told them bluntly they had better prepare for a shock.

The shock came on November 13. Ben-Gurion and Shertok were summoned to the Colonial Office. There they were handed a copy of the statement Foreign Secretary Bevin would be reading to the House of Commons in exactly thirty minutes.

They drove quickly back to No. 77 Great Russell Street, where Weizmann was waiting for them. The three men bent eagerly over the document, reading it together.

This was even worse than what Ben-Gurion had predicted. The international solidarity of labor was a myth. The promises of the British Socialists had meant nothing.

Instead of permitting unlimited immigration, instead of saving at least a hundred thousand European Jews, as Truman had suggested, Bevin was going to let them bring in a mere fifteen hundred per month, and no more.

Instead of a Jewish state they were going to get another commission.

This one would be no different from all the others except that it would include six citizens of the United States, as well as six British members.

Men and women were rotting behind barbed wire in D.P. camps in Europe, but another investigation was to be held. Another chance for Jewish leaders to testify, to plead, to beg.

Then another report.

More words, and words, and words.

Weizmann walked silently from the room. His shoulders sagged, and he looked much older than when he had arrived.

The next morning an emergency meeting was held. The policy of moderation had failed. All eyes were on Ben-Gurion as he stood up to speak. He was the hope now.

"We face the danger of remaining a perpetual minority in our own land. There can be only one possible reply: resistance!"

A few days later Rudolf Sonneborn in New York received a telephone call from a man with a clipped English accent who refused to identify himself.

"I am trying to locate the Sonneborn Institute. I thought perhaps you might help me."

The caller was Sir Simon Marks, a young Londoner who had a message from Ben-Gurion:

"The time has come!"

Acting on Ben-Gurion's suggestions, each of the original group selected a few trustworthy friends and brought them into this odd organization that had no office, no stationery, no telephone, no records, not even a proper name. The first need was funds. Each man made a substantial financial contribution and then solicited money from friends, who often were not even told what the money was for.

The Sonneborn Institute bought the ships Mossad needed for its illegal immigration, more than a dozen in all, including the S.S. *President Warfield,* an old Chesapeake Bay excursion liner that crashed into headlines all over the world a little later as the *Exodus.*

Without thought of ever receiving recognition or reward they created a secret Israel Navy for a state that was still only a dream, and that the British seemed determined would never be more than a dream.

Planes, guns, and all kinds of other material were bought and stored in various parts of the world until the hour of their actual need.

The Old Man was the only authority the Institute ever recognized. The message that had set the wheels in motion had been received from him:

"The time has come!"

CHAPTER TEN

THE Palestine Story in 1946 was rushing towards its denouement, although few of the spectators—or the participants—were certain exactly how it would end.

This was a year of conflict: Ben-Gurion vs. Bevin, Truman vs. Atlee, Irgun vs. Haganah, Truman vs. the Arab bloc within his own State Department, Ben-Gurion vs. Weizmann, moderates vs. activists.

This was a year of lost tempers, confused issues, illegality, rioting, terrorism, and a great deal of sudden death.

This year an acrimonious feud began between the leader of a small state that did not yet exist and the Foreign Secretary of an empire that in some ways had come almost to the end of its existence.

It was David vs. Goliath only if one forgot the two men involved and considered the fight as one between a handful of Jews in a small spot on the east coast of the Mediterranean and the power of Britain.

But one could not forget personalities in this case, for the struggle centered in the personal feud between two individuals.

In some ways it was odd that Ben-Gurion had such admiration for Churchill and such contempt for Bevin. He and Bevin were of the same cut. Both were labor socialists. Both had been general secretaries of powerful union organizations before using that position as a steppingstone to politics. Both were against exploitation of the working class and in accord on the evils of unregulated capitalism.

There was even something similar in their appearance. Both were short, yet large of frame. And both were fighters.

They fought each other for two years, without pause, without politeness. Each assailed the other with adjectives, expletives, and caustic phrases. Each used the weapons of disparagement, denunciation, sarcasm, and ridicule.

Bevin held a press conference at which he said he had gone through all the documents on Palestine, among them the Bible and the Koran, but had been unable to find anywhere the promise of a Jewish state.

Ben-Gurion in answer wrote that evidently Mr. Bevin had never read all of the Bible, and certainly was not very well acquainted with his own state papers.

Bevin said in a statement that ninety million Moslems in India were taking a keen interest in Palestine.

Ben-Gurion replied:

"I challenge the Secretary of State for Foreign Affairs to show that there are even ninety thousand who have ever heard the name Palestine!"

Bevin, speaking more like an angry schoolmaster than a cabinet member, cautioned the Jews that "they should not push themselves to the head of the queue."

Ben-Gurion in his reply said Bevin was guilty of a "remarkable lacuna," that he was "blissfully ignorant," that he was a reactionary, that he had saddled the Labour party with his own antique policies.

Bevin accused Ben-Gurion of distorting the situation by imply-ing that all Jewish survivors in Europe wanted to come to Pales-tine.

Ben-Gurion replied:

"Have British flotillas, planes, and paratroopers been sent to Palestine to prevent the immigration of Jews who did *not* wish to come?"

Bevin, in his anger at President Truman for "interfering," de-clared publicly that the reason Americans wanted the hundred thousand Jews admitted to Palestine was that they "did not want too many of them in New York."

This time Ben-Gurion did not need to reply. The two Senators from New York lodged a vigorous protest with Bevin himself, accusing him of "a false and anti-Semitic utterance."

About this same time Ben-Gurion, weary of being handled like an ugly stepchild, announced:

"We shall treat [with England in the future] only on the basis of a political pact between two independent parties, equal in rights if not in power."

It was Bevin's uncompromising attitude that caused Winston Churchill to speak of his "squalid war against the Jews."

It was Bevin's arrogance that finally caused Ben-Gurion in an-ger to throw down a challenge to him:

"We believe, despite the teachings of Hitler and his disciples, that the Jews, too, are entitled to live as individuals and as a people, just as much as the British and the rest.

"But, again like the British, there are things we value above life itself, things for which we are ready to die rather than sur-render."

This was a cry to battle. This was defiance of the Labour gov-ernment, of the British Army, Navy, and Air Force, and of Mr. Bevin.

Bevin would come out of the fight revealed, to anyone who could read between the lines of a newspaper, as a self-convicted anti-Semite.

Ben-Gurion would come out of it as the undisputed leader of his people, with the prize he was after at last almost within his grasp.

But much had to happen before he would be able to get it.

The afternoon Bevin read his statement to the House of Commons, leaders of the Jewish community in Palestine voted to call a protest strike from noon to midnight of the next day.

Everyone stopped work, and mass meetings were held in the larger centers. In Tel Aviv thirty thousand Jews assembled peacefully and registered their protest in a decorous manner.

But that night small groups of extremists went on a rampage. They broke into government offices, smashed furniture, destroyed files, and even set fire to some of the premises.

Jewish and British police tried without success to check them, and finally British troops appeared and opened fire, killing a number of Jews. Then a curfew was imposed and the 60th Airborne Division took up positions within the city.

During the next ten days there was more rioting, shooting, and deaths. Hospitals reported that most casualties were small Jewish children, and that many had been critically wounded by dumdum bullets which had had shattering internal effects. This resulted in a cartoon in a Hebrew paper showing a surgeon in an operating room remarking to his assistant:

"Good marksmen, these English, not to miss such small targets."

Up to this time there had been only a limited amount of terrorism. Truckloads of dynamite had been hijacked, railroad bridges had been blown up, a few deaths had occurred.

Now Ben-Gurion called for war. He issued the marching orders, directed the opening of a large number of underground munition factories, and was in constant touch with the Sonneborn Institute in New York and other arms-purchasing agents.

By these actions he placed himself in a delicate position. He was by nature a pacifist. His dislike of violence and the taking of human life would soon be well known to all his associates. But the Weizmann policy had failed and he saw no alternative except revolution.

What Ben-Gurion wanted was a bloodless revolution. He wanted to fight the British, but in a gentlemanly manner. His idea of how to encourage the British to go home was massive illegal immigration, widespread sabotage, the blowing up of British installations, perhaps a few kidnapings now and then. But no terrorism, no torturing, no deaths if they could possibly be avoided.

"What does resistance mean? It means applying all our energy and strength to colonization. It means educating the nation and mobilizing it for its redemption, gaining public opinion for Zionist policy, winning the favor of princes and the sympathy of labor leaders, of political parties, of religious bodies, and of all manner of society. It means publishing newspapers, challenging discrimination in law, fighting against any curtailment of our rights, organizing our stand against foes and persecutors, as any nation would that has will, mission, and ability; that can think, poise, and appraise; that is responsible and resolved to protect and defend itself."

But Ben-Gurion had to contend with Irgun and the Stern Gang. Their leaders were mostly recent arrivals from Eastern Europe, bitter young men whom Hitler had taught to hate, and who had seen so many massacres, so much bloodletting, such fiendish treatment of Jews that they had lost all reason themselves. They were goaded into action by what they called the "indifference" of Britain to Jewish suffering in Europe, by the anti-Semitism of Bevin, and by the sight of shiploads of their own people being turned away from the shores of this small piece of land they considered their own.

Most of their followers were young, many of them Oriental Jews without political experience or maturity. No attempt was made to educate them. Instead appeals were made to their emotions, and they were encouraged to live recklessly and die nobly.

At first Haganah tried to work with the extremists. Then to exert some control over their irresponsibility. Finally, to suppress them, in the fear that they would wreck all chance of ultimate success.

Ben-Gurion was the one who ordered these various shifts of policy, although he often was forced to deny it to investigating committees. When he attempted to put checks on terrorism, or to stop it entirely, the extremist leaders used every means to bring him down.

It was terrorism that forced on Ben-Gurion the fifth of his dozen major crises. In 1946 he had to decide whether the end justifies the means. But it could never be the clean, clear-cut decision that a man with a philosophical bent of mind would like to make. This was a revolution, not unlike, in some respects, the one that had been fought a hundred and seventy years earlier by another people who felt the British were keeping them from realizing their own destiny. Now, as then, there might have to be bloodshed. All the weapons that were being assembled might have to be used. But Ben-Gurion felt there were ethics, even to war and revolution.

The terrorists had no interest in philosophical discussion. They argued that the British would leave only if real terror were let loose, horrible enough to frighten the toughest British soldier.

When the Stern Gang assassinated Lord Moyne in Cairo, Ben-Gurion made clear to his people and to the world that this was not his idea of how to fight the British.

From then on, almost every day, he would have to make a decision as to whether some new development, some new act of rebellion was ethical or must be condemned in front of all mankind, even if done by Jews whose goal was the same as his.

There were others in Palestine in 1946 with similar problems. The story was told that at a meeting of Aliyah Khadasha, a progressive party which advocated doing nothing to offend the British, a member declared:

"Haganah has a secret radio station. Irgun has a secret radio station. Why shouldn't we have one, too?"

The meeting voted unanimously for a secret radio station, and a committee was appointed. At the next meeting the committee chairman reported:

"I regret to inform you that I have failed in my mission. The British refused to give us a license for a secret radio station."

In March of 1946 the Anglo-American Committee of Inquiry on Palestine arrived in Jerusalem to take testimony. The twelve members were not in a good mood. The train ride from Cairo had taken sixteen hours. The Holy City looked to them more like an armed camp than the sacred place of three great religions. All important buildings were surrounded by coils of barbed wire. There were pillboxes at the entrance to the King David Hotel, where they were to stay, tanks down side streets, soldiers manning guns on rooftops.

The hotel itself swarmed with white-robed Arab sheiks, private detectives, Zionist agents, innumerable newspaper correspondents, photographers, British army officers.

Before the hearings began, the committee was entertained by the British High Commissioner in his baronial, Moorish-type house on a hill overlooking the Jordan Valley—with machine gunners on the roof.

Ben-Gurion, who was also a guest, wanted to talk to Richard Crossman, Oxford don and assistant editor of the liberal *New Statesman and Nation,* who at thirty-seven became a Socialist member of Parliament and was now one of the six British investigators, so he led the Englishman into a corner and said:

"I read your book *Plato Today* when I was studying *The Republic* in Greek a few years ago."

Crossman was naturally flattered.

Ben-Gurion then asked:

"Why did you make Plato a fascist?"

Crossman reddened and explained that that was not exactly what he had done.

Just then one of the High Commissioner's aides tapped Crossman on the shoulder and whispered something in his ear.

"What did he say?" Ben-Gurion asked as the aide left.

Crossman with some embarrassment said the High Commissioner had sent word that it would be undiplomatic if he, being a member of the investigating committee, remained in conversation with Mr. Ben-Gurion too long.

Ben-Gurion smiled a little sadly as Crossman walked away.

Crossman later said that Ben-Gurion reminded him of a "Pickwickian cherub."

Several days later Ben-Gurion took the stand. By now he and his colleagues were old hands at testifying before investigating committees. This was the eighteenth that had come to Palestine, with its secretaries, cameras, notebooks, trick questions, closed minds, predetermined conclusions.

But this committee might be different. This time the investigators included a California lawyer, a Texas judge who had broken the anti-Semitic Ku-Klux Klan in his native city of Houston, a Boston newspaper editor, and the liberal Mr. Crossman.

Early in his prepared statement Ben-Gurion asked a few questions of his own:

"Why is there this discrimination against us? . . . Jews are not the only people who are different from others. In truth they are not different at all, because difference is a relative concept. The Jews are just what they are. Others are 'different,' but in the eyes of the majority the Jews are always different.

"We are what we are, and we like to be what we are. Is that a crime? . . .

"I know that on the Continent the British people are considered as very different. But no Englishman thinks he is different. To him, the Continentals are different. The Englishman is what he is, but he does not suffer for being what he is or seeming different from others. The Jews suffer not only because they seem different to others, but because they are everywhere a minority. They are at the mercy of others who can do them harm when they dislike this difference."

Turning toward the American delegates, he said:

"More than three hundred years ago a ship by the name of *Mayflower* left Plymouth for the New World. It was a great event in American and English history. I wonder how many Englishmen and how many Americans know exactly the date when that ship left Plymouth, and how many people were on that ship, and what was the kind of bread those people ate when they left Plymouth?"

Some smiled, some shook their heads.

"Well, more than thirty-three hundred years ago the Jews left Egypt. It was three thousand years before the *Mayflower*. But every Jew in the world knows the exact date. It was the fifteenth of Nisan. The bread they ate was matzoth.

"Up until today all the Jews in the world, in America, in Russia, everywhere, on the fifteenth of Nisan eat the same matzoth and tell the story of the exile to Egypt . . . They finish with these two sentences:

" 'This year we are slaves, next year we shall be free. This year we are here, next year we shall be in the Land of Israel.' "

Then Ben-Gurion turned to face the man who had written about Plato.

"It was Mr. Crossman who asked a Jewish witness in London a rather difficult question: 'If you had the choice of getting a hundred thousand refugees from Germany to Palestine or giving up the Jewish state, which would you choose?'

"I want to answer that. I will not sacrifice another fellow

human being, even for the dearest of my ideals. I am entitled to sacrifice only myself. I may ask a fellow human being to do what I am willing to do myself, but it is for him to decide. I will sacrifice nobody else for my ideal.

"Mr. Crossman's question should have been put to the hundred thousand refugees in Germany. If you asked them whether they are willing to buy the 'certificates' to Palestine, as you call them, by renouncing Jewish independence and a Jewish commonwealth, I know what their reply would be. . . .

"Suppose Hitler had in his hand a hundred thousand Englishmen, prisoners, and he told Mr. Churchill, 'Either you give me the British Navy or we will slaughter all these hundred thousand Englishmen,' can you doubt Churchill's reply? He would know he could rely on the hundred thousand Englishmen to answer for themselves. Wouldn't they gladly die rather than buy their lives at the cost of the British Navy?"

The day before they left, Crossman addressed officers of Histadruth in Tel Aviv and then called on Ben-Gurion at his home not far from the sea. He found the "Pickwickian cherub" in his library surrounded by books on ancient Greek. They talked mostly about Plato.

As Ben-Gurion was leading his guest to his car, he said:

"Make up your minds one way or the other, and remember that, either way, we shall fight our Dunkirk."

As Crossman's bodyguard got into the car beside him he made a remark about how dangerous the drive from Tel Aviv back to Jerusalem was going to be.

Ben-Gurion overheard and poked his smiling face through the open car window, saying:

"It's okay. I have already telephoned all the terrorists along the route. Good night."

Amos Ben-Gurion went through the Battle of Tobruk, and then the Italian, Dutch, and Belgian campaigns in the Jewish Brigade without a scratch, but just after the end of the war he had to go to the Sefton General Hospital in Liverpool because of a tropical illness. His nurse was Mary Callow, a dark-haired, attractive English girl from the Isle of Man. Before long Amos wrote home that he was in love. There was only one problem:

she was not Jewish. However, she had agreed to be converted.

Soon after this news reached Tel Aviv, Amos' father had to leave on another trip to Europe. As he packed his bag he slipped in half a dozen pamphlets and several books, all in English, from the shelves of his own library that he thought Miss Callow should read.

When Ben-Gurion met his daughter-in-law in London (he was two hours late for the wedding) he was pleased with her, but said:

"Do you realize what this is going to mean? It will be you who will have to make the sacrifice, not Amos—living in a strange land, among people who talk a language you do not yet understand, and—"

She tried to stop him but he went on.

"Are you sure you are ready to make such a sacrifice?"

She assured him she was.

He smiled and gave her the reading matter.

Ben-Gurion was in Paris when the Anglo-American Committee's recommendations were made public. Bevin had told several of the members (and it was now common knowledge) that if they would present a unanimous report he would respect its recommendations. That was why they had worked so long trying to reconcile their great differences.

"We must flatly reject it!" Ben-Gurion said when he read the report.

The committee had adopted Truman's idea that a hundred thousand refugees should be admitted at once, on the ground that there was nowhere else for them to go, but it had rejected the idea of a Jewish state. Instead the United Nations should run the country until it could be converted into a bi-national state, with equal Jewish and Arab control.

In this way the committee attempted to perform the impossible: write a report that would please Bevin, Truman, Ben-Gurion, Weizmann, the Mufti, and the Arab League.

Ben-Gurion's colleagues did not agree with his proposal of flat rejection. But they were relieved of having to come to a decision by what happened in London. Bevin broke his promise. Instead of attempting to implement the report the Labour government announced it would admit the European refugees only after Haganah and other underground armies had been disbanded, and after the Jewish Agency had suppressed terrorism.

London must have known that its rejection of the Anglo-American report and its violation of Bevin's promise would set off more trouble.

Illegal immigrants were pouring in by the thousands. In trying to get them ashore and hide them from the British, Jewish underground workers often clashed with the British military. Almost every night was full of the noise of battle. Trains were blown up. Bridges were dynamited. Five Irgun men were caught and sentenced to death. Five British soldiers were kidnaped in retaliation.

Bevin made a speech at Bournemouth in which he said he would have to put a full extra division of British troops in Palestine if he were to admit the hundred thousand refugees. This he refused to do.

Defiance increased, until the British who were running Palestine decided on a drastic move. On June 29, which was Shabbat, the Jewish Sabbath, many people in Palestine were awakened by the noise of gunfire. British sound trucks moved through the streets of the cities bellowing the news that a curfew had been imposed.

"No one is to move from where he is at this moment!"

Those who turned on their radios heard the explanation. In Arabic, Hebrew, and English it was being announced that the British High Commissioner had begun "military operations" against the Jewish Agency and Haganah on the ground that they were responsible for the lawlessness.

In Jerusalem, British troops occupied Jewish Agency headquarters, dynamited their way into the offices of other Jewish organizations that were locked because it was the Sabbath, and began a roundup of several thousand men and women, leaders in various walks of Jewish life.

Dr. Weizmann, who was about to go to London for a serious eye operation, was ignored. The active head of Haganah, who was to have been the star prisoner, slipped through the British net and went into hiding. Ben-Gurion, his political secretary, and the Agency's treasurer were in Paris. The other members of the "shadow" government were seized and placed in internment at Latrun.

The Mufti, who had been of such help to Hitler and Mussolini, was enjoying himself in perfect freedom in Cairo, but Shertok, who had helped raise an army of twenty-five thousand men for Britain, was now behind barbed wire at Latrun, along with hundreds of men who had fought in World War II for the Allies.

Ben-Gurion received the first news of the "military operation" in a coded cable from Jerusalem which warned him that neither he nor his political secretary, Shiloah, should return to Palestine for the moment because warrants had been issued for their arrest.

For the next few days Shiloah was busy.

"I must go at once," Ben-Gurion kept saying.

Shiloah would urge him to be patient.

"But if there is danger I must be there!"

Shiloah kept telling him that he would be of much more use to his people if he stayed out of prison.

Ben-Gurion agreed intellectually, but not emotionally. For days he paced his hotel room. He jumped every time the phone rang. He read, nervously, all the newspaper dispatches.

One day Shiloah went out to buy newspapers. When he returned to the hotel he found Ben-Gurion packing.

Like a small boy caught doing something naughty, he confessed he had already reserved a seat in a plane. He unpacked his suitcase reluctantly.

Two nights later Ben-Gurion, looking up from a book he was reading, suddenly said to Shiloah:

"I think the die is cast. Before two years have past, we will have our Jewish state."

In Paris one hot July day friends came to him with the frightening news.

The radio had just announced that the King David Hotel in Jerusalem had been blown up. Or at least part of it. Seventy-five or a hundred people might be dead.

Ben-Gurion spent hours near a radio. He read all the papers they brought him.

This was terrorism at its worst. He knew that it undoubtedly was the work of Irgun.

The "operation" had begun at 12:10 P.M., Jerusalem time, after three warnings had been telephoned: to the hotel itself, to the nearby French Consulate, and to the Palestine *Post*. But the warnings had been ignored. No evacuation of the building had been ordered. One report quoted a British officer as saying:

"I am here not to take orders from the Jews but to give them orders."

The terrorists, disguised as Arabs in white robes, had brought the bombs into the basement of the hotel by truck in milk cans and had planted them in the wing of the hotel that housed the British administration offices. The dead included many Jewish employees of the Mandatory Power, some of whom Ben-Gurion had known well.

Two days later London issued a White Paper. It charged that for many months Irgun and the Stern Gang had been working in co-operation with Haganah, which in turn was under direct control of the Jewish Agency. This clearly put responsibility for the King David disaster on him, for he was the head of the Agency.

Actually Ben-Gurion knew nothing of the plans for the hotel bombing. The Irgun chief, Menachem Beigin, later issued a statement saying that early in the year he had broached the idea of the bombing to the two top officers of Haganah, that they had asked him to postpone the operation for a time, that he had done so twice, and that they had been in agreement with what was finally done.

This was denied by the two men named, who said that they had agreed only if the explosion were to be set off after working hours, when there would be no one in that wing of the hotel.

To make his own position clear Ben-Gurion set these words down on paper in his own hand:

"We do not control the terrorists. We wield no influence over them and we need bear no sort of responsibility, directly or indirectly, for their actions. They have flouted every form of national and communal discipline."

A week after the bombing the radio brought Ben-Gurion the news that twenty thousand British soldiers had turned Tel Aviv into a place besieged. They had cut the seaside city off from the rest of the country. A curfew had been imposed. Except for two hours each afternoon, when women were permitted to go shopping for food, no one could leave home. Violators would be shot on sight.

In four days twenty-five thousand men and women were questioned at interrogation booths set up at street corners. Daubs of different-colored dye were put on the foreheads of those examined, "to separate the sheep from the goats."

Ben-Gurion was incensed by this wholesale mistreatment of his people, but there was nothing he could do. He was still being cautioned against returning, so he sailed for America.

After testifying before a United Nations committee he went to Washington to try to learn the State Department's position on Palestine.

In New York again he was interviewed by reporters, among them Ruth Gruber of the New York *Post*, who offered to let him see what she wrote about him before she turned it in to her editor.

She was proud of the story she showed him. It began:

"There is a man in our town tonight who is to the little people of Palestine what Abraham Lincoln was to the people of America in his day."

Ben-Gurion read the words twice and then made an angry noise.

"How dare you compare me with Abraham Lincoln?"

Miss Gruber tried to explain.

Ben-Gurion interrupted. The anger was gone. Quietly he said:

"When I think of a great man I think of Abraham Lincoln. Who am I? Just a little Jew."

While in New York, Ben-Gurion met Alexander Pekelis, a Jewish immigrant from Italy who had been in the United States just five years but already was editor-in-chief of the *Columbia Law Review*. Ben-Gurion was impressed by his intelligence and intense Zionism, and invited him to attend, as his guest, the first post-war Zionist Congress, which was soon to take place in Basle, Switzerland.

The saddest figure at Basle was Dr. Weizmann, physically ill, bitterly unhappy over what had been occurring in Palestine, yet determined to make one final plea for the moderation in which he so firmly believed.

"I am seventy-two," he said, "and this is probably the last time I shall speak to you."

In the audience were more than four hundred delegates from sixty countries, and a thousand guests. There was probably not a man in the hall who did not have respect for the invalid scientist and would not honor his memory after he was gone, but he was fighting a losing battle when he asked them once more to have faith in Britain.

Bevin had made Weizmann's task impossible. There was no use begging them any longer to have patience and a belief in the nobility of England's purposes.

Ben-Gurion had not wasted his time while in the United States. He had arranged for the support at Basle of a majority of the American delegation, including Rabbi Silver, with whom he had often feuded in the past. Weizmann knew all this before he began his address. That was why he aimed many of his remarks directly at the American delegation.

"Remember it is easy to preach resistance from New York. . . . It is easier to swim in the sea than in the bathtub. . . . You Americans woke up too late."

On the surface the issue was not Weizmann vs. Ben-Gurion but whether they should send delegates to London to continue negotiations with the British.

Ben-Gurion made the speech that decided the issue. He was temperate and polite as far as Weizmann was concerned. He made no direct attack on the ailing scientist. But he did not spare Britain.

"We do not turn to England as beggars seeking a kindness. We demand what is ours by right. Eretz Israel does not belong to England, nor is it part of the British Empire. England has no right to do whatever it wishes there, like someone handling his own property."

He wound up with a call for courage, persistence, and sacrifice.

Ben-Gurion and Silver won their battle by a small majority. This was taken as a vote of no confidence in Weizmann, who promptly walked out of the hall, packed his bags, and returned to London.

Ben-Gurion was now the undisputed head of the Jewish community of Palestine and of the world Zionist movement.

His victory, however, was clouded by reports of new trouble at home, by the sad expression on Dr. Weizmann's face as he left Basle's great exhibition hall, and by the news that his new friend, the Italian Zionist whom he had induced to come to Switzerland from New York for the Congress, had been killed in an airplane crash on his way back.

CHAPTER ELEVEN

BEN-GURION's mind is like an adjustable spotlight. It focuses on a single object with a bright beam, illuminating the most obscure corners. In 1947 he turned the spotlight in a new direction.

During the fifteen years he had been a member of the shadow government he had never asked for a specific portfolio, but at the Basle congress he was put in charge of defense, or "security," as it was then called.

"I accepted the portfolio not because I am a general, or familiar with military science, but because in military matters, as in all other practical affairs, the decisive people are not the experts who are familiar with all the technical details . . . but people with open eyes and level heads, and these are qualities to be found more or less in every normal man."

That was too modest a statement. Ben-Gurion did not go about making himself the supreme commander of an underground army as any "normal man" might have done. He did it with the fanaticism, the singleness of purpose, the spotlight technique of —Ben-Gurion.

Before starting to prepare for war he made one final attempt to deal with the British. The resolution passed at Basle said negotiations should not be resumed "in the prevailing circumstances." Ben-Gurion went from Switzerland to London, accompanied by half a dozen of his colleagues, to see if he could change the "prevailing circumstances."

In their preliminary hotel-room meetings Ben-Gurion suggested proposing partition to Bevin. He even drew a map (almost identical with the map of present-day Israel). The others were against using it.

In London, Ben-Gurion and Bevin finally met face to face. The air was alive with the mutual antagonism.

When Ben-Gurion mentioned the ancient prophets of Israel, Bevin interrupted to ask if he knew how the children of Israel had dealt with those prophets.

Bevin showed no interest in Ben-Gurion's dream of reviving the splendor of ancient Israel. He threatened to drop the whole Palestinian matter into the lap of the United Nations.

At a private luncheon a British official said Bevin was counting on the antagonism of Russia, the vacillating attitude of the United States, the voting power of the British Commonwealth, and the opposition of the entire Arab bloc.

In the midst of the London negotiations an English businessman in Jerusalem and a British judge in Tel Aviv were kidnaped, which did not increase Bevin's affection for Ben-Gurion and the Jews of Palestine.

The attempt at a solution ended with Bevin proposing a U.N. trusteeship plan, which was immediately rejected by Arabs and Jews alike.

So Ben-Gurion went home. The Latrun prisoners had been released after five months behind barbed wire and the warrant for his own arrest had finally been torn up.

He had been away almost a year. He found Paula and his daughters well but exhausted, as most Tel Avivians were. Just a few weeks earlier there had been riots, more clashes with the military, more deaths, and a million dollars in property damage. Walking along the streets of Tel Aviv, Ben-Gurion could see the scars.

While he had been away, his sixtieth birthday had occurred. It is incorrect to say that Ben-Gurion ever "celebrates" a birthday.

"What is there to celebrate?" he once asked a Palestinian friend. "You didn't have anything to do with your own birth. If you want to celebrate, do it on the anniversary of a day on which *you* did something; something important, like settling in Palestine."

At sixty he was going to teach himself what a supreme commander should know about military matters.

Despite his age he began devoting himself to this new interest with the energy and enthusiasm of a very young man. He read all the books he could find in all the languages he could understand on all facets of military science.

He summoned the heads of various branches of Haganah to his Tel Aviv home and took them, one by one, to his library, where he asked them penetrating questions. He focused the spotlight on the most minute details.

First, Yaacov Dostrovsky, Haganah Chief of Staff, who was just back from a secret arms-buying trip. Then Israel Galili, Haganah commander, a stocky young farmer who had never seen a day of regular military service, but whose ability Ben-Gurion respected. Galili was a member of Mapam, the pro-Soviet political party, which was second in strength to Ben-Gurion's Mapai and which had supplied most of the young men in Palmach, the commando branch of Haganah.

Then Yigael Yadin, who had been born in Jerusalem and had learned the terrain of Palestine by digging it up. His father was a celebrated archaeologist, and the son was following in his father's path.

Yadin and Ben-Gurion would have long and acrimonious arguments during which the future Prime Minister would pound the table until the glasses would rattle and sometimes bounce off. At such moments others would have said, "Yes, Ben-Gurion," but Yadin, who was exceedingly slim and almost a foot taller than his superior, spoke his mind freely. Ben-Gurion liked him for it, and named him Haganah's chief of operations, although he was then only thirty.

Then, Yigal Allon, a sandy-haired young sabra, a farmer's son born in Galilee one year after the Balfour Declaration. He was now only twenty-nine, yet he was commander of Palmach, a tough-talking soldier who once described his relationship with Ben-Gurion as being "always on the edge of rivalry and most cordial relations." During World War II he had lived in Arab disguise in Syria and had led the Palestinians who paved the way for the Australian incursion.

Ben-Gurion called these key figures by their first names, and they called him "Ben-Gurion" to his face and "the Old Man" or "B.G." when he was not there.

He would sit with notebook on his knees, pencil in hand, writing hundreds of pages in neat Hebrew script on what they told him.

"Ben-Gurion's seminar," they called it.

They explained to him Haganah's commando technique, the tricks they had been taught in Wingate's day, the military psychology of their potential enemies, the dangers, the problems, the solutions.

Then Ben-Gurion left his library and began to move about the country, visiting Haganah camps and training places.

"What do we need the most?" he kept asking.

Palmach had several thousand men and girls, a headquarters of its own, a few Piper Cub planes nicknamed Primuses, after a locally used kerosene stove, and a naval unit that had no ships but helped bring in illegal immigrants.

Haganah had fifty thousand soldiers, an artillery unit with no artillery, an air force with six obsolete reconnaissance planes hidden in a kibbutz, and a few British planes that could be used to drop supplies to settlements or as bombers, with the bombardier carrying a fifty-pound bomb on his knees.

This makeshift army had ten thousand rifles and a few hundred light and heavy machine guns, mortars, and homemade Sten guns, but no tanks, flame throwers, or other modern devices of war.

Even if someone had offered tanks, planes, and artillery in 1947, they could not have been accepted. Palestine was a small country and a tank is not easy to hide. They had to equip themselves with what could be buried in the earth in an emergency or concealed under a woman's skirt.

Haganah had been one of the most "used" and persecuted armies in history. During World War II its men were employed by the British in commando operations on the western desert, on suicide missions into the Balkans, and as parachutists behind enemy lines.

In 1941, when there was danger of a German invasion, the British planned to evacuate Palestine and leave the Jewish underground armies to try to hold the country, so a military school was opened to which picked Haganah men were sent. When the danger passed, the British returned to their policy of arresting Jewish underground soldiers.

Shortly before the British-Free French operation against the Vichy French in Syria the Haganah men imprisoned for illegal military activity were released and used as the spearhead of the Syrian attack. One of them, Moshe Dayan, lost an eye and would have to wear a black patch the rest of his life.

In only one field did this army of amateurs have undisputed supremacy. Its intelligence was beyond criticism. An aerial survey had been made of most of the country, from a plane rented for twelve dollars an hour from a commercial firm.

Haganah had a file on every town, village, and settlement, containing local maps and a dossier on every resident.

Soldiers in this underground army wore khaki shirts and khaki shorts, but this was also standard dress for a large percentage of the Palestinian non-Arab population. After World War II the British had sold shiploads of surplus war goods in the Middle East. Khaki shorts and shirts could be had for a few shillings, making them the cheapest and most practical clothing for this part of the world. So doctors, truck drivers, and lawyers wore khaki, and underground soldiers as well.

There were no badges of rank, no patches to distinguish units.

The underground volunteers were from sixty countries and spoke almost as many languages. Some had not yet learned Hebrew. There was no common language in which they could be instructed.

Palmach members worked half a month and trained half a month. There was no definite rule for the men and girls of Haganah; they gave what time they could afford to military pursuits.

Books on military matters were stolen, ordered from abroad, smuggled into the country. It made no difference whether they were in Russian, English, German, or some minor language, for there was always someone who could read and translate them, even if they were in Aramaic. They were studied until they were thoroughly thumbprinted and their pages worn thin, then passages would be copied into the notebooks that each officer kept.

Ben-Gurion knew they had only a few months to turn this band of dedicated amateurs into a real army, so he devoted all his intelligence and most of his time to the task. He slept fewer hours than ever. Paula and his daughters caught glimpses of him only occasionally.

Because most of the military terms that had existed in ancient days had been lost during the centuries that Hebrew was a dead language, new terms had to be created. They needed, first, a Hebrew word for "chief of staff." Ben-Gurion searched the Bible. In Genesis 36:15 he found *alouf*, which has always been translated into English as the "duke," and in II Kings 25:19 he found *sar hazova*, which in English was called, clumsily, the "officer that was set over the men of war." Either would do. Ben-Gurion chose *alouf*. This led to a gentlemanly row with his good friend Rabbi Fishman (later Minister of Education), who preferred *sar hazova*.

Under Ben-Gurion's direction scholars compiled a three-thousand-word military dictionary with Hebrew words for such non-Biblical terms as parachutist, anti-aircraft gun, spark plug, half-track.

Ben-Gurion attended almost every officers' course, listening quietly to the instruction and writing in his notebook, aware that the time might come when the future of his people would depend upon whether he had been a good student.

The most advanced officer course was given at a kibbutz called Ein Haschofet, which had been one of the chief Haganah bases for years. Those who came for training drifted in, by twos and by threes, until almost two hundred were there. The course lasted four months.

These days of intimate work with the military rejuvenated the sixty-year-old supreme commander partly because he was having a new intellectual experience, partly because he was among young people, with whom he always felt more sympathy than with his conservative contemporaries.

At times when there were fresh Arab troubles, or friction within the shadow government, or new political problems with the British, he would walk into a room of Haganah officers and in a few minutes drop his worries, relax the muscles of his face, and seem completely happy.

This man without friends (the Teacher was dead and Plato was only a name on a book) made the Army into a friend.

He liked it because it was the one army in which sheer ability brought promotion and in which "Follow me!" took the place of "Forward march!" as a normal officer command. This would make for the highest rate of casualties among officers that any army had ever suffered, but it would also make for the best morale any army ever had.

The love of Plato and the love of an army were not generally compatible. But Ben-Gurion decided that Haganah, with its stress on self-discipline, might have been comprehensible to the Greek.

The rapport between Ben-Gurion and his soldiers was not one-sided. They developed an affection for him, and he became their spiritual leader as well as one of the Army's founding fathers.

In Jewish Palestine young people, especially sabras, did not have much respect for the thinking of the older generation. Spiritually and intellectually they felt little in common with Jews brought up in Warsaw, Berlin, Minsk, Bucharest, Sofia.

But this man spoke their language and had their dreams, so that when he talked to them the thirty-five or forty years separating them melted away. He had once been a kibbutznik; they were kibbutzniks, too. He had once composed poetic prose as he stood watch with a rifle in the lonely night. So had they. He was not afraid to deviate from a pattern. He was a spiritual leader in khaki, and that was what they wanted, and a military leader with vision. He was the chief of a state that might soon come into existence, yet he could take time off and mix with them as an equal.

Ben-Gurion was what one associate called "a very closed-up man"; when he cried he generally cried inside. Yet whenever he was told about Haganah casualties, his suffering became evident. Death bothered him, especially the death of young people.

In the photographic section of the Government Press Office in Tel Aviv there is a file of hundreds of photographs of Ben-Gurion. When pictured with diplomats, statesmen, and men of importance he usually looks as if he were in a hurry to leave. But when surrounded by Haganah soldiers, whether during hostilities or moments of peace, he seems relaxed and at ease.

During the Bevin years a young Jewish underground soldier was arrested and tried by a British military court.

"Do you have anything to say for yourself?" he was asked before sentence was imposed.

In his prison cell the young man had prepared a statement in which he expressed his attitude toward war, killing, the British, the future. The statement explained the hold such young men had on Ben-Gurion.

"We are sons of a certain family. It is not only a Hebrew family. Properly speaking, it is a universal family. Its age is eternity; its home is the globe; its secret is faith; its fate is suffering; its happiness is self-sacrifice; its enemy is oppression; its banner is liberty, and its name is resistance. . . .

"We are not overestimating our strength. It is inconsiderable in comparison with yours. But there is a great principle of history: a large force aiming at despoiling and oppressing is inconsiderable; a small force aiming at freedom and justice is powerful.

"We belong to the international and universal family of resistance. One tragic feature marks the way of that family. It is compelled to use force, but it despises physical force. It holds a rifle or pistol, but its desire is to work with a spade or a pen."

Ben-Gurion's idea of relaxation has never been to read a detective story, go to a film, listen to music, drink alcohol, or in any other way try to shut off mental activity. He keeps his brain functioning at top speed every waking hour. When one subject tires, he merely turns the spotlight onto another.

During his 1947 seminar he sought relaxation from military problems in a study of Oriental religion and philosophy. This kept his mind from growing dull and broadened once more the field of his interests.

In the early months of 1947, in quick succession, the Officers' Club in Jerusalem was blown up, the British shut down all postal service for Palestine in retaliation, an order was issued that nothing on wheels would be permitted to move until further notice, martial law was declared in Tel Aviv, the oil tanks at Haifa were set afire, two Jews sentenced to death for terrorism blew themselves up rather than be hanged, and the prison at Acre was bombed, enabling more than two hundred Arab and Jewish prisoners to escape.

In April, Ben-Gurion was asked to testify at Lake Success. He went by way of Cairo, where an Egyptian customs official, knowing who he was, gave him a half hour of insulting treatment. Turning to a companion, Ben-Gurion said:

"They'll be sorry for this someday."

It was the remark of a man normally not easily provoked.

Ben-Gurion was traveling on the expense account of the shadow government but, as usual, he stayed at a modest uptown hotel in New York. He brought two cases of books with him. When he returned he had three cases. The extra books were purchased after he had discovered that New York has an equivalent of Charing Cross Road: several city blocks on the edge of Greenwich Village lined with secondhand bookshops.

This time he visited Paula's sister, whose son, Will Maslow, was an official of the American Jewish Congress. There was little time for conversation because someone had insisted that Ben-Gurion should have a new suit of clothes, and a tailor came to take his measurements. Besides, most of the time the house was full of Zionists who had hunted him down and wanted to ask questions.

His nephew asked what his salary was now. Together they figured out it was the equivalent of thirty-five dollars a week.

"On such a salary how can you afford to buy even secondhand books?"

Ben-Gurion's eyes twinkled mischievously.

"Did you ever hear of an expense account, Will?"

A special session of the U.N. on Palestine opened at the end of April. Bevin asked the U.N. for the appointment of another investigating committee.

The five Arab states in the U.N. tried to keep Ben-Gurion and his colleagues from being heard at Lake Success. The stratagem failed, and the Jewish representatives had one more chance to beg for justice.

Then one day Andrei Gromyko told his colleagues that the Soviet Union, which had gone to such extremes to stamp out Zionism within its own frontiers, now favored a solution in Palestine that would in some measure "compensate for what the Jews had suffered in Europe."

The next day an investigating committee was appointed, with

one member from each of eleven small countries. When the group reached Palestine, Ben-Gurion was one of its witnesses. In answer to a question he said:

"We feel we are entitled to Palestine as a whole, but we will be ready to consider the matter of a Jewish state in an adequate area of Palestine."

The eleven committee members leaned forward.

"Then you are not opposed to partition?" the Czechoslovak member asked.

"We are ready to consider it."

Ben-Gurion had pointed the way to what would be the ultimate solution.

While the U.N. committee was still in the Holy Land, the Haganah ship *Exodus 1947*, which had been purchased by the Sonneborn Institute, arrived off the coast of Palestine with forty-five hundred Jews from the D.P. camps of Germany. She was boarded by British sailors, and after a unique battle (the British were armed with rifles and tear gas, the Jews with cans of food and broomsticks) she was brought to Haifa Harbor, where the forty-five hundred were transferred to three British ships, put in cages below decks, and were then transported back to detention camps in Germany.

The U.N. committee reported unanimously that the British must go. A majority favored the suggestion Ben-Gurion had made: partition; an Arab and a Jewish state.

Britain indicated that she was ready to leave Palestine whether she was forced out or not, but in case she needed more prodding the terrorists, who a month ago had hanged two British sergeants, stepped up their anti-British activities. British prestige in this part of the world had reached its lowest ebb and British popularity had reached its nadir.

But Ben-Gurion, with all the other matters there were to discuss, took time out to say in a public address:

"If the hour of parting between us and England has come—and it has—we would wish the parting to be one of honor. We know there is not only an England of Bevin, but an England of Balfour, of Wedgwood, of Wingate, too."

In another address he said:

"I must record occasions when numerous British soldiers carried out the painful duty of searches, arrests, and expulsion of refugees with disgust and with tears in their eyes. . . . There are cases of British soldiers and sailors risking their lives to save refugees. . . . It is not the soldier and sailor who are to blame . . . it is what Mr. Churchill called the 'squalid war against the Jews.'"

Thirty years to the month after that other bright November day when Lord Balfour made his declaration, the United Nations Assembly approved by a vote of 33 to 13 the partition plan, and ordered Great Britain to leave Palestine in eight months at the latest. Jewish and Arab states would come into existence two months after that.

Ben-Gurion was in Jerusalem when the news came. From the windows of the Jewish Agency headquarters he watched the crowds beginning to form in King George V Road, named after the English monarch who had been on the throne in Balfour's day. At last they had something to celebrate, so they danced the *hora* and waved their blue-and-white flags, and sang "Hatikva," but Ben-Gurion went to his desk and began to write.

"The miracle of the U.N. decision for the resurrection of the Jewish state is not in itself a shield against the dangers which may still await us."

There was music in the street now.

"We should not forget that if the age of miracles has not passed, neither has the age of aggression and violence, which need no miracle to occur. Even after the Jewish state is established, we dare not delude ourselves that all our troubles will have been resolved and that henceforth life will be all joy and festivity."

Dr. Chaim Weizmann, working on his memoirs in a mountain village of Switzerland several months later, wrote his reaction.

"It is proper to ask whether we have the men needed for our task."

CHAPTER TWELVE

FEW MEN in history have had to face so many problems, such intensity of opposition, such diverse discouragement.

During the six months between promise and fulfillment it seemed to David Ben-Gurion that almost everything and everybody had turned against him and his people.

First, there were the forty million Arabs of the surrounding states. He had been warning everyone for months that they would probably attack the moment the Jewish dream became a reality. There were sixty-two of them to every Palestinian Jew. They lived on almost a hundred times as much land as the Jewish state would have. They had at least the moral support of three hundred million Moslems.

Then there were the one million Arabs inside Palestine. Already they were causing trouble. They might turn out to be Enemy No. 2 if they listened to the voices that were coming from Amman, Beirut, Damascus, Cairo.

The U.N. resolution had been a signal for the worst Arab outbreaks Palestine had ever known. In most cases the Mandatory Power had merely watched as Arab bands roamed the countryside committing murders, arson, robbery; attacking convoys en route to desert settlements; killing drivers and passengers; harassing Tel Aviv from Jaffa; running wild in Safad, Haifa, and Lydda.

In Haifa, Palestine's second-largest city, Haganah began military operations after many of the seventy thousand Arabs there, under the leadership of their own military commander, had harassed the city's eighty thousand Jews for four days. Then suddenly the Arab leader announced that all seventy thousand were going to become voluntary refugees. Haganah sound trucks toured Haifa broadcasting an appeal from Ben-Gurion to the Arabs to remain where they were and promising them fair treatment in the new Jewish state. But orders had come from the Mufti, so they left.

Then there were the British. Ben-Gurion had tried to be fair. He had delivered speeches saying, "Let's not be intolerant; let's not judge all by some; let's not blame individuals." But the closer it came to May 14, the more bitter he personally became. Privately he used the expression "perfidious Albion," and the British unfairness became an obsession with him.

It was not just that British soldiers blew up the plant of the Palestine *Post* and three weeks later drove a lorry loaded with dynamite into a narrow thoroughfare in Jerusalem called Ben Yehuda Street and set it off, blowing arms and legs and heads off a hundred and twenty Jews who had been sleeping. This was terrorism, but if there were fanatical British Jew-haters who would do such a thing as this there were also Anglophobes among the Jews who had already been guilty of similar deeds.

It was more than this. It was more than the anti-Semitism of Bevin. It was something Ben-Gurion had not anticipated. He had been certain that the British, as upholders of the "democratic processes," would honor the decision of the United Nations, reached by a majority vote democratically taken, and would retire in good grace. Bevin had encouraged him to believe this by telling Parliament:

"I am not and His Majesty's government is not going to oppose the U.N.'s decision."

But Bevin then turned around and did exactly what he denied he would do.

"The British Government is in fact using every possible device to frustrate and nullify the U.N. decision," Ben-Gurion said angrily, in February, and of this he had proof.

London had said that until the mandate ended the British would maintain law and order. But all the instruments of death necessary for making war were given to the Palestinian Arabs, while they were taken from the Palestinian Jews whenever possible.

In Jerusalem one day British troops disarmed four Jews and then handed them over to well-armed Arabs, who mutilated, then murdered them.

Ben-Gurion accused London of encouraging the Arab states to move against the Jews by sending them ever increasing quantities of arms, and by opening the frontiers of Palestine to any Arabs who might like to come in, singly or en mass.

In Iraq there was a twenty-eight-man British military mission, and Iraq was getting ready to attack.

In Transjordan there was the Arab Legion, British-trained, British-armed, British-supported, at a cost of ten million dollars a year to British taxpayers. And Transjordan was prepared to march.

In Saudi Arabia forty-five British officers were helping with military plans that included action against the new Jewish state.

Egypt was receiving continuing shipments of aircraft, bombs, guns, tanks from Great Britain, for use against the Jews.

London upset the U.N. timetable by announcing she would terminate the mandate, whatever Lake Success said, on May 15.

A U.N. commission was to have come to Palestine to help Arabs and Jews set up their separate free states. Britain refused to permit it.

But it was not just British terrorists in Ben Yehuda Street and British political defectors in Whitehall.

In its insecurity the Mandatory Power had built great stone fortresses in scattered parts of Palestine. Except for a few structures in the cities, they were the most formidable buildings in Palestine. Teggert forts, they were called, after the Englishman who had conceived them. The Mandatory Power could have blown them up, or given them to the governing body of the state in which they would be located (Arab or Jewish as the case might be). It did neither. It gave fifty Teggert forts that lay within the perimeter of what was to be the Jewish state to the Arabs.

The United Nations had said Britain should evacuate a seaport and a large reception area in the center of the country by February 1 to permit the Jews to engage in extensive immigration. London refused to comply.

The British Treasury blocked all Palestine bank accounts and excluded the country from the sterling bloc.

British taxpayers had a substantial investment in Palestine: land, military equipment, buildings, stores of supplies, vehicles, equipment. Some of this tangible wealth was sold, generally to Arabs, at bargain prices. If a Jew obtained permission to purchase something, the sellers often found a technical difficulty that prevented delivery.

In the past the Mandatory Power had punished the Jewish community occasionally by suspending postal services for a brief period. Now, weeks before the end of the mandate, the entire cable, telegraph, and postal system was dismantled, cutting the 650,000 off from all communication with the outside world.

Ben-Gurion had hoped that the British might turn over to him and his colleagues at least the skeleton of the government they had built up during the past quarter century. It now became apparent that not a lawbook, a calendar pad, not the slightest accouterment of government would be left. Files that would have been of great value to anyone trying to organize a new government were burned by the British themselves in public bonfires.

It is not often in history that a state disintegrates while the world watches. Each day another branch of the Palestinian administration would stop functioning and become lifeless.

Ben-Gurion knew the weakness of Haganah. He knew, too, how few trustworthy friends the 650,000 had in the world. He knew that their several planes could fly only eighty miles an hour, that much of the underground ammunition would go in a straight line for only about twenty-five yards, that the Czech armament order had not yet arrived, that there were hardly any shells for the three-inch mortars, and that they had only 186 heavy machine guns in the entire country.

Jerusalem was another of Ben-Gurion's problems. He had been taught in his childhood the words of the Haggadah:

". . . next year in Jerusalem."

This love of Jerusalem was something few non-Jews could understand. To Christians, Bethlehem, Nazareth, and the shores of the Sea of Galilee were much more important than Jerusalem. Mecca was the Moslems' holy city. But the Jews had never allowed themselves to forget that the First and Second Temples stood in Jerusalem, and that in this city all Jewish history, Jewish sentiment, Jewish memories had centered. Millions of Jews through the centuries had shed their blood there.

To Ben-Gurion, Jerusalem had always been a symbol of Jewish continuity, the heart core of Jewish life, the eternal city of going home.

It should have been the hub of the new Jewish state, but at

Lake Success they had denied it to the Jews, partly in order to appease others. Their holy city was to be internationalized.

There were a hundred thousand Jews in Jerusalem completely surrounded by Arabs. Most were elderly. Few were of fighting age. Many were ill. The ultra-orthodox refused to do military service because it violated their religious beliefs. The Haganah commander had few trained fighters and fewer weapons. Convoys from Tel Aviv had to run a gantlet of death, for the road lay through villages of Arabs who had obtained an abundance of arms from some friendly source and would permit no Jew to pass. Jerusalem depended on water piped from distant places. The Arabs had cut the lines. Jerusalem normally bought its food from Arabs in the surrounding villages. That was impossible now. There was acute danger of famine.

Ben-Gurion was not what the world called a religious man. The external forms of religious observance were not important to him. Yet the love of Jerusalem was in every fiber of his being. So when a cold-minded military adviser suggested evacuating the city he resolutely shook his head.

"How will you supply it?"

"We will find a way!"

"How will you defend it?"

"I believe in miracles."

Hadassah Hospital, the greatest in the Middle East, built with money contributed by Jewish women in America, and the Hebrew University, with its hundreds of thousands of priceless books, were on Mount Scopus, within sight of the center of Jerusalem, but Palestinian Arabs controlled the road up the famous hill.

Three weeks before May 15 something happened on that road which left a deep hurt in the hearts of all six members of the Ben-Gurion family.

Seventy-seven professors, doctors, and nurses started up the hill in a convoy to visit the isolated institutions, for strictly non-military reasons. Officers of the Mandatory Government had given them an assurance that the road on this particular day was safe. They talked eagerly together and were happy that they were going to have a brief chance to set foot inside the hospital and the university buildings.

Part way up, Arab irregulars attacked the convoy.

British troops were in the neighborhood, and were informed of the trouble.

For six and a half hours the British maintained a never explained hands-off policy while the Arabs tortured and then massacred all seventy-seven.

One of the doctors was the fiancé of Ben-Gurion's younger daughter, Renana. They had been deeply in love.

Then, in the supercharged atmosphere of the period, Beigin's Irgun went wild. Without orders from Ben-Gurion, it mobilized several thousand shock troops and attacked Jaffa, the largest Arab community in Palestine. The British military came quickly to the rescue of the Arabs with tanks, artillery, planes, flame throwers. By the time the three-sided battle ended, a majority of the Arab population had fled to neighboring countries.

Ben-Gurion was annoyed because Haganah had an over-all plan and if each splinter group went its own self-determined way chaos might soon be at hand.

What happened at Deir Yassin was worse.

Convoys of food, water, medicine, and military supplies were being pushed through to Jerusalem. Often the lorries would be shot up by Arabs along the way and the drivers killed.

During a Haganah attempt to clear the Tel Aviv–Jerusalem road Irgun offered to be responsible for the Arab village of Deir Yassin. Before Irgun left the village, 254 Arab men, women, and children had been killed.

Ben-Gurion reacted with instinctive anger. That Jews could be guilty of such behavior shocked him, even if the excuses Irgun gave were true; even if done under the stress of war; even if done with provocation. He promptly sent a message of sympathy to King Abdullah of Transjordan, denying all responsibility.

Then the United States, after supporting partition, made a swing of 180 degrees and proposed a U.N. trusteeship for Palestine, an idea acceptable to no one.

There were those cautious ones within his own ranks, some even within Mapai and Histadruth, who now decided that because of developments this was no time to think about declaring a Jewish state. It might be more prudent to wait. Even Dr. Weizmann at one point took this view. Gradually, however, Ben-Gurion's determination won them over.

As the elected head of Palestine Jews, Ben-Gurion had the task of keeping up morale, trying to create unity among people whose great strength had always been their individualism, conducting the diplomatic campaign so that the U.N. would not suddenly give in to Washington and reverse itself, endeavoring to create good public relations around the world, spending hours each day with his military leaders planning the defense of this little country that existed so far only on paper, presiding over meetings of what was still properly called a "shadow" cabinet, seeking to chart a safe course between the ideals of the moderates and the extremists, helping organize a government machine to take over when the British left, preparing his people for the death and destruction he knew would certainly come, steeling them to the possibility of famine, to the probability of having to go for long periods without water, and to the certainty of air raids, artillery bombardments, a naval blockade, loss of settlements, and long casualty lists.

He had had his sixty-first birthday, and he grew tired more easily now, but this was no time to consider the body. It was to Paula's credit that he had energy enough to keep going. She insisted he eat nourishing food at least once a day, and when he paused to sleep she watched over him so that neither people nor noises would disturb him.

But Ben-Gurion saw little of his home, his wife, his daughters, or his books in these days.

Besides his other responsibilities, he had an agreement with a weekly magazine and a Hebrew daily newspaper to write political articles at regular intervals. Often he would write them slowly in longhand at two or three o'clock in the morning, propped up in bed after a hard day and a long evening of other work.

During the six months many things went wrong.

Three Messerschmitts arrived, but one crash-landed and the second cracked up in another accident.

Golda Myerson, one of the shadow government's key figures, suddenly suffered a slight heart attack.

Chief of Staff Dostrovsky became too ill to sit in an office or to come to staff meetings, so he had to do his part of planning the war from a *pension* in Haifa.

Yadin, who substituted for Dostrovsky, came every day for consultations with Ben-Gurion. Once he brought news of an exciting but non-military nature. His father had just had an experience no other archaeologist in the world could equal.

An Armenian antique dealer had sent a message to Dr. Sukenik (Yadin was the son's secret military name, which he later adopted officially) to come at once to the gateway of Military Zone B, Jerusalem. There he and the Armenian talked across rolls of barbed wire.

The Armenian had a piece of parchment, a sample of many scrolls that some Bedouin herdsmen had found when one of their goats wandered into a dark cavern, near the Dead Sea, and they went after it. The rolls of parchment had been in earthenware jars. The Bedouins took them to Bethlehem, where they now were. Would Dr. Sukenik care to buy them for his Hebrew University?

He consulted his son. Was it safe for him to go to Bethlehem in view of the current Arab uprising?

As a high-ranking member of the Haganah General Staff, Yadin said "no" to his father, but several days later Dr. Sukenik went anyway and brought back three scrolls that he had purchased for not much over a hundred dollars. (Several years later his son would buy four more in New York for a quarter of a million dollars.)

Ben-Gurion had his office in a house on Hayarkan Street, on the sea front in the heart of Tel Aviv.

Yadin was the most frequent visitor. He and Ben-Gurion spent hours poring over maps. Often it was necessary for the man with the fringe of white hair to make an irrevocable military decision. Sometimes, wanting to avoid a commitment immediately, he would suddenly switch the conversation to the matter of the scrolls.

"Does he know yet the significance?"

At such times Yadin, towering over his commander, would look into the older man's twinkling eyes and say:

"Ben-Gurion, I must have answers to *my* questions, *now!*"

Others came with problems about transportation, immigration, emergency water supplies, communications, secret food dumps, prisoner camps, the British, when should the next cabinet meeting be held, and please, his wife, Paula, was on the phone, and taxes—what about taxes after May 15, and how about passports, and where could they get their hands on printing presses and mimeograph machines—how could a government even come into existence without mimeograph machines?

One day the Jewish official who had been placed in charge of communications came and asked Ben-Gurion if he wouldn't, please, do something about a name for the new state. He wanted to order postage stamps, but how could he even consult with the artist who would make the design unless he knew the name by which the country would be called?

Ben-Gurion waved him away. There was no time for the luxury of discussion about such matters.

The first postage stamps bore only the words Doar Ivri (the Jewish Postal Service).

Ben-Gurion was much concerned about the public services. He told the shadow government:

"When the time comes, there will be enough men who will eagerly make themselves available for positions of importance in the government. What worries me is the public services— locomotive drivers to run our trains, operators to man our telephone exchanges—the hospitals."

At his suggestion an emergency committee of thirteen was appointed. Each man would prepare a plan for the reorganization of a certain number of government departments that would be put into effect the moment zero hour arrived.

But where was a new state overnight to get trained administrators, experienced public servants, organizers, price control experts, a ration board, men to head all the bureaus and departments?

Ben-Gurion knew that the Jews were now facing the great problem of all revolutionaries. During these years in Palestine, Jews had been teaching themselves to be rebels, underground soldiers, masters of subterfuge, propagandists, politicians. Such training would be of little use in setting up a bureau of taxation or figuring out what the controlled price of sugar ought to be.

One day the emergency committee met to discuss where the

immediate provisional center of government should be established. Jerusalem was out of the question. Haifa was discarded because the British said they might remain in the seaport for six months after the end of the mandate.

Natanya, on the sea coast between Tel Aviv and Haifa, was considered because it had been a British leave camp, with buildings containing seven hundred rooms.

Another plan was to scatter government departments over a wide area.

Ben-Gurion had an idea of his own. He nominated Kurnub, an abandoned Nabataean place in the heart of the Negev Desert, also known as Mamshit.

He forgot about everything else as he talked to his colleagues about Kurnub.

Once it had been a busy town on the caravan route across the desert. Men paused at Kurnub to rest themselves and their animals, and there had been a toll collector who demanded a fee from every caravan.

Later a Roman Byzantine citadel had stood there.

Ben-Gurion admitted rather sadly that it was now nothing but a forlorn place in the desert that many Palestinians had never heard about, desolate and deserted, but in the surrounding valleys signs could still be found of ancient agriculture and there were the remains of Byzantine dams, which proved that the soil had been rich and rainfall plentiful in winter.

Ben-Gurion was almost unanimously opposed by his colleagues, and so, being a good democrat, he sat back in his chair, half closed his eyes, and accepted defeat.

The place they finally chose was Sarona, a community of gabled stone farmhouses built by German Templars on the edge of Tel Aviv. The owners had been taken away by the British during World War II because of their Nazi sympathies. (The man to whom Hitler entrusted the entire program of exterminating the Jews of Europe was a German Templar born in Sarona.)

Sarona was renamed Hakirya (The City). One by one and in pairs men of the shadow government went out to inspect the houses and decide which government department would get which farmhouse, and whose secretaries and typists would occupy which kitchen, and whether the wine cellars would do as air raid shelters.

Desks and chairs and filing cabinets would have to be made and stored secretly somewhere in preparation for the Day.

Seven weeks before May 15, Ben-Gurion and his colleagues issued a statement. A Jewish state would be declared. It would come into existence the moment the mandate ended. The hand of peace was extended to Arabs within and without the country. The Jews still wanted to co-operate with the British to make the withdrawal as orderly as possible.

It had taken weeks of discussion and hours of pleading by Ben-Gurion to get agreement on that statement. There were still those who were frightened by the situation, nervous over the price that might have to be paid, not quite sure that Ben-Gurion was a prophet with clear vision.

In those last days Ben-Gurion was everywhere, visiting underground munitions factories, making a reckless trip to Jerusalem in the last convoy that got through safely, inspecting front-line positions, passing along words of encouragement, bolstering morale.

He issued orders to Haganah's high command that if real war should suddenly come they must plan their campaign in a way to keep Jewish casualties to the minimum.

At the same time he overruled his military advisers on a major tactical point. They wanted to abandon a certain number of Jewish settlements that they considered indefensible and consolidate Jewish forces. On a map it looked sensible, but Ben-Gurion said:

"We shall fight for each Jewish spot, foot by foot, house by house."

This Churchillian stubbornness antagonized a few realists, and to some seemed in conflict with his hatred of casualties, but it inspired more confidence than resentment.

As the hour of decision drew near, with tension greater than it had ever been before in this land of taut nerves, a policeman appeared one rainy gray morning at a chemical laboratory in Tel Aviv with a pat of butter on a glass plate.

The receptionist looked at the butter and then at the policeman.

"It's to be analyzed," he said.

A chemist was called.

"Analyzed for what?" he asked.

"For Paula Ben-Gurion," the policeman replied.

The chemist smiled and telephoned Mrs. Ben-Gurion.

"I want it analyzed because I think the place it came from is cheating my David and sending him poor-quality butter. He's a busy man these days, and he must have the best food there is, to keep him going. You analyze it and tell me the truth."

There was good news and bad news in the last days of the mandate.

The United States ordered an embargo on the sale and shipment of war material to any Middle Eastern country. Because the Arabs already had one very good source of free war material they were little affected, but this was bad news for the Sonneborn Institute.

Then Secretary of State Marshall sent a message suggesting that it would be wise for Ben-Gurion to reconsider his decision to declare a Jewish state, despite U.N. permission. It was even reported that President Truman's private plane, the Sacred Cow, would be placed at the disposition of the Jewish representatives in Washington if they would fly home and try to persuade Ben-Gurion to change his mind.

The one piece of good news was that during the darkness of a certain night a Haganah ship slipped through the British blockade. It carried the first consignment of weapons purchased in Czechoslovakia, which were brought ashore and hidden quickly in distribution centers.

A short time before May 15, Ben-Gurion addressed a closed meeting of Zionist leaders. Eight months earlier he had tried to tell them the truth, but most of them had remained unconvinced. This time he used strong words.

"Not for over eighteen hundred years have we been so grimly circumstanced."

He said the Jewish community would have to "mortgage every scrap of its economy, its manpower and transport, its science and techniques, its financial resources and moral strength, its press and public life."

Even then he could not guarantee them anything.

"The determinants of victory are logistics, money, morale, and intellect."

His peroration was:

"Flouting the experts, I dare believe in victory."

At the last minute Irgun and Haganah signed an agreement that they would co-operate fully in all military matters.

Now, at last, moderates and extremists, anti-Zionists and pro-Zionists, the ultra-religious and those who observed no religious practices at all, city dwellers and kibbutzniks, European Jews and Oriental Jews, the left and the right, sabras and those who had come off the last boat were as united as such diverse people ever had been.

Jewish Palestine was ready. Not properly prepared. Not satisfactorily armed. But ready. And it had a leader.

Dr. Chaim Weizmann, seriously ill, had been in New York all this time. Jabotinsky and Katzenelson were dead. Others had vacillated. One man alone had kept his head clear, his hand steady, and his eye always on the spot on the horizon that had sometimes seemed like a mirage.

During these six months Ben-Gurion had grown in stature from a shrewd statesman to a world figure, showing an ancient people the way back to their lost homeland.

But still he had to prove that he had the ineluctable qualities of the shepherd boy after whom he had been named.

CHAPTER THIRTEEN

THE BRITISH said they would relinquish their mandate and start leaving at midnight on May 14-15, which would be Friday-Saturday.

On Wednesday morning of that week Ben-Gurion called the thirty-seven-man National Council into session.

The most important question was whether a majority still agreed that this was the time to declare the state. Ben-Gurion wanted no accusation, later, that he had dictated the decision or shouted down the opposition.

But first he had news for them. It was about Gush Etzion, a

group of four settlements fourteen miles south of Jerusalem completely surrounded by Arab villages. Not long ago thirty-five Haganah men had been killed on the way back from taking supplies to the besieged settlers. Since then airplanes had been used to drop food to them. But Arab irregulars had been harassing the settlements continuously.

Ben-Gurion's news was that two columns of the Arab Legion, under British command, had opened a large-scale assault on Gush Etzion, though the mandate had not yet expired.

There was stunned silence.

Then Moshe Shertok, who had returned only a few hours earlier from the United States, told of the insistence in Washington that a state not be proclaimed at this time.

Golda Myerson reported on her visit to King Abdullah. Once they had held a secret conference inside Palestine, but this time she had to go to him; to Amman. Very surreptitiously, disguised as an Arab woman. The King had been personally friendly, but nervous and depressed.

"Why are you Jews in such a hurry to proclaim a state?" he asked.

"Would you call waiting two thousand years hasty?" she replied.

He was against any division of Palestine. He wanted it all, and did not deny that he intended using the Arab Legion to get it.

Then Yadin told them that intelligence reports indicated the armies of all the neighboring Arab states were moving rapidly toward the frontiers. An invasion from all directions could be expected on Saturday, as well as air raids on Tel Aviv. In spite of this, after Ben-Gurion spoke, they voted overwhelmingly to proceed with their plan of independence.

The next question was exactly when the state should be proclaimed.

Technically, as one legal expert pointed out, it could not be done until midnight of Friday-Saturday. But at sundown on Friday, Shabbat would begin and after that Orthodox members of the Council would not be able to sign their names, travel by automobile, or violate any of the other rules.

Orthodox members consulted the charts carried by all Jews who wish to be exact in their religious observances and figured out that if they started the proclamation ceremony promptly at 4 P.M. on Friday, it would be finished well before the official time of the setting of the sun.

After the Council adjourned, a meeting was held of the future Cabinet, which first considered a tentative declaration of independence drafted by four lawyers. One member objected:

"How can we declare the independence of a state without telling what its boundaries are? First you must define the Jewish state—say where it is—how far it goes—where it begins and ends."

Ben-Gurion silenced him simply by referring to the Declaration of Independence of the United States of America, which makes no mention of boundaries.

The last matter on the agenda was choosing a name. Many had assumed that the new state would be called Judea (Yehuda in Hebrew). But since Judea technically is only that area immediately surrounding Jerusalem, "Judea" would not do.

"Zion" was then debated and discarded because it is the name of a hill overlooking the Old City of Jerusalem.

" 'Ever,' " proposed one of the ministers, but no one else liked this suggestion, even though it was the root word of *ivri*, meaning Hebrew.

"Eretz Israel" was discussed for a long time. This was what the Jewish homeland had always been called, but technically it meant all of ancient Palestine, and its use might lead to accusations of irredentism.

"I suggest 'Israel.' "

It was Ben-Gurion himself who had spoken.

The word sounded strange at first. They kept saying it, half aloud, trying it out.

"Israel."

"The Israel Government."

"The navy of Israel."

"Israel Consul."

"An Israel citizen."

(Israel philologists say that the only correct use of the word "Israeli" is to indicate a citizen of Israel, that the adjective is "Israel.")

Ben-Gurion suggested they take a vote. He and six others were for it; three were against it; the other four were absent.

Thus a state was named by the man who had worked harder than any other to bring it into existence, with the approval of half his Cabinet.

It was after midnight when they adjourned. Zeev Sharef, the future chief of the government secretariat, said to the stenographers:

"I know you have had a hard day, but I must ask you to transcribe your notes before you leave."

When they finally finished, Sharef took the completed transcript with him. Years later he explained:

"I knew that Tel Aviv would probably be bombed on Saturday, and I thought that if the government leaders and the stenographers and all the rest of us happened to be killed the world would never know the story of how Israel was created, so I buried the records of that night's session, and also of the meetings on Friday, in the deepest cellar in Tel Aviv until the danger was over."

Ben-Gurion devoted Thursday almost exclusively to military affairs.

He was at G.H.Q. until 4 A.M. Friday.

On Thursday invitations went out to about two hundred Palestinian Jews to present themselves at the Municipal Museum on Rothschild Boulevard half an hour in advance of 4 P.M. on Friday, May 14. They were asked to wear "festive dark clothes," and were severely cautioned to keep both time and place a secret. If the Egyptians were able to land bombs on the museum at the right moment, Israel might be born with its entire leadership dead.

The most important day in the life of David Ben-Gurion began at 7 A.M., when he left his bed, ran his hands through his white hair, dressed, greeted Paula with a few affectionate words of Hebrew, and then sat down in the kitchen to have his coffee while he went through the Hebrew morning newspapers and the English-language Palestine *Post*.

"Have there been any telephone calls about Gush Etzion?" he asked.

"No. What's happened there?"

He told her that during the night news came of the fall of the principal settlement. A few hundred poorly armed settlers had held out as long as possible against thousands of well-equipped legionnaires. The slaughter had been great.

"There was a call that you must be at headquarters for another meeting at nine."

Outside the house a military jeep was waiting.

At headquarters a dozen officers were already bending over maps.

He listened more than he spoke. There was a frown on his face most of the time. He kept opening and closing his fists nervously.

Messengers came and went. Some of the reports they brought from field commanders were encouraging; some were not.

At Latrun enemy artillery had bombarded Jewish positions all night. The only piece of artillery in Haganah hands had been captured.

Suddenly there was the noise of a plane. Ben-Gurion ran to the window. It was flying low, heading north.

"British," someone reported.

"It looks as if the British are really going," someone else said.

Yadin suggested that Ben-Gurion issue a general order calling on the population to prepare air raid shelters, dig trenches, help build roadblocks.

The Old Man went to work.

At noon a jeep drove him home. Paula opened the door.

"What news?"

He told her briefly.

Shertok was waiting in the kitchen. As Ben-Gurion ate the vegetables Paula had prepared for him, the expert on foreign affairs volunteered his opinion that the opposition of Secretary of State Marshall to the declaration of a Jewish state would not extend to military intervention.

Amos Ben-Gurion arrived with his wife and child just as Shertok was leaving. He was now a regimental commander. With his father he discussed the possibility of air raids the next day.

"Why are there no shelters in Tel Aviv?" the father asked. "I have been warning for a long time about the danger of raids, but no one listens. Everyone thinks my predictions are too black."

His English daughter-in-law asked:

"Is it true that we have only one piece of artillery?"

Ben-Gurion smiled at her use of "we." She was no longer a stranger among alien people.

"We expect artillery any day, and if it does not come we will steal artillery from the enemy."

He went to his room to change his clothes, putting on a dark blue business suit, a white shirt, dark shoes and socks, a dark silk tie. Suddenly he called to Paula:

"Has anyone done anything about Rabbi Fishman?"

Rabbi Fishman, who had been imprisoned at Latrun and had been connected for many decades with the fight for a state, lived in Jerusalem, now a city besieged. No one from there would be able to get to the afternoon ceremony, but Ben-Gurion wanted his old friend in the hall. A Primus (one of the Piper Cubs) must be sent for him.

Ben-Gurion was concerned with small details. Would the meeting place be properly guarded? Would the secret be kept? What about chairs, flags, a picture of Herzl?

He telephoned to Sharef, who said he had found, hidden in a cellar, a large and impressive picture of the author of *The Jewish State* and a bank had lent them a mimeograph machine for the day so that copies of the proclamation and the first resolutions of the new government could be made for the press.

Then a messenger came from headquarters. Chief of Staff Dostrovsky had just been taken to a hospital in Haifa. Yadin would now have to assume all his responsibilities. And a munitions ship that had been approaching Tel Aviv had been caught by a British destroyer. It was now being towed to Haifa.

At one o'clock he convened the National Council. The chief interest at the meeting was the Cabinet's decision about a name.

"What is it to be called?" someone shouted.

"Israel!" Ben-Gurion replied, bellowing the word proudly.

There was a babel of comment.

Ben-Gurion pounded the gavel.

Shertok and Rabbi Fishman defended "Israel," and in a few moments the opposition melted away.

Then the tentative draft of the independence resolution was read. A member of Mapam, the political party with Soviet leanings, objected to the use of the word "God" in the last sentence, beginning: "With trust in God, we set out hands . . ."

He argued that this was offensive to freethinkers and that it had better be settled at the start whether Israel was to be a theocratic state.

Ben-Gurion looked at his watch. In less than three hours the public ceremony would begin. If a religious argument got started it might last for days.

Someone suggested that "Almighty" be substituted for "God." The concession satisfied the Mapam freethinker, and they went on to discuss the rest of the declaration.

Then Ben-Gurion put the entire proclamation to a vote. It passed with only a few "nos."

"Now I will put it to a vote again," Ben-Gurion said, "in the hope that for the sake of history it will be passed unanimously." It was.

On the way from the room Rabbi Fishman stopped Ben-Gurion and asked:

"Are we going to war with the Arabs?"

Ben-Gurion nodded.

"And do we have anything to use in the air against them except that broken-down cart?"

Then the aged rabbi told of his trip from Jerusalem.

"A man came to me and said he had orders from the future Prime Minister that I was to come with him. He took me to a field where there was a broken-down old cart."

The rabbi never referred to the Piper as a plane. He insisted it was a broken-down old cart. The pilot tied him in with ropes, and they "flew in twisting ways, sometimes north and sometimes south, one way and then another." He was sure it took "a few hours" to go the forty air miles.

He kept shaking his head and saying:

"I don't see how we can beat the Arabs with flying carts like that."

Ben-Gurion went home to rest for an hour. As he drove through the city, the streets were crowded. People stood in clusters, some with newspapers reading about the battle that had begun at Bab-el-Wad, not thirty miles away, for control of the road to Jerusalem. The cafés were packed. Trucks loaded with young soldiers, men and girls mixed, raced through the streets on their way to frontiers.

Orange juice stands and boys selling flags were doing a lively business.

When Ben-Gurion arrived home, Paula gave him two more messages. The munitions ship had reached Haifa, but the British had not searched it yet and apparently were unaware of the nature of the cargo, and there was no news at all of the airplanes that had been ordered weeks ago from a certain Latin-American country.

A few seconds before 4 P.M. a fleet of shining new American automobiles (rented for the occasion) drew up in front of the museum.

The secret had not been very well kept by the two hundred invited guests, for the street was crowded with people. Many carried blue-and-white flags emblazoned with the star of David. They cheered as each dignitary stepped from a car.

Inside, the paintings that normally filled the building had been removed. Herzl's portrait hung over the dais, where the cabinet members took their places. Before them were members of the National Council, the two chief rabbis of Tel Aviv in tall silk hats, the guests, and the largest assemblage of reporters and photographers ever seen in any one place in this part of the world.

Three of the left-wing council members had come without ties, but otherwise everyone was dressed for a formal and festive occasion.

Ben-Gurion was the last of the officials to enter. He gave an impression of strength and dignity. The reporters started to scribble in their notebooks.

Otte Wallisch, a Tel Aviv artist, rushed in with the independence proclamation. He had finished the decoration and embellishment of the piece of parchment, but not the words, which would have to be put in later.

Then a man in khaki pushed through the crowd and beckoned to a short, stocky figure. Israel Galili, Haganah commander, followed the soldier from the room. They whispered together in a corridor, and then Galili wrote something on a piece of paper and handed it up to Ben-Gurion, who read it and smiled.

Not until the ceremony was over were the others told what the message said. There had been an impressive victory in western Galilee, and most of that part of Israel was now securely under Haganah.

The Tel Aviv Philharmonic Orchestra in an adjoining room played "Hatikvah," which would automatically become the Israel national anthem.

"The Land of Israel was the birthplace of the Jewish people. Here . . ."

The hand in which Ben-Gurion was holding the text trembled. He obviously was trying to keep his voice from sounding melodramatic.

The declaration started thousands of years ago, at the dawn of Jewish history, and moved forward, sentence by sharp sentence, through the centuries, to Herzl's time, Balfour's time, Hitler's time, and finally to the time of Ben-Gurion and the living prophets.

Israel was to be a state based on liberty, justice, and peace. There would be social and political equality, without regard to race, sex, or religion. Freedom of conscience and freedom to worship as one pleased would be guaranteed. Israel would cooperate with the United Nations and uphold the principles of its charter. Christian and Moslem holy places would be protected. The hand of peace was held out to Arabs everywhere.

Ben-Gurion's voice grew stronger. Some of the spectators began to choke up with emotion. The way had been so long; the price had already been so great.

". . . on this Sabbath eve, the fifth of Iyar, 5,708, the fourteenth day of May, 1948."

It had taken seventeen minutes for Ben-Gurion to read the proclamation.

Now he announced the new state's first decrees. The British White Paper of 1939 was hereby annulled. So were all laws restricting Jewish immigration or purchase of land. Otherwise all Mandatory laws were declared valid and in effect until the time came to revise them or establish an all-Jewish legal code.

The founders of this newest state put their signatures to the piece of parchment, which had a typewritten text of the declaration pinned to it.

At exactly 4:37½ P.M., Ben-Gurion rapped his gavel and said dramatically:

"I hereby declare this meeting adjourned. The State of Israel has come into being."

As he walked proudly from the room with head erect, jaw jutting forward, he passed a British reporter he knew and whispered:

"You see, we did it!"

The ceremony was broadcast, and soon crowds gathered along Rothschild Boulevard, Ben Yehuda Street, Allenby Road, Hayarkon Street on the sea front, in the cafés and popular restaurants.

At home Ben-Gurion said to Paula:

"I feel like the bereaved among the rejoicers."

He was thinking of the battle fronts.

He changed immediately into khaki and went by jeep to G.H.Q.

"How is the situation in the capital?"

It was the first time any of his associates had ever heard him use the word "capital" about Jerusalem.

During the evening he joined with four other labor members of the government in sending a cable to Dr. Chaim Weizmann, who was ill in New York. In it they extended their greetings to the man "who has done more than any other" for the creation of Israel.

That night Ben-Gurion also talked by telephone with his daughter Geula. Not one of his children had been at the ceremony. Amos was with his military unit. Renana was in besieged Jerusalem, a student at the university, and Geula had been unable to leave her three-month-old baby. Ben-Gurion described the proceedings for his oldest child. Later she told friends:

"He seemed happier than I had ever known him to be."

About the time he was going to sleep, a message from America was received at the Haganah secret radio station, located in a private residential building not far from G.H.Q.

Yaacov Yanai, head of the Haganah Signal Corps, who was working the night shift, pulled the message out of the air by accident. It was a request for Ben-Gurion to do a broadcast to the United States.

Yanai called one of Ben-Gurion's aides.

"It's out of the question. The Old Man has gone to bed."

Several hours later—it was then only early evening in New York—the Haganah station picked up a news broadcast telling of Truman's recognition of Israel.

Instead of going through "channels" this time Yanai drove directly to the Ben-Gurion house in Keren Kayemet Boulevard and banged on the front door.

It was an angry Paula Ben-Gurion who finally answered.

"What do you mean by making such a noise? You will wake up Ben-Gurion. He is——"

Yanai explained what had happened.

She said it made no difference; no one was going to bother her husband.

Yanai pleaded, and at last was admitted to the house and shown to Ben-Gurion's room.

The white-haired man sat up in bed and blinked as Yanai excitedly told him the news.

"I don't believe it!" the Old Man said at first.

But as he said it he was getting out of bed.

"If it is true, I must broadcast to America."

He put his coat on over his pajamas, while Paula found his socks and shoes.

In the car on the way to the station he was quiet, composing what he wanted to say.

It was 5:20 A.M. Tel Aviv time (10:20 P.M. the night before in New York) when Prime Minister Ben-Gurion began his first broadcast to the United States.

Five minutes later, while he was still on the air, the walls of the building suddenly trembled and the air was filled with a great noise. The microphone shook. Lights flashed on the engineer's control panel.

Ben-Gurion paused for an instant and then, as calmly as a professional war correspondent, interrupted his own train of thought by saying:

"The noise you just heard came from bombs dropped by enemy aircraft which are flying over our heads."

By the time the talk was finished, Yanai had learned by telephone that Egyptian planes had bombed Dov Airport, the secret Haganah landing strip.

"I must go there and inspect the damage," Ben-Gurion declared.

They were just getting into Yanai's car when Ben-Gurion saw an automobile approaching from the direction of G.H.Q. He flagged it down. In it was Yadin.

"Are you going to the airport?"

"Yes."

"I'll go, too."

"No!"

Yadin insisted like a stern parent that his Commander-in-Chief should get some rest in preparation for the strain of the days ahead. Then Yadin drove off alone.

Half an hour after the first raid another flight of Egyptian planes came over Tel Aviv and headed again for Dov airfield. As they swooped low, Yadin and the other Haganah men who were there threw themselves onto the ground and held their breath.

After the planes had gone and Yadin was getting to his feet, he saw a man with a fringe of white hair coming toward him.

"Ben-Gurion!"

The Old Man grinned.

"How did you get here?"

Like a naughty schoolboy, the supreme commander explained that after Yanai left him at his door he commanded one of the guards on duty in front of his house to drive him to the airport. He had arrived just at the right moment.

By now it was time to begin the day's appointments, so he asked to be driven to the waterfront. The first immigrants to set foot on the soil of a free and independent Jewish state in nearly two millennia were being brought ashore from a transport ship. It was fitting that they should be greeted by the Prime Minister of the new nation, even if under his overcoat he wore pajamas.

When Ben-Gurion finally reached home, Paula had his breakfast ready. She also had a few messages.

His old friend Joseph Baratz had sent him an urgent appeal for guns to defend the kibbutz of Degania.

The munitions ship the British seized had now been released and was on its way back to Tel Aviv.

Ben-Gurion telephoned Geula. He had thought of her when he heard the bombs drop. Were she and the baby all right? Did they have a good shelter to go to?

"Give my love to the children."

Then Yadin arrived, looking distraught.

"The Egyptian Army has crossed the frontier and is bombarding our settlements."

"We expected it," Ben-Gurion replied.

"The Arab Legion is moving, too. The Syrian Army as well."

"I had better go to headquarters with you."

Yadin nodded.

The Old Man went upstairs to change into battle dress.

Yadin waited.

Paula began washing the dishes.

CHAPTER FOURTEEN

FROM the moment the first Egyptian bombs fell on Dov airfield until a cease-fire was arranged twenty-seven days later, Prime Minister Ben-Gurion concerned himself with almost nothing but war. Paula saw little of him. He would sometimes come home for a few hours' sleep, but there were nights when he used a cot at G.H.Q. to get what little rest he felt was essential.

Soon after the state was declared, Zeev Sharef approached him with some urgent questions about the organization of new government departments.

"You mustn't bother me with these things," Ben-Gurion said, waving his hand in annoyance.

"But we must organize a civil service——"

"I am not interested in such matters at this time," Ben-Gurion said tartly.

Sharef lost his temper.

"Then you are not a Prime Minister!"

Instead of getting angry the Prime Minister replied:

"You are right. I am not. I am only the commander of the

Army. Nothing else matters just now but winning the war. Bother me with these other things later."

For fifty years he had had a single, all-consuming desire—to help create a Jewish state. Now that the goal had been reached, he had a new one: to try to live up to his given name—to try to be the modern David who would help bring down the Arab Goliath. And it *was* a Goliath. On that Sabbath day in May the armies of Egypt, Lebanon, Syria, Transjordan, and Iraq had all swarmed across the borders. The young people of Haganah had held them, at some places. But the Goliath was still threateningly there, with at least one foot on Israel soil.

Ben-Gurion took time out from war for a gracious gesture. Forty-eight hours after the declaration of the state he called the Provisional Council into session to pay tribute to the man who had been almost forgotten in the fast rush of history.

It was Ben-Gurion's idea that Dr. Chaim Weizmann be unanimously elected President of the Provisional Government of Israel, but he knew it would probably mean more to the ailing chemist in New York if the motion were made by Dr. Felix Rosenblueth, the Minister of Justice, who had been Dr. Weizmann's intimate friend since World War I.

In his seconding speech Ben-Gurion did not conceal the many differences that had divided them in recent years, yet he said:

"I doubt whether the presidency is necessary for Dr. Weizmann, but the presidency of Dr. Weizmann is a moral necessity for the State of Israel."

As soon as the cable went off to Dr. Weizmann, Ben-Gurion turned back to war.

One night a messenger came running into G.H.Q. with an envelope of captured documents. A translator read them out in Hebrew. One gave a timetable. Haifa was to have fallen on May 20, Tel Aviv and Jerusalem five days later. On May 25, King Abdullah was to have entered the Holy City and been crowned king of all that his troops surveyed.

As Ben-Gurion listened he opened and closed his fists.

Jerusalem was another great crisis in Ben-Gurion's life. The United Nations said it was to be an international city. He had accepted that verdict. This apparently was the price he and his people would have to pay for a state.

But when the Arabs attacked and tried to make Jerusalem theirs alone and not a finger was lifted by anyone to stop it, he felt he was no longer obligated to respect the pieces of paper that others had torn up. He decided Jerusalem must be defended and made part of Israel, despite the Arabs, the British, the United Nations.

But Jerusalem was encircled, besieged, cut off from Israel. The problem was to clear a corridor. He kept insisting that the Arab Legion be met head on at Latrun, where it dominated the Tel Aviv–Jerusalem road.

It was to satisfy him that the 7th Armored Brigade was formed and thrown into battle. It was neither armored nor a full brigade. Many of the men had been in the Army only a few days. Some had been in the country only a few weeks. They spoke eight languages. Many understood no Hebrew. Three days after they were brought together in one unit they were started off for Latrun. The discovery that they had no water containers forced a twenty-four-hour postponement.

Yadin was convinced it was a mistake. He argued with Ben-Gurion until two o'clock in the morning, and at one point pounded the table so violently with his fist that several glasses crashed to the floor.

Ben-Gurion insisted that the brigade commander be called in. "The entire fate of Jerusalem rests with you," he told the young man. "Do you think you can take Latrun?"

"We will carry out any orders you give us," came the reply.

Ben-Gurion was thinking hard. There was talk of a cease-fire. This was like a game of musical chairs. When the music stopped —when the U.N. forced an armistice—the final boundaries of Israel might be just where the lines were when the shooting suddenly ended. If the road to Jerusalem had not been opened by then, all chance of claiming even part of the Holy City might be lost—forever.

So the 7th Armored Brigade went forward by buses to within five miles of Latrun and prepared for the attack. It was four hours behind the revised schedule.

Ben-Gurion's General Staff was angry with him by now. Yadin went to the front and sent back a telegraph message:

"I beg you to order a delay of twenty-four hours."

The reply he received was brief:
"No."

'So the 7th Armored Brigade attacked that night, suffered eight hundred casualties, and was forced to retire.

The next night Ben-Gurion ordered the 7th to try again. Another failure.

It was not stubbornness. It was Jerusalem. It was his knowledge of history. It was his love of the Bible. It was also the messages with which Dov Joseph, military governor of the Holy City, was besieging him.

"Jerusalem is starving . . ."

Yadin finally brought in Yigal Allon, the best field commander the Army had, to help mount a third attack, which also failed.

Latrun was never captured, and it is still in Arab hands, but as a result of Ben-Gurion's obsession part of Jerusalem is today in Israel, for the Arab Legion was forced to divert men and guns from the Holy City, and while military eyes were on Latrun hundreds of Jewish men and girls set to work on a path running parallel with the Latrun–Jerusalem road that had been used for centuries by donkeys and goats. They widened it and linked it up at either end with the main road. They worked in the blackness of night to avoid detection, under the guns of the Arab Legion. They made a six-mile road over the granite hills, laboring mostly with their bare hands. They called it the Burma Road, and soon heavily loaded lorries, herds of cattle, and pack mules were moving in an almost endless line—and hundreds of Tel Aviv civilians with sacks of flour on their backs—helping to lift the siege of an ancient city.

Because of Ben-Gurion's militarily unsound obsession Jerusalem was thus connected by a corridor with what the U.N. said should be Israel. '

In those first twenty-seven days of war Ben-Gurion's Anglophobia was intensified.

"We must now re-establish touch with the world," Ben-Gurion told his Cabinet, "for the Mandatory Power was so evilly disposed that it made known to the Universal Postal Union that after May 15, Palestine would be sponged from the map."

The case of Sarafand further embittered him. Ten miles southeast of Tel Aviv during World War II the British had established their largest Palestinian military installation. Even before the ending of the mandate was announced, the Jewish Agency made an offer for the land, buildings, and equipment. A six-figure price was finally agreed upon. But at the last minute the Colonial Office in London vetoed the transaction, with no reason given. Thereupon Sarafand was presented to the Arabs as a gift—free.

It was with satisfaction one night in May that Ben-Gurion read a report at G.H.Q. that said:

SARAFAND TAKEN

"How many Jewish lives did it cost?"

No one knew the exact number.

One week after independence Ben-Gurion sent an S O S to Marcus Sieff, a young Englishman who had had a brilliant military career in the Middle East during World War II, asking him to take three or four months' leave from his business affairs in London to help reorganize the Quartermaster Corps.

Sieff was given an office near Ben-Gurion's room at G.H.Q., and they conferred almost every day on military matters. As they talked, the Commander-in-Chief often indicated his admiration of British ways.

He frequently went down the hall to Sieff's office to ask about the British method of taxation, the British economic system, or "How is it that a Tory government and the British trade union movement can get along as well as they do?"

Although Israel had been recognized by the United States, the Soviet Union, and many lesser nations, London addressed diplomatic messages to "the Jewish authorities in Tel Aviv," refusing, along with the Arabs, even to use the name of the state. The Israel post office marked the letters, "No one of that name and address known," and returned them.

Yet Ben-Gurion said one day to Sieff:

"I consider Great Britain the most highly civilized nation in the world."

Sieff's first military survey covered fifteen closely typed pages. Ben-Gurion took it home from headquarters late one night. He brought it back early the next morning. Apparently he had taken it to bed and spent hours studying it, for he knew every detail.

"You are very critical, Marcus."

"Yes," the younger man replied. "I know I am."

"You are critical of some of my General Staff."

"I know."

"Also of the Commander-in-Chief."

"Yes."

"You know, of course, that I am Commander-in-Chief?"

"I do, sir."

The white-haired man leaned back in his chair and spoke almost wistfully.

"Marcus, I've been a man of peace for almost sixty-two years. That is a long time. You have got to let me make some mistakes during my first few months of war."

One day Sieff told the Commander-in-Chief that some cargo ships should do their unloading in Tel Aviv Harbor, to establish an international precedent.

"But there is no law by which I can command the ships that are now unloading at Haifa to come to Tel Aviv," Ben-Gurion replied.

Young Sieff hesitated a moment, and then said:

"Winston Churchill would have found a way to do it."

Ben-Gurion blinked as if hit between the eyes. Then he reached for his telephone, put in a call to David Landman, chief of the Haifa Port Authority, and said:

"Look, I want four cargo ships that are unloading now in Haifa down here in Tel Aviv by tomorrow."

As the man at the other end began to explain why it was impossible, Ben-Gurion hung up.

The four ships arrived the next day.

Sieff was forced to make several quick trips back to London. Each time he went, Ben-Gurion would say:

"Marcus, before you go, let me give you the titles of some new books I want you to bring back for me."

When Sieff would ask Ben-Gurion how he knew what new books were coming out, in the middle of a war, with Israel cut off as she was, the Commander-in-Chief would smile like a "Pickwickian cherub" and say nothing.

The first cease-fire came into effect at the end of the twenty-seventh day of fighting. It was arranged by Count Folke Bernadotte. Several weeks earlier Bernadotte and Ben-Gurion had met for the first time at G.H.Q. Sharett (who had by now Hebraized his name from Shertok) was present. Also Dr. Ralph Bunche, Bernadotte's American Negro assistant.

The tall, blond member of the Swedish royal family, cultured and self-possessed, and the short, tough Jewish bulldog did not instantly appeal to each other.

Ben-Gurion eyed his visitor suspiciously.

"I have come only to discuss a truce proposal," Bernadotte said in English with a heavy Scandinavian accent. "I cannot deal with the whole problem of the future of Palestine."

There was something about the way he said it that antagonized Ben-Gurion.

On his part, Bernadotte decided that the Israel leader was showing "a very bitter spirit."

"Twice my government has agreed to an unconditional truce," Ben-Gurion declared. "The Arabs have refused. In spite of that, the Security Council has applied no sanctions against the Arabs."

They argued over many technicalities. Then Ben-Gurion said:

"If there is a truce, Jews now separated from their families in Jerusalem must be permitted to be reunited with them."

When Bernadotte made no reply, Ben-Gurion went on:

"My own daughter Renana is in Jerusalem. I would like to see her. I have not seen her for a long time."

Bernadotte quickly answered:

"Your official position as Commander-in-Chief will place obstacles in the way of such a visit."

The argument went on for a long time. At last the mediator looked at his watch and said he must leave; he had an appointment to attend a concert in Tel Aviv.

It was during the truce which was finally arranged that Ben-Gurion had to face his next major crisis.

The truce had been in effect nine days when a ship called the *Altalena* approached the shores of Israel. Many people knew about her already.

She had been a decommissioned LST, bought for seventy-five thousand dollars in Brooklyn by the American League for a Free Palestine, headed by Playwright Ben Hecht, which had enlisted the support of hundreds of prominent Americans, many non-Jews, who wanted to help Israel in some tangible way, not all of them aware that the league was the fund-raising American front for Irgun.

At Port-de-Bouc, France, the *Altalena* had taken on five hundred tons of arms, ammunition, and other military equipment for which the American League had paid four million dollars, and had started for Israel. Part way she received an order by radio to turn back because a truce had been signed. A second order countermanded the first. A third told her to put in at Kfar Vitkin, up the coast twenty-four miles from Tel Aviv.

Many people knew of the *Altalena's* approach.

Count Bernadotte and his U.N. trucemakers knew of it because they had received a full report from Port-de-Bouc on what had been taken aboard the ship and when she had sailed.

Ben-Gurion's Deputy Minister of Defense, Israel Galili, knew of it, for he and Beigin, the Irgun leader, had held several conferences about what should be done with the arms.

Several weeks before the mandate ended, Irgun had signed an agreement to submit to Haganah discipline and serve under Haganah leadership. Ben-Gurion's first order after independence had abolished private armies and established one sea, land, and air force under government control. Twenty days ago Irgun had agreed to end all independent activities aimed at obtaining arms and military equipment.

Galili insisted that the *Altalena* cargo be turned over to the government. Beigin said Irgun supporters had bought and paid for it, that the ship was Irgun property, manned by Irgun followers, and that the weapons would be doled out by him and by him alone.

Finally Beigin offered to compromise. He would send 20 per cent of the cargo to Irgun in Jerusalem, then equip the six Irgun battalions serving in the government army with what they needed, and turn over the balance to Galili.

Galili, on Ben-Gurion's orders, rejected the offer.

The debating continued right up to the hour the *Altalena* approached Kfar Vitkin.

While most of the eight hundred German refugees taken aboard in France were being put ashore, ultimatums were flying back and forth.

Ben-Gurion at G.H.Q. said:

"This is a frightful threat to the state, and may set off the fuse of a disastrous civil war."

Some of the military men at headquarters who knew how badly arms were needed tried to figure out a compromise. But Ben-Gurion was firm.

"No state can countenance private citizens or organizations importing . . . wholesale consignments of rifles and machine guns . . ."

So word was sent to Kfar Vitkin that the *Altalena* was to be handed over to the government.

By this time almost a fifth of the cargo had been put ashore. Irgun men were deserting their military units on several fronts to help with the unloading. The regular army was standing by for orders, puzzled by the peculiar situation.

Bernadotte sent one of his U.N. observers to verify the report that arms were being landed in violation of the truce. His man was refused admittance to the area.

Late that warm June evening Ben-Gurion called his full Cabinet into emergency session, explained the situation, and asked for approval of the order he felt must be issued.

His ministers were not in perfect agreement. There was what Ben-Gurion himself later called "heart-searching debate."

But he had made his decision. He was certain that this was the moment in which the authority of the state had to be established, even if what might ensue would give aid and comfort to Israel's enemies and bring tears to the eyes of millions of Jews.

If the dream had been worth twenty centuries of struggling and waiting it was worth securing, now, by bold action.

So, with the approval of the majority of his Cabinet, he ordered the Army to disarm Irgun forces at Kfar Vitkin and Israel naval units to take control of the *Altalena*. In both cases force was to be used, if necessary.

The unloading was stopped. The *Altalena* moved out to sea, flanked by two Israel corvettes. It looked as if Ben-Gurion had won a bloodless victory.

But the next morning, after the *Altalena* had anchored within sight of the sea-front hotel at Tel Aviv occupied by Bernadotte's staff, a small boat of Irgun men came ashore, set up guns on the beach, and announced defiance of Ben-Gurion, of the regular army, of the United Nations, and of anyone else who might try to take from them their ship or its cargo.

Ben-Gurion called his Cabinet into another emergency session. He asked for and received authority to issue an ultimatum to the *Altalena*: surrender or face "military measures."

Civil war began early that morning. First Irgun and regular army men and girls were firing at each other on shore.

Then Yigal Allon, Palmach commander, was called to G.H.Q. Ben-Gurion himself gave him his instructions. He was to bring up an artillery piece and direct his fire at the munitions ship.

After Allon left, Ben-Gurion issued an order for the evacuation of all civilians from the waterfront area. His own house was not far back from the sea, so he telephoned Paula and explained the situation.

"Tell the neighbors to leave their houses until the trouble is over, and be sure that you go, too."

It was typical of Paula Ben-Gurion that she carried out only half her husband's order. She went from house to house warning her neighbors. Then she went back to her own kitchen and continued her household chores.

It was typical, also, that she did not answer the telephone when it rang that afternoon.

"I was afraid it might be Ben-Gurion, and I knew he would worry if he thought I was still here."

Early in the afternoon Allon brought his military piece into play. One shell made a direct hit and set the cargo on fire. It was like a Fourth of July fireworks display. The ninety men and girls still on board tried to swim for shore.

By nightfall the dead and wounded numbered close to a hundred. Among the dead was Abraham Stavsky, who had been tried for the murder, fifteen years earlier, of Chaim Arlosoroff only a few yards down the beach from where he himself now met death. He had been in charge of the *Altalena* from the day she was purchased in Brooklyn.

Tel Aviv was stunned, bewildered. The breathing space in the war with the Arabs had been a relief. Why did this have to happen?

With the *Altalena* still burning on the waterfront and with the streets full of confusion, Beigin made a broadcast that evening over Irgun's secret station, screaming oaths into the microphone, using hysterical language for more than two hours, until his voice gave out.

Ben-Gurion knew his people well enough to be sure that that broadcast would cause no stampede in support of Irgun. He felt certain that the majority would support him if he continued to give them bold leadership, so he ordered a roundup of Irgun members. Hundreds were jailed.

The next day he went before the Provisional Council, making no apologies. Two of his ministers resigned, hoping to start a stampede against him. He stood firm.

"I am hardly among the cowards of Israel, yet I am very much afraid of an armed minority . . . Arms are for killing, literally killing and nothing else. Alas for mankind that it must produce weapons of destruction! . . . More than once Irgun spilled Jewish blood . . . with five thousand rifles the whole Jewish community is at your mercy, and unless mass murder is in your mind you cannot want five thousand rifles."

He wound up the report with words for which Irgun never forgave him:

"So praise to the gun that sank the unsurrendered ship!"

The Council voted him its confidence, 24 to 4.

The two ministers who had resigned returned in a short time to the Cabinet. One was Ben-Gurion's aged, Orthodox friend, Rabbi Fishman, who resigned on so many occasions that Ben-Gurion nicknamed him "the Minister of Resignation."

The spectacle of Jews killing Jews on the beach of the only all-Jewish city in the world less than a month after the creation of the first Jewish state in nearly two thousand years had distressed many people, but gradually the world came to see that Ben-Gurion's firmness had broken a potential revolution and brought under control a terrorist organization that for years had successfully defied everyone.

Notice had been given to the world that henceforth Israel would be a country in which law and order would prevail and in which responsible government would demand respect and obedience.

What his critics had started to label as Ben-Gurion's first major blunder was actually the most brilliant and best-timed political act of his career—as long as no one raised the philosophical and ethical question of ends and means.

In early July the war began again, with Saudi Arabia joining in, which made it six to one instead of five to one. But by now Israel had an Air Force, with planes smuggled out of the United States, into Mexico, across the ocean, into Czechoslovakia, down to the Middle East; flown by young American, Canadian, and Australian pilots, some not even Jews.

Lydda Airport fell. So did the Arab city of Ramle. Then Nazareth. Israel planes bombed Cairo, Damascus. Israel warships bombarded the Lebanese city of Tyre. The "unbeatable" Arab Legion was driven back. The corridor to Jerusalem was broadened.

After ten days of fighting, in which Israel forces gained everywhere, a second truce went into effect. Ben-Gurion agreed to it, over the objection of most of the military leaders, but under pressure from most of his political advisers.

In June, President Truman appointed the first American diplomatic representative to Israel. Professional diplomats had never been especially to Ben-Gurion's liking, but he was delighted with this man. James G. McDonald had not held a diplomatic post before. He was an open-faced, good-natured Middle Westerner with a Scotch-German background. He laughed when he told Ben-Gurion that he "didn't wear the old school tie of the State Department."

McDonald made no secret of his friendship for Jews and for Israel.

Ben-Gurion liked the frankness and honesty of this tall, thin man (McDonald was six feet two) with hair as white as his own, which he kept brushing back with his hand when it fell over his eyes.

Violating protocol, Ben-Gurion invited him to tea even before he had presented his credentials. They were engrossed in conversation when the shrill sound of a siren interrupted them.

"An air raid!" Paula announced excitedly. "You must all go to the next room. That's our shelter. It's got a reinforced ceiling."

Ben-Gurion went reluctantly.

"Egyptian planes, probably. The Egyptian front is only thirty-five miles away. That's why the planes sometimes get here before the sirens go off."

He continued his conversation with McDonald in the next room, unconcerned about whether it was really a raid or not.

One day when it was so hot that even old-time Palestinians remembered it, the new Soviet Minister, Pavel Yershov, presented his credentials. This was Ben-Gurion's first experience with diplomatic protocol as the head of a government. Those who knew about such matters advised him that Yershov and his aides would wear heavy woolen formal uniforms. Ben-Gurion's uniform as Commander-in-Chief (formal and informal) had been an old pair of khaki trousers and a khaki shirt. But that would never do, so he, Sharett, the chief of protocol, and all the rest of the Israel delegation wore formal morning attire, from striped trousers to stiff collars and ties, while the Israel military band was required to wear battle dress.

The ceremony was stiff and unpleasant for Ben-Gurion. The Russians, unaccustomed to desert heat, seemed several times on the point of physical collapse. Even the Israelis were uncomfortable. But protocol was followed to the last gasp. The Russians left a few minutes after the final note of the band.

Several days later American diplomatic authorities called to make arrangements for McDonald to present his credentials. Ben-Gurion was delighted when told that McDonald had suggested that everyone wear "seasonable summer clothes and protocol be damned."

Because McDonald had had no experience in such matters, Charles F. Knox, his first counselor, who had spent his life in the diplomatic service, explained normal procedure to him: eight or at the most ten minutes after the end of the formal ceremony McDonald must leave. This was important. In the meantime absolutely no serious talk of any kind.

When the formalities were over, fruit juice and cakes were served. The junior diplomatic officers of the two countries went to one end of the room to exchange non-serious pleasantries, strictly according to protocol, leaving the two principals alone.

Ben-Gurion took McDonald by the arm to a quiet corner and invited him to sit down.

"I hope you will forget protocol and let me talk frankly for a few minutes," McDonald said.

Ben-Gurion's eyes twinkled. Nothing the tall Middle Westerner could have said would have made him happier.

Forty minutes later they were still sitting in the corner, while Sharett and Knox were using all the diplomatic sign language they knew to bring the meeting to an end.

In September, Ben-Gurion felt his suspicion of Bernadotte's friendliness justified when the U.N. mediator finished work on his own plan to bring peace to the Middle East. Israel was to give up all the Negev, Ramle, and the New City of Jerusalem; Haifa was to become a free port and Lydda a free airport, and all Arab refugees were to be taken back.

Ben-Gurion was at G.H.Q. on September 17 when he received a telephone call from Jerusalem.

"Bernadotte has been killed."

The mediator had been on his way to keep an appointment with Dov Joseph, military governor of the New City.

Four men in a jeep blocked the road. Using Sten guns, they killed Bernadotte and a French U.N. observer sitting in the car beside him.

The four men in khaki escaped, but the Stern Gang had already publicly taken "credit" for the assassination, and had sent notes to consulates in the Jewish part of Jerusalem threatening similar action against anyone who "interferes with the interests of Jewish nationalism."

Ben-Gurion did not vacillate. The instructions that went out from G.H.Q. to the military commander in Jerusalem were his:

"No. 1: Arrest all Stern members.

"No. 2: Find and surround all Stern bases and confiscate all arms.

"No. 3: Kill all resisters.

"No. 4: Impose a curfew, close borders and all roads leading out of Jerusalem.

"No. 5: Take no action against Irgun unless they help the Sternists.

"No. 6: Act as soon as forces are available."

That evening the Cabinet approved the Prime Minister's suggestion to give Irgun until Tuesday noon to disband as a military unit. A twenty-thousand-dollar reward was posted for the capture of Bernadotte's murderers.

The Stern leader, Nathan Freidman-Yellin, was caught at Haifa port about to flee the country. Hundreds of other Sternists were rounded up. Irgun accepted the ultimatum and disbanded.

The murderers were never caught, but another crisis had passed and Ben-Gurion had come out of it more of a world leader than ever, respected, now, even in Whitehall, and with his own country fairly well united behind him.

An apocryphal story told in Tel Aviv at that time illustrated a new problem Ben-Gurion was facing.

One day an aide informed him that the great number of radio and telegraph messages from the United States were jamming Israel communications, to which he replied:

"Please inform my friends abroad that all suggestions as to how to run Israel should be transmitted by less urgent methods of communication."

Two weeks after the Bernadotte assassination Dr. Weizmann finally came home. Although he was improved in health, after an eye operation at Geneva, he walked slowly to the podium to preside for the first time over the Provisional Council, with Ben-Gurion walking beside him, holding his arm.

This would have been another crisis for the Prime Minister if Dr. Weizmann had had the desire to make himself a President with extensive powers, such as the President of the United States has.

Ben-Gurion thought of Weizmann's role as that of an elder statesman, a President in the French sense, with dignity of office but little voice in running the country.

If Weizmann had been younger and politically more ambitious, there might have been a clash, for Israel did not yet have a constitution and division of political power had not been established.

But it was obvious as they walked in side by side that the feud was over. Ben-Gurion did not even seem to mind that physically Weizmann still towered over him.

"This is a great and sacred moment for me," the half-blind chemist said in mellow tones.

Dr. Weizmann accepted the homage of his people and then

went back to his institute and his magnificent home at Rehovoth.

Ben-Gurion went back to G.H.Q.

The second truce was still in effect, but old Jerusalem was in Arab hands. So was Latrun. Also the road up to Mount Scopus, where the university and hospital stood, worthless and abandoned. Jerusalem was still bordered on three sides by the enemy. A huge Arab wedge almost split Israel in two.

If military operations began again, Ben-Gurion wanted his army to make one more attempt to free all of Jerusalem.

"If we try and are defeated, the consequences may be catastrophic," said the young acting Chief of Staff, Yadin, who argued that Egypt was Israel's principal enemy, and if there was another round of the war every effort should be aimed at crushing the Egyptian forces.

Ben-Gurion called a staff meeting. Yigal Allon, who by now had been appointed commander in the south, took a pointer and turned to a map.

"If we defeat the Egyptians in the Negev we will be able to come to Jerusalem from the rear. This way . . ."

He grew excited as he mapped the operation.

"We could skip Latrun and any more head-on disasters. We could cut around this way . . .

"But first we must clear up the Negev."

Allon knew that Ben-Gurion would always listen to a man who had a dynamic idea, and Ten Plagues, as the Negev operation came to be called, was certainly dynamic.

After Allon went back to his desert post he loaned a small plane he had at his disposal to any desert settlers who would agree to go up to G.H.Q. and beg Ben-Gurion to do something to relieve the situation in the Negev.

The situation in October 1948 was that the entire Negev had been awarded to Israel by the U.N., but fifteen thousand Egyptian soldiers were in physical possession of three strips of the desert, including the ancient cities of Gaza and Beersheba. Israel was cut off from all contact with her settlements in the south Negev because the only road down to them went through one of these strips. Egypt, similarly, had difficulty supplying her forces in Bethlehem because the Israel Army controlled an area through which the east-west road ran.

As a result one of those peculiar agreements between belligerents was worked out with the assistance of the U.N. truce commission. For six hours out of every twenty-four Egypt would permit Israel convoys to go north and south, and for six hours each day Israel would permit Egyptian convoys to move east and west.

It was Egypt's violation of this agreement that gave the Israel Army its excuse to begin Operation Ten Plagues.

Foreign Minister Sharett was firmly against a resumption of hostilities, fearing what it might do to Israel's standing abroad.

But Ben-Gurion was learning an unhappy fact about world politics, that possession is nine points of the law. Under the Bernadotte Plan, Israel would have been permitted to hold all of Galilee, not because she had any more legal right to it than to the Negev, but because it was firmly in Israel's hands.

So the Prime Minister personally gave the order for the campaign to begin.

Ten Plagues was a complete success. Beersheba fell. In one week the Egyptians were put to rout, except for a pocket of twenty-five hundred Sudanese at a desert spot in the north Negev called Faluja, in charge of an obscure young Egyptian captain named Nasser, who was writing a book he called *The Philosophy of the Revolution.*

During November, Ben-Gurion had a chance to do a little reading and writing. In one article he pilloried the British again.

"The British Army, Navy and Air Force, the entire police force of the Palestine government, all the pressure of British diplomacy and all the resources of the British secret service—in fact almost the whole might of the British Empire—was mobilized and deployed in order to prevent arms reaching the Jews and to deprive them of the means of defense . . .

"In the end the British, although they succeeded in associating many other powers with the blockade against Israel, were no more successful than the Philistines."

The success of Ten Plagues had been so great that the Israel military now persuaded Ben-Gurion to risk one more action.

To overcome the objection of Sharett and others concerned with world opinion Egypt was provoked this time into starting hostilities herself. This was done by refusing to permit food supplies to go across Israel-held territory to the Nasser pocket. Egypt had a choice of allowing the captain and his men to starve or to attack. She attacked.

That was the signal for the start of Operation Ayin. Again Yadin the archaeologist and Allon the farmer planned and executed the operation. Allon was to set out from Biblical Beersheba and swing down to the Negev-Sinai frontier as quickly as possible, wiping out Egyptian resistance as he went.

Yadin had an archaeological as well as a military interest in this campaign. The only road from Beersheba to the Sinai frontier swung in a wide arc. It was heavily patrolled by Egyptians. On each side of the road the land was barren and trackless, passable only to camels.

But Yadin, the archaeologist, discovered from a photographic survey the remains of an ancient Roman road that crossed the desert in a straight line.

Israel engineers went to work and soon had the old road in condition to support trucks and light military equipment.

Just before zero hour Yadin announced at G.H.Q. that he was leaving at once by jeep for Beersheba.

Ben-Gurion said he would like to go, too, to see the beginning of the operation. He, Yadin, an aide, and a driver started out in a jeep. Because there had just been a heavy rain and the road was in bad condition, the driver decided to take a short cut across country. They were within twenty miles of Beersheba when they came to a brook too swollen for the jeep to cross.

"We must build a bridge," Yadin announced.

So the Israel Chief of Staff, his driver, the Commander-in-Chief, and his military aide walked back to a deserted Arab village, Kaukaba, which they had just passed, ripped some wooden doors from farm buildings and hauled them back to the brook. As they attempted to get the jeep onto the improvised bridge, it became so deeply mired that they were unable to extricate it.

With the zero hour for Operation Ayin not far off, the four men set out on foot for the main highway, five miles away. Ben-Gurion, twice the age of any of the others, puffed and grunted a little, but he did not fall behind.

When they reached the highway they flagged down the first

military vehicle they saw. It happened to be going in the direction of Tel Aviv.

"Would you be so kind as to take us to Beersheba?" Yadin asked.

"Can't you see that I'm——"

The young driver stopped in the middle of the sentence. His jaw dropped. He rubbed his eyes. Then he stammered an apology to the Commander-in-Chief and to the acting Chief of Staff.

When they reached Beersheba they were told that every building in Kaukaba was heavily mined and that some kind providence must have saved them all from being blown to bits.

Operation Ayin was so successful that Allon and his men were deep into Sinai long ahead of schedule. They halted seven miles from the main Egyptian headquarters and air base, and were getting ready to mount an attack that would have freed the Gaza strip and crippled the Egyptian Army, perhaps for years, when a message came from G.H.Q.:

"Cease all operations."

Allon told his subordinate officers:

"You continue to prepare for an attack in the morning."

Then he jumped into a jeep and drove across the Roman road to Beersheba. From there he flew in his private plane to Tel Aviv.

He would have been less puzzled by the order if he had known what had been going on elsewhere in the world while he was planning the obliteration of the Egyptian Army.

Ben-Gurion had gone to Tiberias with his wife for a few hours of relief from the strain. G.H.Q. kept him informed of developments, but between calls it was good to be able to see the blue water of the lake, to read a book, to enjoy the quieting effects of natural hot-spring baths.

On Friday afternoon, the last day of the year by the Christian calendar, Sharett telephoned excitedly. McDonald had just called on him and read him the text of a coded telegram from President Truman.

The British Foreign Office (which still did not have diplomatic relations with Israel) had asked the United States to transmit to Israel a message that Great Britain would invoke an old treaty with Egypt (even without Egypt asking) and would make war on Israel unless Israel's soldiers withdrew at once from Egyptian soil.

The United States itself also demanded that the Israelis withdraw, and intimated that unless this occurred immediately Washington might find it necessary to reconsider her entire attitude toward the Jewish state.

Sharett's explanation had not satisfied McDonald, so he was going to drive the 115 miles over dangerous roads from Tel Aviv to Tiberias by rented automobile in order to see Ben-Gurion himself.

Late that night McDonald arrived. He was received by the Prime Minister and his wife in a small room off the hotel lobby. They talked for an hour and a half. Ben-Gurion assured McDonald that Israel forces had already received orders to withdraw.

McDonald wanted a military escort for the return trip. During the hour it took to arrange it, they talked of irrelevant matters.

Finally the escort arrived and the tall, lanky American started back for Tel Aviv.

Meanwhile at G.H.Q., Allon had found only a duty officer. He asked where Yadin was. He had gone to bed. Allon woke him up.

"We're losing a wonderful opportunity to destroy the entire Egyptian Army," he said intensely.

"This is not a military decision," Yadin replied. "President Truman has threatened to reconsider the Israel-American relationship unless our troops withdraw from Sinai."

"I must see Ben-Gurion," Allon said.

"He's in Tiberias."

So Allon woke up Sharett instead.

"Please let me take El 'Arish!"

"Impossible," Sharett said curtly. "We have made a promise to the American Government and we cannot possibly go back on our word."

"Then let me call the Old Man."

So a call was put through to Tiberias.

Ben-Gurion listened in silence to all of Allon's arguments. Then he gave him a four-word reply, hung up the receiver, and went back to sleep.

"Withdraw within twenty-four hours!"

Once more Ben-Gurion had tried to guide a middle course between the desire of his military for freedom to clear Israel of all enemy troops and punish the invaders so they would never be able to do it again and the caution of Sharett, who insisted that Israel, now that she had her independence, must behave like a responsible member of the family of nations.

Egypt asked for an armistice. It was granted, and fighting ceased almost at once. The Arab-Israel War of 1948 was over.

When Israel held her first election, to fill the hundred and twenty seats in a unicameral parliament or Knesset, twenty-one parties put up candidates, proving that nothing had happened to kill individuality and political independence in this new state, which led Ben-Gurion to say to his friend McDonald:

"Please ask Mr. Truman to share with us the secret of the American two-party system."

Ben-Gurion's Mapai won forty-six seats, twice the number any other party gained. Beigin's Irgun followers, calling themselves the Herut (Freedom) party, filled fourteen. Three Arabs and eleven women were among the winners.

Parliament elected Weizmann President, and one of his first acts was to call on Ben-Gurion to form a Cabinet, which he did after some weeks of negotiating, allying Mapai with four Orthodox parties and two minor groups to get a majority.

Thus the labor leader with a dream became the first Prime Minister of Israel, and the world began to express curiosity about this strange little man with such a fanatical belief in the future of a mere seven hundred thousand people (fifty thousand had come in during the war) who under his guidance had won their right to a piece of desert smaller than Massachusetts.

CHAPTER FIFTEEN

BEN-GURION has always been more popular with painters than sculptors, because no one could ever reproduce in stone, metal, or wood his hair and the peculiar quality of his eyes.

Writers have found words for his hair:

"His hair foams up on each side of a bald spot."

"A shock of white hair rises in an undisciplined fringe."

". . . an aureole of bushy white hair frilling a softly wrinkled pate like a ruff upon a pudgy Elizabethan neck."

But they are always making mistakes about his eyes. Within a few months of each other a reporter for a New York newspaper, a staff correspondent for an American magazine, a diplomat-turned-writer, and the author of a radio script all called them blue, while a celebrated literary figure who had just visited him described them as green, and a weekly news magazine made them brown in one of its cover portraits and blue in another. No one was to blame. Although his eyes are brown, they sometimes seem to have a blue-green glint—the color of hard metal. They are friendly eyes, but not soft. Softness and gentleness are not Ben-Gurion's most pronounced qualities.

Sometimes after he has been alone for an hour or two, thinking or reading, his eyes seem like those of a poet who has detached himself from the world of materialistic considerations.

His gray shaggy eyebrows often seem to bristle.

His jaw is as firm and determined-looking as if it were made of marble. His skin is ruddy, almost russet-colored. His lips are thin, and he often purses them tightly together, but when his mouth relaxes and his eyes twinkle and the crow's feet begin to show, his smile is enchanting.

His forehead is wrinkled now, and there are two sharp lines from his nose to the corners of his mouth.

His hands, small and slim, are never still when he is talking. He uses them to thump his desk, tap the arm of a chair, point accusingly, or mold a thought, as if he had clay in his hands.

He rarely sits upright in a chair. He either lounges back, listening, or bends forward, talking.

When he walks he gives the impression of being on his way somewhere and of knowing his exact destination.

Most of the time, even when delivering a public address, he speaks softly, in a conversational register, almost as if he were tired.

He dresses as he pleases, and puts comfort above convention-ality. On a few occasions there has been no way of avoiding a tall silk hat, striped trousers, and cutaway, or black tie and dinner jacket, or even tails. But photographs taken on these occasions leave no doubt that he wanted to be back again as quickly as possible in loose-fitting trousers, comfortable shoes, and open-necked shirt.

During the 1948 war Ben-Gurion wore "battle dress," and continued to wear it for several years, until one night he and Nasser appeared on the same American television program (on film) and some viewers criticized him for not having dressed for the occasion like "a man of peace." After that he seldom wore battle dress.

Shortly after independence he was scheduled to speak at a morning session of a Histadruth Congress. He arrived a little late, out of breath, wearing striped trousers, cutaway coat, silk hat, and gloves, having just hurried from a reception for a newly appointed ambassador. As he took his place at the podium and unfastened his tie he said:

"Comrades, please excuse my working clothes."

The official arrival of spring and fall are declared in Israel by the Prime Minister. One day word spreads that Ben-Gurion has appeared with his shirt open at the neck, which signifies that spring has come. When he buttons up his shirt collar, summer is over.

The salary he receives as Prime Minister comes to four hundred dollars a month, less than the income of the average New York taxi driver.

One morning during the days of food scarcity in Israel, a woman in Tel Aviv pushed her way to the head of a queue of people waiting to get their monthly ration of chickens. There was a roar of anger until someone said:

"Ladies, this is Ben-Gurion's maid. She gets paid by the hour. Ben-Gurion can't afford to pay her much. If you are good Israelis you'll let her go in first."

The Prime Minister does not own an automobile. The government supplied him with a large Dodge, which had little value because of its age, but which he finally decided was too pretentious. He wanted to change it for a jeep. His physician objected.

"A jeep will be very bad for your lumbago."

"But how can I set an example to other government officials,"

Ben-Gurion demanded, "with people like you telling me what I have to do?"

A compromise was reached. The Prime Minister agreed to a small European car after he was told it would actually be cheaper to buy and run than a jeep. But he still would have preferred a jeep because of the absence of chrome and frills.

The austerity that Ben-Gurion preaches and practices has made it almost impossible for Israel extremists to foment ideological hatreds and has helped in creating a degree of brotherhood in the multi-lingual, multi-racial, multi-party state.

It was Ben-Gurion, as the first head of government, who had the opportunity to set the pattern. He could have bedecked himself with medals, as Tito did, or put his picture on stamps and coins, as the first head of Ghana would soon be doing, or ridden at state expense in high-powered motorcars with bullet-proof glass and armed bodyguards, as many another new ruler has done, or he could at least have surrounded himself with some of the glamour that is part of the compensation many modern states give their rulers. But instead he set a pattern of almost monastic simplicity.

For Ben-Gurion music, painting, and sculpture are unrewarding. After McDonald's arrival he would often send the American diplomat's wife and Paula to a concert while he went to bed with a book.

When Leonard Bernstein, the American conductor, came to Israel on his first visit he told Ben-Gurion:

"This is one time you *must* attend a musical affair."

He went, and neither fell asleep nor seemed bored. But after Bernstein left, he returned to his books.

Once he was a patient for a short time in the Bodenheimer home for convalescents in Haifa and was assigned to a room that had walls covered with large and vivid German expressionist paintings. The director, proud of his art, after three days asked him:

"How do you like it?"

"What?" the Prime Minister replied.

"Our collection of paintings."

"How do I know? I haven't been outside this room."

"But they are on your own walls!" the director said, more amazed than hurt.

Two days later Ben-Gurion sent for the director.

"I'm sorry. You'll have to take out these paintings. I can't stand them."

He has never tried to impress people. They must accept or reject him as he is, for what he is. He once said:

"I see no reason for ever pretending."

Films and plays have little interest for him because he feels they generally deal only with problems of a personal nature.

Chess is the only game he has ever played. He feels it acts to the brain as a whetstone to a steel tool. He has never had any use for games of chance or parlor gambling. He does his gambling with life—his own life and the lives of hundreds of thousands of others. When engaged in such gambling he is always daring and usually successful.

Before he became Prime Minister he never gave cocktail parties, luncheons, dinners, or receptions and rarely accepted invitations to such functions.

Sometimes Paula would invite a few people in for the evening, and would ask him to leave his books and come down for half an hour and be sociable. But unless the guests included someone Ben-Gurion thought could make a contribution to his fund of knowledge or stimulate his thinking, he would make excuses long before the half hour was up and return to his room.

When Jorge Garcia Granados, who had been such a good friend of the Jews as a member of the UNSCOP, was appointed his country's first Minister to Israel, Ben-Gurion's secretary said:

"We must make something for him."

"What do you mean?" the Prime Minister asked.

"A reception, a dinner, a cocktail party—something to welcome him."

Although Ben-Gurion had great respect for the Guatemalan he shrugged his shoulders. A cocktail party finally was arranged, and he was persuaded to attend.

The first person he saw on entering the room was the Mexican Minister, whom he knew and liked, so he took him into a corner and began firing questions:

"What is your export-import situation?"

"How is it with your neighbors?"

"How about the Communists?"

To Ben-Gurion's annoyance, his secretary frequently interrupted, bringing up guests to whom he felt the Prime Minister should speak.

After ten minutes, Ben-Gurion excused himself and left.

With great effort his protocol officer forces him to accept one invitation a year from each ambassador or minister, generally on the country's principal national holiday.

"It is my duty and desire," he once told an aide, "to spend as much of my time as possible outside office hours either reading or thinking."

The force that drives Ben-Gurion has nothing to do with nervous energy. Rather, it is an inner will that has the quality of electricity, energizing his brain, kindling sparks in his eyes, even making the fringe of white hair stand on end.

Extremists have occasionally called him a dictator, among other reasons because he has control of the Army. (So has the President of the United States, who is Commander-in-Chief of all the armed forces.)

It is true that he tries to get his own way within the framework of democracy. When the tenth anniversary celebration was being planned, he made this typical remark:

"I will insist that the main events take place in Jerusalem, but of course there is a competent authority in the Knesset which will decide."

In 1949 one of Tel Aviv's favorite jokes was that a delegation went to Ben-Gurion just before the mandate ended and suggested that he permit himself to be named King of Israel, but that he refused because he could not tolerate the thought of being David II.

He has never looked on power as an end. He has given evidence during the first ten years of the state that he has wanted authority only to help achieve the dream.

He has humility without self-effacement, meekness without weakness, shyness without fear.

He demonstrates his humility whenever he laughs at jokes about himself, which, from the start, have been many. He was even able to smile over the story being told in Tel Aviv in 1949 about the man who was so sick of standing in queues that he bought a pistol and told a friend he was going to shoot Ben-Gurion because he obviously was to blame for all the country's troubles.

Several days later the friend met the unhappy man again and asked him what had happened.

"I bought the pistol and went to Ben-Gurion's office, but there were so many people already standing in line waiting to shoot him that I got discouraged and went home."

He objects to streets being named after living people.

"Wait and see if they are still famous after they are dead."

He becomes quickly impatient with those who interrupt his trend of thought and with sloppy thinkers who use such expressions as "and so forth." He also dislikes those who use clichés and are unable to state their thoughts or desires in simple, straightforward sentences.

He agrees that small minds discuss people; average minds, events; great minds, abstract concepts.

Casual conversation even on subjects in which he is interested annoys him. That is why he considers cocktail parties a waste of time. He wants to plumb a subject to its depths or not approach it at all.

He has always thought shaking hands a "barbarian habit" which has no utilitarian purpose now that men no longer need to prove to each other they are not carrying daggers.

He greets people with "*Shalom,*" but he dispenses with "How is your wife?" and "Isn't it a pleasant day?" He feels that such remarks impede thought, waste time, and delay intelligent conversation.

He attempts to increase his own store of intellectual wealth by each human contact he makes and has the capacity to incorporate into his own thinking the best of the ideas he gleans from others.

He is an excellent judge of solid worth. Flashy minds put him on his guard. He considers brilliance alone not enough.

He has scant respect for experts, although he often makes use of them.

"Experts know facts," he once said, "but they seldom know their purpose."

On another occasion he said to an aide:

"If an expert tells you something is impossible, it probably means that he just does not know how to do it. As soon as an expert uses the word 'impossible,' it is time to get a new expert."

He is receptive to criticism only if he thinks the critic is as well versed as he himself in the matter under criticism.

His power of concentration is legendary.

During 1949, when he had thousands of problems pressing in on him, a friend gave him a four-hundred-page book of philosophy. Two days later he returned it.

"Maybe you would like to borrow it later when you have more time," the friend said.

The Prime Minister smiled. He had read it to the smallest detail, and proved it by engaging in a long discussion of the book.

His mind operates like an artillery piece rather than a rifle. Especially during the war, he made decisions that seemed strange to many people because they were unable to see the target. Before an artillery piece can be fired, many exact calculations are necessary, and the success or failure of the shot is not immediately discernible—except to the target.

Flashes of wit, jokes, anecdotes about people rarely amuse him, but he will listen by the hour to a man like McDonald telling "inside stories" about how and why an event or a decision came about.

The vigor of his personality is so great that no one could ever say, after a gathering:

"I think Ben-Gurion was there."

He has no interest in personal publicity. He told a journalist associate:

"I would much rather read an article *by* myself than *about* myself."

Yet he is always unconsciously creating perfect press-agent situations.

During the 1948 war he accepted an invitation to attend the marriage of one of his messengers, but at the last minute a military emergency prevented his going.

When Josef, the messenger, returned from his honeymoon, Ben-Gurion said to him:

"I've missed your wedding, but at least I will not be deprived of having wine and cakes with you. I will come to your house tomorrow at ten."

At nine forty-five the next morning the Prime Minister looked at his watch, then turned to the thirteen members of his Cabinet, with whom he was having a serious discussion, and said:

"I am sorry but I must go now to see Josef and his wife. I will be back in an hour."

He has intellectual as well as physical courage, which he has demonstrated by his many self-conducted tours into remote fields of thought, and by his willingness to champion unpopular causes and defend unwelcome decisions.

The loneliness that he has had to suffer most of his life has come partly from being ahead of the thinking of his people. It is a loneliness that great men always suffer. When other Jews were using Yiddish, Ben-Gurion began to speak Hebrew. When others were content to wait for messianic guidance in recovering the Holy Land, he started fighting for it. While others retained their galuth names, he took one with a Biblical sound. When self-defense was still a foreign concept, he helped introduce it into Jewish life. When terrorism was still popular, he put a halt to it. After 1948 there would be many other times when he would risk political annihilation for the loneliness of being a leader.

When he knows he is right he can resist public clamor, even to riots and threats on his life. This has kept him from ever becoming a demagogue.

He not only admits to being somewhat of a mystic himself, but he encourages it in others. He once wrote:

"Let us not treat realism and mysticism as mutually exclusive . . . We must be realists, critical realists, toward every concrete step which we are taking in the present and near future. And we must be mystics, full of a deep and boundless faith, and having a tremendous and resolute will with regard to the future."

While he has not been happy about the splintering of the electorate into so many political parties, the necessity of ruling by coalition has never seemed to distress him. The hurly-burly of political activity is not distasteful to him. He is a master at the commutations and permutations of party politics.

Although he has been a socialist from boyhood, there is nothing doctrinaire about his political beliefs. On many occasions he has been willing to drop a party principle if it has been proved impractical.

He can be as stubborn as an army mule when he thinks his opposition is wrong. He believes in democracy and the right of the majority to decide, but when he is in pursuit of his main objective he will argue, cajole, storm, and philosophize until enough of his opponents have seen the error of their ways to make the majority into a minority.

His favorite characters, living and dead, are men and women with dedication: zealots, searchers after something.

He dislikes mediocrity, and takes little interest in people who are primarily concerned with money, food, houses, automobiles, getting, spending, accumulating, possessing.

Although he will give a second chance to a man who has made a mistake he will never forgive lying or the telling of half-truths.

Insincerity he finds as irritating as a mosquito buzzing in the ear.

Stupidity makes him spread his hands in a helpless gesture, shrug his shoulders, and shake his head in despair.

He strongly objects to people shouting at each other because he says the victim of the shouting is being humiliated and no one has the right to humiliate anyone else, even a friend.

On the rare occasions when his wife raises her voice to him, she always quickly pats his shoulder and says:

"But you know I love you!"

Ben-Gurion's reaction to people and events are often spontaneous and warm, but they are rarely personalized. If Paula tells him that So-and-So has just had a baby, he is likely to say with great sincerity:

"Good! Another strong Israeli to help build the country!"

He lives every moment for the cause. Whatever happens is important only if it advances the dream.

Although he inspires hero worship, there is little warmth in his relationship with those around him. He might know that the wife of a close acquaintance was critically ill, but it would not occur to him to say:

"How is she today?"

His associates often complain that his attitude toward people is erratic and illogical. If he likes a person he is capable of hurting him, just as a man can hurt the woman he deeply loves. If he dislikes a person he refuses to listen to him, even when he may be talking sense.

His basic interest in people is in people collectively, not individually.

The older he grows, the more he speaks the thoughts and dreams of the new generation in Israel. He is the spokesman for the sabras, although he is not a sabra himself. He is the spokesman for youth, although he has passed three score and ten. He chooses only young people for his personal staff, and delights in putting them to physical as well as intellectual tests.

At a conference he attended a few years ago, the delegates were billeted ten miles from the agricultural training center where the meetings were being held.

"I think I will walk to and from the meetings," he announced.

Teddy Kollek, one of his favorite young political assistants, was forced to walk the twenty miles with him rather than admit his physical inferiority to the much older man.

"I feel more free when I am walking than at any other time."

He has almost no petty qualities. Although he has foretold almost every important event in the past half century of Jewish history he has rarely indulged in saying:

"I told you so!"

After Dr. Weizmann became President, Ben-Gurion seemed to lose all trace of his old inferiority complex. Without ever appearing either arrogant or self-important he developed an ability to mix on an even footing with other world-important figures, although he was the leader of only a million or two people in a country smaller than Albania.

Reading the Bible keeps him from feeling insignificant. By steeping himself in the long history of his people he renews his faith in their historical importance and becomes acutely aware that Israel is something more than just a small group of people Hitler missed, trying to make a life for themselves on a desolate desert.

At an American Fourth of July celebration on the seashore of Tel Aviv one year, he began his address in Hebrew. Then he suddenly stopped and said in English:

"Excuse me if I talk in a language spoken on this shore four thousand years ago."

With this one short remark he mobilized history to enhance his position and put Israel on a level with the great English-speaking nations. When a foreign dignitary comes to call, he prepares himself by sitting quietly for a few minutes before receiving his guest, thinking about the man, his background, his country, its history. If the guest is an American, he may start the conversation by saying:

"It is amazing to think that there were only 102 passengers on the Mayflower . . . yet from that beginning grew up this great phenomenon called America . . . you have given the world a new concept of democracy."

Gradually and adroitly he leads the talk from the visitor's country to his own.

"Do you know how many immigrants have arrived in Israel since the state was formed? Do you realize how many people this would mean proportionally for the United States?"

Many a visitor has gone from his office feeling intellectually refreshed.

His life has been ruled from the start by symbols:

The Soldier.

The Mother.

The Worker.

The Pioneer.

To him these are symbols of strength. He wants his people to be strong so they can realize the dream. Often he makes speeches to the symbols. Or about them. He has made all of them important and respected in Israel.

Although he is a Jew—every milligram of him—he has many qualities that are distinctly un-Jewish.

He can sit in a political meeting for hours, silent, while everyone else fumes, splutters, and expostulates. When the others have finally exhausted themselves, Ben-Gurion, as fresh of mind and spirit as when he arrived, will quietly make a speech, pointing the way.

It is not a Jewish trait to be economical with time, yet Ben-Gurion rarely wastes a moment. He is always prompt himself, and complains if a meeting is late in starting or someone appears behind schedule for an appointment.

"The only thing you can never recover is time," he has often said.

Another of his non-Jewish characteristics is conciseness. It is traditional for Jewish speakers and writers to ramble. Ben-Gurion's words can always be fitted neatly into an outline, with none left over. Although his speeches are long and his articles run to many thousands of words, there are neither wasted words nor irrelevant thoughts.

It is not typically Jewish to maintain an icy calm in a moment of crisis, yet that is what Ben-Gurion has always done.

Family ties are not of as much importance to him as they are to most Jews. A brother, Nahum Green, for years operated a cold-drink kiosk at the corner of Ben Yehuda Street and Nordau Boulevard in Tel Aviv. Once he was overheard to say:

"What was I asking for that he should turn me down? All I wanted was a better location!"

Then he shrugged his shoulders and said:

"He always was *meshuge* [crazy]."

On another occasion a visitor asked him why he was selling cold drinks while his brother was one of the world's great statesmen.

"Never mind what people here say," he replied. "In Plonsk *I* was the one who was considered bright."

As an intellectual Ben-Gurion is a creature of many paradoxes. He is a three-dimensional man, living simultaneously in the past, the present, and the future.

When Yadin, as acting Chief of Staff, would go to him with an urgent problem, Ben-Gurion would often force him to discuss ancient Israel for an hour before giving him five minutes to state his twentieth-century military difficulty.

He is an intellectual with an almost compulsive instinct to escape into action. Yet as a man of action he is always trying to escape into the provinces of the spirit.

Because he is essentially a lonely man and communicates his innermost feelings to no one, he seeks companions in history.

Ibsen said that the strong man is mightiest when he is alone. This seems to be true of Ben-Gurion.

A sense of history is the dominant force in his life. For him history is not something static or dead. It is like a great river, surging from there to here; a river with distant sources that can be traced, if anyone cares.

Most of his intellectual energy goes into trying to keep the river flowing freely, trying to make his own people aware of historical continuity. This is not difficult in a land where almost anyone can scratch in the earth and find a piece of pottery two thousand years old, and where the starter in the bus depot shouts, "Last call for Nazareth, Beersheba, Jerusalem!"

For him the Bible is not only Israel's history book, but her Encyclopaedia Britannica, Baedaker's Guide, Blackstone's Commentaries, Bartlett's Familiar Quotations, World Almanac, and the genealogy of every Jew in the world.

He is convinced that no one can understand today's headlines or yesterday's battles without knowing the Bible, and that it is ignorance of this history book that has caused some foreign diplomats and statesmen to make errors in the Middle East.

His sense of the past is emotional as well as intellectual, patriotic as well as practical.

While driving back to Tel Aviv from Tiberias, where he had been bathing in the hot springs, he saw a cedar tree and began a long monologue addressed to his wife and Zeev Sharef, who accompanied him.

"Do you realize that the cedars of Lebanon are five thousand years old? It was from these same cedars that the Temple was built. Five centuries! Do you realize that that was before Noah, before——

"I know that the problems we will be discussing this afternoon in the cabinet meeting will be important, but those cedars! They have seen the conquest of Judea, the Kings, the Maccabees. Just think of all they have seen!"

There was a pause for a moment as he slumped back in the seat. Then he leaned forward again.

"Someday when there is peace—real peace, and not just a cease-fire—I want to go up to Lebanon and tell them, 'See here, give us just one of those great cedars of yours so we can plant it in Israel.'"

Ben-Gurion has the emotional and intellectual ability to live as if the days of the First and Second Temples were back just a few years—as if he might walk down a street in Jerusalem tomorrow and meet some man who had just had a conversation with King David.

To him the people of the Bible are not dusty historical characters—figures in a wax museum—creatures of wood or stone. He knows them better than he knows most of the ministers in his own Cabinet. He speaks of Joshua and Isaiah more intimately than he does of Eisenhower and Macmillan.

Other men quote history; Ben-Gurion evokes it.

He is spokesman for the Biblical past, a leader of today's struggle, and the voice of the future, all at the same time.

One day a member of his own party, coming from his office, made a helpless gesture and said:

"I can't discuss anything with him. I speak of yesterday and he talks about three thousand years ago. I speak of tomorrow and he discusses two thousand years from now. It is like trying to talk about today's meat shortage with Moses and some man who won't be born for another few thousand years."

One of the reasons he is so satisfactory as a leader of Israel is that his people recognize in him a truly Biblical character. He not only knows the Bible, he is a figure directly out of it.

He has not confined his historical research exclusively to the Biblical era. He has explored many of the streams of thought that have flowed into or out from his own great river. Because the Greek stream was the widest and deepest, he made that his second specialty, but he is in a constant state of search, exploring the lore, the history, the thinking of the great ages of man, looking for wisdom and eternal truth.

He is not an ivory-tower intellectual. One moment he may be conversing with Plato, and the next reading a Russian or American scientific magazine, and the next going out with the Army on maneuvers.

He is probably the only head of a government who surprises his official guests by swinging the conversation casually from the current problem under discussion to life at the bottom of the sea, and then to a subject as abstract as the relationship between matter and the spirit.

Even his closest associates who know what he reads and whom

he sees are awed by the breadth of his ever expanding knowledge.

As he turns from the present to the future he has a passionate belief in the limitless potentialities of man and a sense of frantic urgency.

Many a reporter, coming to interview him, finds a tired old man until some question about the future is asked; then his eyes light up, he throws off his weariness, his hands begin to make characteristic gestures, his voice takes on new fire, and he is Ben-Gurion, one of the great visionaries of his age.

When he talks of the future he thinks not only of Israel and her role in making deserts bloom and an old culture flourish again in the Middle East, but also of setting an example in social justice to people who have rarely known any. He talks also about atomic energy, converting the sun's rays into power, distilling fresh water from the sea. He looks hundreds of years ahead and sees Asia and Africa as the dynamic centers of the world.

Other men make predictions about the future, but Ben-Gurion conjures up the future, projecting himself and his listeners into it, creating visions for his people to see.

When they were beset by food shortages, enemy attacks, lack of friends in high places, he would tell them his prophecies—hills barren no more, a land of green instead of brown, a part of ancient Israel restored to the flourishing fertility of another day. The sun would be put to work. Science might even change the climate. There was no limit if there was faith enough. Israel would become the fountainhead of a rich new way of life. The Renaissance in the Middle East!

This was Ben-Gurion the Prophet, direct lineal descendant of Isaiah, Jeremiah, Daniel, Hosea, Joel, Amos, Obadiah, Jonah, Micah, Nahum, Habakkuk, Zephaniah, Haggai, Zechariah, and Malachi.

He observes none of the dietary laws and follows none of the other Orthodox religious practices. At times he has had to cooperate, for reasons of political expediency, with the religious political parties and approve legislation that has made Israel a slightly theocratic state, but Mapai is anti-clerical and he himself is more anti-clerical than the party.

Yet he is a deeply spiritual man, with a touch of fatalistic mysticism and faith in the stern ethical values of the Hebrew religion.

One of his close associates of recent years, Yaakov Herzog, son of the Chief Rabbi and an extremely religious man himself (he is now Minister in Washington), has often told Ben-Gurion:

"You behave as if you believe in miracles more than most Orthodox Jews do."

Ben-Gurion seems to be groping always in the province of the spirit for something he will probably never find. This explains some of the paradoxes. It explains his long friendship with Rabbi Fishman (Maimon), with whom he has had bitter philosophical and religious arguments.

He has made it clear to those around him that he would like to go down in history as a contemplative man.

Philosophy for him started out to be what fishing was to Coolidge and Hoover, or golf to Dwight Eisenhower, but it soon developed into a deep and serious study.

Once a professor of philosophy from Athens came to Israel to discuss political problems with Ben-Gurion. He had no trouble obtaining an appointment, but after a two-hour session he left, extremely unhappy.

"The Prime Minister discussed Plato and Socrates for the entire two hours and then showed me to the door."

From Plato, Ben-Gurion learned that a philosopher is "a man perfect in wisdom, understanding, and knowledge, with the virtues of justice, truth, and humility, the love of good, the avoidance of power." In the seventh decade of his busy life he set out to become, as nearly as he would be able in the time left, a philosopher in the Platonic sense.

He is by nature a man of peace. He told a reporter:

"I am the Minister of Defense. This is the worst thing I have to do in my life, because I am wasting the best of our youth and I am wasting money—hundreds of millions. Why? Do you think I like to spend money on tanks and planes? Do you think I like to send our best young people to be soldiers? I prefer to use money for construction and education. I hate what I do, but I am forced to do it."

He has never been lacking in enemies. There were the British, then the Arabs, then vacillating great-power politicians, anti-

Zionists, skeptics, fainthearted friends, terrorists, Communists, potential fascists, those who opposed a planned economy, exploiters, religious fanatics, materialists, idle dreamers—the list was long.

He has weaknesses and has made mistakes. One of his severest critics in the Knesset once said, after listing some of the grave blunders he had made:

"But after all, only a great man can make great mistakes."

His opponents have used such words as "wild," "unrestrained," and "daydreamer" about him. When his daydreams come true, they call him "lucky."

One of his weaknesses as the head of a government has been his lack of diplomatic sense. There have been times when he has undone with a single overly frank sentence plans on which his own Foreign Office had been working for months.

He has been criticized for putting political friends in government positions (an accusation not infrequently leveled at leaders of older and larger nations), for having a messianic complex (one unhappy phrase in a speech lent weight to this charge), and for wasting his time with inconsequential people just because they are old Zionist friends.

Palmach leaders still criticize him for not exploiting the military successes of 1948. They argue that if he had ignored pressure from the United States and the U.N. he could have liberated all Palestine.

But most critics admit that there might not be an Israel today had it not been for David Ben-Gurion and that when the time comes he will be difficult to replace.

The secret of his leadership is partly that he is the synthesized product of three thousand years of Jewish history, that he is perfectly in rhythm with the surging movements of his own time, and that he has a universal appeal.

Yemenite Jews, deeply Orthodox in their religion and untouched by Western civilization, recognize in this freethinker from Poland the personification of their dreams.

A highly educated and British Jew like Marcus Sieff acknowledges his superiority.

Americans who are not Zionists and may not even be Jews see him as one of the ten contemporary leaders, in a world in which nations are managed by managers and real leaders are few.

A wise man from across the sea said of him:

"After talking with Ben-Gurion for five minutes you know he knows.

CHAPTER SIXTEEN

ONE of Ben-Gurion's office assistants asked him:

"When do you ever have a chance to rest?"

"Do you mean sleep?" he replied.

"No, rest."

"Well, I read a lot."

"No, I mean a complete rest."

Ben-Gurion looked at the young woman as though he thought her a little mad and said:

"If you mean just sitting staring at a wall, I never do that."

Besides being Prime Minister, Ben-Gurion at that time was Minister of Defense and the head of eighty-two government departments, and devoted from twenty to thirty hours a week to serious reading and intensive study.

His normal day began about 7 A.M., after four or four and a half hours' sleep, which for years has been all he has required. By this time Paula was up and had a simple breakfast ready for him. He spent an hour with the morning newspapers and part of the next hour on state papers. In those days he would often walk the mile and a half to his office (after the Defense Ministry had been moved to a two-story stucco building at Hakirya, on the edge of Tel Aviv) and be at his desk by nine o'clock. For four and a half hours he conferred with the chiefs of military departments.

At one-thirty he went home for a light lunch and a half-hour nap, after which he would work on government papers in his brief case until returning to his office at 4 P.M. For the next four hours he was Prime Minister, meeting distinguished guests, being interviewed by reporters, conferring with department heads, receiving foreign diplomats, writing speeches and articles, and performing the other functions of the head of a government.

He walked home at 8 P.M., taking with him, always, a brief

case full of work, and sometimes a colleague in the government with whom he wished to talk.

Paula would have supper ready; generally cheese, bread, sour cream, and salad. No matter who the guest was, they ate supper in the kitchen.

Watching Ben-Gurion at his own table, many guests decided that his wife could have put a beefsteak or a piece of herring in front of him and he would have eaten it without knowing the difference.

Were it not for Paula, he would ignore food entirely. It is her concern about his bodily needs that keeps him alive.

For years there was a rule in the Ben-Gurion home, even after he became Prime Minister, that he and Paula would take turns washing the dishes. On evenings when it was his turn he would hurry through his meal, even if a guest was present, wash his own dishes, and then stand waiting impatiently for the others to finish. If the guest insisted, he would be permitted to join in the cleanup. A list of the distinguished Israel citizens who have washed dishes in the Ben-Gurion kitchen would read like a Who's Who of Israel.

After supper and the departure of any guests Ben-Gurion turned to his brief case and worked on state business until midnight. The hours from midnight until 2 or 3 A.M. were always the favorite time of his day. Propped up in bed with a small light over his head, he would read for pleasure, book after book, the subject usually determined by his current philosophical interest. This was "rest" for him, as refreshing as sleep.

The Ben-Gurion house in the north part of Tel Aviv, about half a mile back from the sea, is a two-story, boxlike stucco building, no different than hundreds of others around it except for the wooden sentry box in front of the door. During the war first-floor windows were bricked up in case bombs fell in the neighborhood.

On the ground floor are living room, dining room, a small library, two of the walls covered with books, and Paula's room; on the second floor, four rooms, three of them packed with books from floor to ceiling; at least four thousand; one of the best private collections in the Middle East. There are hundreds of volumes on Indian philosophy alone. Ben-Gurion has his desk in the largest of the three rooms, which also contains a globe of the world. In the smaller of the two connecting libraries are a few chairs. Here he sometimes receives intimate acquaintances or diplomats. His own simply furnished bedroom leads off this third library.

In the winter in Israel many men wear overcoats, the temperature often drops to the uncomfortable thirties, and most modern houses turn on their central heating. But for years the only heating device the Ben-Gurions had was an old-fashioned, portable kerosene burner.

One day Ambassador McDonald was invited for lunch, and found Paula bundled up in heavy slacks and a sweater. The oil heater that day was first used to raise the temperature in the dining room slightly above that of the interior of a refrigerator, and later the Prime Minister and the American Ambassador huddled over it, rubbing their hands together, as they talked of matters of grave import.

On another occasion McDonald received a message to call on Ben-Gurion in the early evening for a conference. Paula admitted him and said:

"He's upstairs working. Go up."

He found the Prime Minister in bed, under three or four blankets, signing state papers.

Looking over the top of the spectacles he wears when reading, he said:

"It's either freeze downstairs or be comfortable in bed."

His Tel Aviv office in those days was starkly simple. One of the most functional objects it contained was an old-fashioned black iron machine for punching holes, which he always kept on his desk. Whenever he saw a piece of printed or written matter that was of special interest to him he used the machine to punch holes in it and then slipped it over the two paper fasteners in a file that he never let anyone else handle.

Foreign Office cables in which he was interested were marked "Return to B.G.," and eventually he punched holes in them and put them in his file.

On the last day of every month, just before 8 P.M., Ben-Gurion bent over the end of the two paper fasteners, wrote the month and the year on the cover, and said to one of the office assistants, as if he were well satisfied with the way he had performed his role of archivist:

"Well, now it's time to start a new one!"

He carried the current month's file with him in his brief case wherever he went.

As Minister of Defense, Ben-Gurion had an adjutant or military secretary, and as Prime Minister he had a director of the Prime Minister's office (Teddy Kollek, product of a kibbutz on the Sea of Galilee), an adviser on public relations (Moshe Pearlman, an experienced British journalist and the author of many pamphlets and books), a private secretary (his first was Elkana Gali, who had been trained in the Foreign Office and who had also come from the shores of the Galilee lake), and two "office assistants," as well as a stenographer who did little else but help him with his speeches and literary work, and several typists.

From all of these young people Ben-Gurion demanded self-sacrifice, which they gave him in varying degrees.

It was the military secretary who set the pattern of a devoted subordinate. Lieutenant Colonel Nehemiah Argov was twenty-eight years Ben-Gurion's junior. He was almost a sabra, having come from one of the Baltic countries as a small child. He had grown up in Ein Gev, and had been married and divorced in his youth, a subject he mentioned only once in his years of association with those in the Prime Minister's office.

Argov had been suggested for the post by Chief of Staff Dostrovsky because during his ten years with Haganah he had been adjutant to one officer after another, and finally to Dostrovsky himself. He came to Ben-Gurion one month before the 1948 Arab invasion.

Argov was exactly the Prime Minister's height, five feet four. His dark hair was in striking contrast to his chief's white fringe. He had an angular face, sharp-pointed nose, unhappy eyes. He seldom smiled. He was slim, with a wiry, athletic build. He would often amuse himself while waiting somewhere for his chief by chinning himself on a door.

His devotion to Ben-Gurion soon became known in every corner of Israel.

On nights when Ben-Gurion stayed late at his desk, the staff would sit in the outer office laughing, telling stories, perhaps talking about a film they wanted to see "if B.G. leaves soon enough." Argov would pace the floor nervously. After seeing that Ben-Gurion reached home safely he might join the others at a cinema, but halfway through the film he was likely to excuse himself, saying:

"I'm sorry but I'm worried about B.G. I must see that everything is all right."

As an A.D.C. he was the connecting link between Ben-Gurion and the Army. In addition he performed the duties that the United States Secret Service does for a President, worrying twenty-four hours a day about "security." With so many Arabs in the country, with the frontiers so close, with surprise air raids always a possibility, and with terrorists at hand who specialized in assassination, Argov had to be on the alert. But he gave his role a much more personal interpretation. His devotion was so great that he finally became almost a personal servant, bringing the Prime Minister a glass of water before he addressed the Knesset, seeing that he had his afternoon cup of tea, and waiting on him like a valet.

Argov resented the title "adjutant," and whenever a newspaper referred to him in this way he would telephone the editor and say:

"Please be informed that I am the Prime Minister's military secretary."

One of the compensations for his devotion was the power that accrued to him. He became more than just a go-between. He passed on anyone who wanted to see the Prime Minister, and if he said "no" there was no court of appeal.

Argov quickly developed a sixth sense about his superior. He seemed to be able to *feel* Ben-Gurion's most casual reactions to people, remarks, and events. If he suspected the Prime Minister disliked a man he hated the man.

Argov was a definite personality, but he converted himself within a few years into a perfect shadow. At times he would walk a step or two behind Ben-Gurion, as if he actually were a shadow. He geared his personality to his superior's, and became his alter ego. Ben-Gurion had no hobbies, so he had none. Ben-Gurion was informal in his manner of dress, and so was he. When Ben-Gurion had his shirt open at the neck, so did Argov.

Ben-Gurion has a singleness of purpose, so Argov developed one also, only his was his commander's happiness. He was willing to be ridiculed and misunderstood in order to keep the Old Man free of worries.

Anything that was not connected in some way with Ben-Gurion was of neither importance nor interest to him.

At first Argov intentionally mimicked the gestures and the manner of speech of the man he served. Gradually it became unconscious and he began to talk, gesticulate, and even walk like him.

There was no selfish motive in all this. Argov neither sought nor gained wealth, social distinction, or public acclaim. He neither drew a large salary nor had a comfortable life.

He was jealous of only one person, a man long dead. He knew of the close bond there had been between Berl Katzenelson and his chief. He once told a Tel Aviv friend of his frustration at not having the capacity to make an intellectual impression on Ben-Gurion.

In the first few years of independence the Prime Minister changed his civilian secretary three or four times, but Argov's position was as secure as his own.

There were many explanations of the older man's interest in the younger. One was that it was a perfect father-son relationship.

Another, that he saw in this young pioneer from Galilee, so fine of feature, so devoted and loyal, the average man of the future—a pattern of what all young Israelis might someday be like.

Others in the office knew that Ben-Gurion told Argov things he mentioned to no one else, not even Paula. But there was no give-and-take. Argov listened while Ben-Gurion talked not so much *to* him as *at* him, often using him as a sounding board. It was the Prime Minister thinking aloud.

The young man sat at the older man's feet, figuratively and sometimes even literally, and as he listened some of the vision of the master reflected itself in the face of the disciple.

Because Israel is so small a country, where almost everyone knows everyone else, Nehemiah Argov became one of the favorite subjects of conversation, between battles and frontier incidents.

The importance of the relationship between the young army officer and the white-haired leader was deprecated by old-time Zionists and by intellectual labor leaders who resented anyone mentioning a military adjutant and the great Katzenelson in the same sentence. There was nothing at all in common between these two men except—they were the only two friends Ben-Gurion ever had—friends for entirely different reasons, yet the only two men who ever came really close to him.

Argov may have been influenced by the story of the man whose name he bore. The original Nehemiah twenty-four centuries ago had been cupbearer to a king; this Nehemiah would see that a Prime Minister got his tea. The old Nehemiah had been guardian of the royal apartment, responsible for protecting the ruler from harm. This Nehemiah would take on the same responsibility for another head of government several millennia later. The Nehemiah of the Bible had been a socialist, championing the cause of the poor and taking strong action against exploiters; an ardent advocate of Hebrew at a time when another language was used by the people; a writer whose pen had great facility. The Biblical Nehemiah had come to the Holy Land from a distant place, had rebuilt Jerusalem, and had organized a great migration of Jews from abroad. Argov's parents may have had a dream that he could someday become a twentieth-century Nehemiah. He would fail them if that was their dream. But at least he could help the man who was going to succeed in doing it, the man who resembled in so many more ways than he did his own namesake.

Nomenclature was always a problem. The Prime Minister called all his youthful associates by their first names, including Nehemiah. He insisted that they call him plain "Ben-Gurion." One of the young typists was always making a mistake and saying "Mr. Ben-Gurion." Each time she did he would say, "Yes, *Miss* Mina!" sarcastically emphasizing the Miss.

The first day a new private secretary began work, he made the error of saying:

"Mr. Prime Minister——"

The Prime Minister interrupted.

"If you want me to call you by your first name you had better call me Ben-Gurion."

After that every time the young secretary slipped and said, "Mr. Prime Minister," Ben-Gurion would reply, "Yes, Mr. Private Secretary."

When Ruth Havilio, who became one of the office assistants, was waiting in the outer office to be interviewed and Ben-Gurion came through the room, she respectfully jumped to her feet. The Prime Minister turned on her and said:

"*Shvi* [Sit down]!"

When she hesitated, he smiled in the direction of Argov and said:

"He's a soldier and I am his commander, so I can order him to sit down. I suppose I must *ask* you."

One day Ben-Gurion called Miss Havilio to his desk and asked if a certain member of his Cabinet had been to see him.

"Yes, the Minister was here yesterday," Miss Havilio replied. Ben-Gurion said:

"What do you mean, 'the Minister'? You are talking about a man. Call him by his name."

Miss Havilio felt argumentative and answered:

"But it is a fact that he is a Minister."

Ben-Gurion's eyes danced.

"What is your father's name?"

"Nissim."

"And so you are Ruth, daughter of Nissim. That is a fact, yes?"

"Yes."

"But is it necessary for me every time I wish to speak to you to say, 'Ruth, daughter of Nissim'?"

Once, to welcome a new member of the staff, Miss Havilio and the private secretary bought some flowers and put them on the new man's desk, with a card, already printed, which said:

With the Compliments of
The Prime Minister's
Personal Office

Then, to make it seem a little more personal, they signed their own first names. Ben-Gurion, passing through the outer office, saw the flowers, read the card, and then asked:

"Where is my name?"

"You are the Prime Minister," Miss Havilio said.

"What do you mean, I am the Prime Minister? Were you never taught what colleagues are?"

"I was also taught what a Prime Minister is."

"A Prime Minister," replied Ben-Gurion intently, "is an office, not a man. Someday there will be another Prime Minister. But I am a man!"

Then he took a pen and wrote on the card a signature he rarely used, "David," a name by which hardly anyone ever called him.

The office routine was simple. The private secretary, Miss Havilio, and the other office assistant would take all the incoming mail, put the highly important or personal letters on Ben-Gurion's desk, and answer the others themselves. In those first days of independence it seemed that a majority of the citizens of Israel had complaints, wanted something, or found another excuse to write personally to the Prime Minister, expecting a personal reply.

A man whose water pipes had burst—a wife whose husband had run away—people wanting to tell the Prime Minister how he should run the country—letters that should have gone to individual ministries.

It would have taken many Ben-Gurions to have answered them all, so the staff did it, signing the replies, "From the Prime Minister's Office." The system would have worked well, except for the Prime Minister's habit of wandering into the outer office and picking letters at random from the pile on Miss Havilio's desk, and walking off with them. Every letter interested him, and he felt cheated at not seeing them all.

Soon after independence a letter came from three Arabs, nomadic Druses. Now that there was a state, they were writing to the Prime Minister to say that they would like jobs. Ben-Gurion saw the letter on Miss Havilio's desk, took it to his own office, and spent most of the afternoon and early evening conferring by telephone with officials in various government departments, trying to find suitable employment for three out-of-work Druses.

After that the staff played a continuous trick on their chief. If anyone had a letter he was especially eager for Ben-Gurion to read, he would put it on the top of the mail at the corner of Miss Havilio's desk, and Ben-Gurion was almost certain eventually to pick it up and walk off with it.

Another trick was to slip a letter they wanted him to see, urgently, between the pages of a book catalogue that had just arrived by mail.

The staff could always tell when Ben-Gurion was especially worried about something by his increased interest in books. He would stalk into the outer office and say:

"Haven't those books I ordered weeks ago come yet?"

Ben-Gurion reads most of the coded cables that come from Israel's diplomatic representatives.

He never dictates to a secretary, although he could do so in seven languages. Instead he has a notebook in which he scribbles his replies to communications in pencil in Hebrew, and then tears the sheets out and walks to the outer office and hands them to a typist.

His letters are always in simple language, with few long words or complicated constructions. Regardless of what language the answer is finally to be in, he always writes in Hebrew. The office assistants do the translating. Ben-Gurion will often correct or improve the translated versions.

One day a British author, well known for his literary style, came into the outer office just as Miss Havilio finished making a rough translation of a letter Ben-Gurion wanted to go out in English. She gave it to the Englishman and asked him to "polish it up a bit." He graciously obliged, making many improvements.

That evening Ben-Gurion came from his office holding the finished letter in his hand.

"Whose English is this?"

Miss Havilio confessed.

"It's very beautiful," Ben-Gurion said, "but it's him, not me. Now you translate it over again into my kind of English."

The Prime Minister writes his speeches and articles in Hebrew on three-by-five cards, which he rarely numbers, thus causing frequent distress for the stenographer who types the words onto manuscript-sized paper.

He prepares each speech as if it were his first—or his last—as if it were the most important speech in his career. He verifies every fact he is going to use, checks every quotation, knows the source of every claim he is going to make and the proof of every assertion.

Anyone who writes an article attacking Ben-Gurion's concept of modern Zionism is apt to find himself in sudden correspondence with the Prime Minister of Israel.

An obscure Los Angeles Jew several years ago wrote Ben-Gurion a letter on whether an American Zionist ought to immigrate to Israel. The correspondence flowed back and forth for three and a half months—thousands of words—until finally both sides got tired.

Often writers who cannot get into print any other way start a correspondence with Ben-Gurion and then sell the letters and replies to a magazine.

Words are important to Ben-Gurion, no matter what happens to them. The printed word takes on for him almost a sacred value. While Prime Minister he has often written for a Yiddish paper in the United States with a circulation of five thousand.

He has written many books and millions of words of magazine and newspaper articles. He has been generous in the number of introductions he has written, without compensation, for other men's books.

He has the writer's occupational illness of wanting to see his words in print as quickly as possible. His first question when he turns in an article is:

"How soon will it appear?"

His style is somewhat staccato. What he writes for Hebrew papers reminds some Americans of Brisbane at his best. His sentence structure is Biblical. Few if any Hebrew writers have as large a Hebrew vocabulary. He always seems to use exactly the correct word. His writing is forceful but not flowery. His sentences often strike like successive hammer blows. Hebrew is the perfect language for him because it is a language of action (even the abstract is tied up with the concrete).

Twenty-five years before he became Prime Minister, Ben-Gurion started writing what may be the most valuable unpublished book in existence. It has already grown to thirty-five volumes containing at least five million words. Few people have ever seen him working on it, and he has never, as far as anyone knows, permitted anyone to take a volume and read it through. Few have even had the privilege of glimpsing the exteriors.

It is technically a journal, rather than a diary, for it contains profound thoughts culled from his reading, provocative remarks made by visitors, his own reactions to events and ideas. He writes it every evening at home, usually just before or just after midnight.

His associates call it simply "his book." He never discusses it with them, and he keeps all the volumes in his Tel Aviv library.

In his office he has another continuously growing book, which is less personal but which in some distant day may become source material for a definitive history of modern Israel.

Whenever Ben-Gurion is talking with a visitor he sits with a block of note paper on his lap, writing constantly. If the person is a stranger, he may start off by asking:

"Exactly how do you spell your name?"

Then in Hebrew characters he writes a complete résumé of the conversation. After the guest has gone, he copies his notes himself into a cheap six-by-eight-inch notebook with a black cover. At the end of each of these notebooks he makes his own index.

Two years later, if the subject comes up again, he is likely to send for the proper book, turn to his previous notes, and say:

"You are wrong. What you said last time—and I have your exact words—was . . ."

He even enters what he himself said, so there can be no misunderstanding about any commitments he has made.

Once Baruch Tal, a Mapai party associate, asked him:

"Why do you go to all that trouble?"

Ben-Gurion replied:

"Often I have other more important matters on my mind, but if I sit taking notes I compel myself to pay attention to my visitor and his problems."

Except when he is reading, Ben-Gurion is nowhere happier than when at the podium. He delights in barraging his opponents with logic, pinning them down with irony, then demolishing them with historical bombshells.

He prefers to speak without a public address system, having learned oratory in the pre-mechanical age.

On one occasion when a chairman advised him to make his remarks brief, he asked with simple honesty:

"And what is the value of brevity?"

He never equaled Dr. Weizmann's record (of taking part in a debate at Basle, Switzerland, that lasted three days and two nights), but has often spoken for hours without a pause. One Histadruth conference at which he did the major part of the speaking began at 10 A.M. and continued until 5 P.M. without a break.

By comparison with the shining Biblical oratory of Abba Eban, Israel Ambassador to Washington, Ben-Gurion speaks in a rich but simple style. He knows no forensic tricks and rarely changes the pitch of his voice.

Yet when he gets to his feet in the Knesset, there is a hush and almost breathless expectancy because of the personality of the speaker and the importance of what he generally has to say. He rarely delivers a "minor" speech. Each one seems like a pronunciamento. He is not a master with the rapier, nor is his sarcasm generally light. He is a philosopher more than a politician.

He does not strive for picturesque language, yet he is capable of saying:

"In the Diaspora, Jews are human dust, whose particles try to cling to each other . . ."

And:

"Israel makes everything that is Jewish human and everything that is human Jewish."

CHAPTER SEVENTEEN

ONE SABBATH afternoon several years ago Ben-Gurion and his wife attended a reception at the Sharon Hotel on the sea at Herzlia for visiting United Jewish Appeal delegates from the United States. Halfway through the afternoon the Prime Minister arose and started to say good-by. Then his wife whispered something in his ear and he sat down again, saying:

"Paula tells me we should stay a little longer, and I always do what Paula says."

This was not an exaggeration. In certain departments of his life his wife has always had the last word.

Paula Ben-Gurion is devoted, energetic, and unconventional; a shadow and a protector; a woman with few inhibitions. She has a personality of her own as strong as her husband's.

During more than four decades she has darned his socks, washed his shirts, borne and brought up his children, seen to their education, cared for the grandchildren.

Once she explained why she has always done at least the light laundry:

"I am very particular about Ben-Gurion's shirts."

No matter whether he was a labor organizer, secretary general of Histadruth, member of the shadow government or, finally, Prime Minister, she has treated him like a child, making him wear his scarf when the weather is bad, seeing that he has on his rubbers when it is raining, giving him milk to drink periodically, and feeding him the food he has needed for energy.

When she knows he is going to address the Knesset she equips herself with a thermos bottle of hot tea and a cup, and seats herself behind a curtain near the podium while he is talking. The moment he has finished, she pours the tea and makes him drink it.

She answers every telephone call that comes to the house, and no one gets to talk to her husband unless she thinks the matter is urgent.

"It's a bother for me and sometimes I get tired of so many calls, but it saves him a lot of time."

She also protects him by never discussing family finances with him.

"If he had known how poor we were sometimes he would have been very worried."

When he is taking a nap, she tells the sentries guarding the house to keep the children in the street quiet. If they do not succeed, Paula herself will storm out, shouting, "*Sheket, sheket* [Quiet, quiet]!"

One day while the Prime Minister was napping, a crowd of children gathered in front of the house and began to chant:

"We want to see Ben-Gurion! We want to see Ben-Gurion!"

They kept it up until Paula chased them down the street with a broom.

As far as their father ever knew, Amos, Renana, and Geula went through their childhood with virtually no illnesses. Paula arranged it so he never was aware that they were sick.

A member of Ben-Gurion's government who has been associated with him since he was a young man says:

"Catholic culture was spread throughout the world by members of monastic orders, who were free of worry about all the petty family problems that beset other men, and therefore were able to concentrate all their energy on the job at hand.

"Paula in her wisdom and devotion has provided Ben-Gurion with all the advantages of a family life without any of the worries or encumbrances. She has let him live like a monk or hermit just as much as he has wanted to."

Several years ago Paula wrote an article, "My Life with B.G.," for *Rimon*, a monthly magazine that published two editions, the first in Hebrew and then a week or so later an English translation.

The Hebrew edition, telling of their marriage in New York, described the civil ceremony just as it took place, in an office at City Hall before a civil official.

After the magazine came out, someone pointed out to Paula and her husband that this might be offensive to some Orthodox Israelis. The reaction of husband and wife was typical. The Prime Minister, instead of scolding his wife, brushed the criticism aside, saying in effect:

"It's the truth, isn't it?"

But Paula, worried over having unwittingly caused her husband embarrassment, went to the telephone, called the magazine, and asked that the offending sentences be removed from the story when it appeared in English.

On the wall of the Ben-Gurion living room there is a photograph of Helen Keller. If anyone even glances at it, Paula will say:

"When she met Ben-Gurion she felt his head with her fingers and kept saying, 'What a head! What a head!' She knew he had the head of a great man."

Forty-two years ago, when she was still Paula Munweis, she began saying to friends:

"Someday Ben-Gurion is going to be a great man."

Before long she had dropped the "someday."

After a few more years she changed the tense of the verb and made it a simple statement of fact instead of a prediction.

At first people looked at her a little oddly when she said it. Some even laughed behind her back. She told everyone—clerks in shops, neighbors, foreign diplomats, her own children, Jews, Christians, and even Arabs:

"You know, Ben-Gurion is a great man."

Paula's unconventionality has given birth to hundreds of stories that Israelis repeat with amusement, yet with no malice; with amusement rooted in affection.

Paula herself has never objected to these stories and is contantly adding to the saga.

In the *Rimon* article she wrote:

We received visits from internationally known statesmen, such as Dag Hammarskjold and Dr. Ralph Bunche. I did not hesitate to express my views to Mr. Hammarskjold, whose bachelorhood affects his political attitudes. I said to him: "Why don't you get married? Then you would have troubles of your own and you would forget to make trouble for us." Dr. Bunche was even told by me that lately he had changed for the worse.

Mr. Hammarskjold and Dr. Bunche knew Paula well enough not to be offended. They knew the remarks were based on friendship and were made without ill will. But the Israel Foreign Office holds its breath for fear of the effect her forthrightness will have in a world in which "diplomatic" has come to be synonymous with not speaking out in uninhibited honesty.

In 1948, Henry J. Morgenthau, Jr., former Secretary of the Treasury, came to Israel in his capacity as chairman of the United Jewish Appeal and was given royal treatment for days. Near the end of his visit he held a press conference in a Tel Aviv hotel. Paula Ben-Gurion sat beside him smiling her approval as he told how the funds being raised in America for Israel would help prevent the spread of Communism in the Middle East.

Suddenly a shrill voice shouted:

"We don't want your dollars. You can't buy us. We know the friendship of the Soviet Union for Israel."

It was the young editor of a Communist paper. As the others tried to silence him, Morgenthau calmly said:

"This is a democracy, and you have the right to your own opinion."

That seemed to end the matter. But not for Paula. As soon as the conference was adjourned she sought out the Communist and told him exactly what she thought of him for insulting Israel's distinguished guest.

No one has ever tried to suppress Paula, and it would be a foolish man who might think he could.

"By nature I am a frank person," she says, "and I do not hesitate to say what I think to anyone, no matter what his position or standing."

When Paula comes into a room full of people making "polite conversation," it is as if someone had opened a window and let in fresh air.

Once when she was attending a session of the Knesset, Menachem Beigin walked past her without speaking. She wheeled around like an artillery piece, caught up with him, and in the presence of many parliamentary members began by saying:

"Look here, Mr. Beigin, political differences are no excuse for rudeness . . ."

He finally apologized and fled.

Strangers are often taken aback by her sharpness and frankness. She has the independent spirit of a pioneer. She knows none of the finesse of high society. She likes plain talk as much as her husband does.

Her unconventionality comes out in other refreshing ways. One day some American visitors who had met the Prime Minister and his wife were about to leave their hotel for the airport when an Israel policeman appeared at their door and said Mrs. Ben-Gurion had sent him to ask an important question: the Prime Minister during his various visits to the United States had become fond of hamburgers and was always asking her to make them, so please, would they give the policeman the recipe?

After one of the few cocktail parties ever given in the Ben-Gurion home, Paula looked at the mountains of unconsumed sandwiches, fruit, and cookies and said to her husband's secretary as he was about to leave:

"I'll get a bag and you take them home."

The secretary managed to escape without taking anything, but half an hour later a uniformed sentry appeared at his door with a large platter of leftovers from the party.

Paula Ben-Gurion is about her husband's height. She has a mass of black hair, which she often parts in the center and which is strikingly in contrast to her husband's white wisps.

She wears no make-up, little jewelry, and almost always dark clothes.

"That is the way my husband wishes it."

She buys one pair of shoes a year, except that once when she went abroad she admitted to reporters that she had indulged in an extra pair for the trip.

She sometimes wears a tam, but more often goes bareheaded, as her husband does.

She keeps a neat house.

"That's because I was once a nurse. I like order."

She has been a devoted mother and is a proud grandmother. Her favorite story about her family concerns Geula's son, Mushik, now eleven. The boy's father, Immanuel Ben Eliezer, is the head of a department in the Ministry of Defense. One day Mushik said to him:

"Dad, you're so tall and good-looking, but you're only an officer. Grandpa is old and short, but he's Prime Minister. Why is that?"

One of Paula's little jokes is that "we are a United Nations family because Geula was born in New York, Amos in London, and Renana in Israel."

At the end of 1948, on Ben-Gurion's suggestion, the government introduced a system of identity cards, each of which had to bear a new photograph of the holder.

One day Argov instructed David Anderman, chief of the government photographic department, to go to Ben-Gurion's house during siesta hour with his camera, lights, tripod, and other equipment to photograph the Prime Minister.

At first Paula refused to admit him.

"Ben-Gurion is sleeping."

"But Argov commanded it," Anderman protested.

"All right, but it doesn't make any sense. You have hundreds of pictures of him already."

Ben-Gurion was also difficult. He has never had much patience with photographers. If they can snap something and go away he is content, but if there is any posing, adjusting of lights, or wasting of time he becomes impatient.

When he appeared from his bedroom he had a jacket over his pajamas. Anderman suggested he should put on a shirt and tie.

"What's the matter with what he has on?" Paula asked angrily.

While the Old Man was upstairs getting on a shirt and tie, Anderman started setting up his equipment in the living room. As he put his tripod on the rug, Paula said:

"You're going to ruin my carpet with all your mud."

Thereupon she rolled it up.

Important government and political conferences are often held in the Ben-Gurion home, but the doors are never closed to Paula. She walks in and out while the discussion is going on, with cups of tea or clean ash trays. Her husband trusts her completely. He knows that she will gossip as eagerly as the next woman about personalities but that she will never tell anyone any of the state secrets she knows.

Her gossip is penetrating, unrestrained, and often demolishing. It is usually directed against those people she calls—using an idiom she learned in America—"phonies." She is able to spot an insincere person the moment he enters a room, an ability her husband does not have to the extent she does.

Her heart is as large as the Negev and as warm as a July afternoon on the desert.

During the days of austerity she would often stand in a queue talking about the problems of being a Prime Minister's wife with the other hausfraus. Sometimes she would use the Yiddish diminutive about him.

"I must get such-and-such for my Dovidle."

Paula's warmheartedness is nothing passive. It has a fierce, active quality, just as her devotion to her husband has.

Once when the wife of a government official was ill, Paula sent one of her uniformed sentries to the official's house two or three times a day to get a report on the wife's condition and find out if anything was needed. When the official tried to thank her, she became gruff and almost angry. Gratitude embarrasses her.

The intellectual difference between husband and wife might have led to separation years ago if the devotion on both sides had not been so intense.

Paula's favorite author is Longfellow. Once she knew many of his poems by heart. Her favorite fiction writer is Jack London. She has no intellectual pretensions. She likes to go to movies and listen to entertainment on the radio. Ben-Gurion's world of Plato, Buddha, the Oriental philosophers, and the mystics is an intellectual place with which she has never become acquainted. At midnight when her husband retires to his room, turns on his bed light, and enters this world, their paths separate for a few hours. But in the morning he will be down in the kitchen at seven, ready for his cup of coffee and his morning greeting.

Just as Ben-Gurion has set a stimulating example to the leaders of the new Israel in how to stay humble though holding high office, so Paula has given the wives a few lessons. She has changed almost nothing about her way of life in forty years. She chats with the sentries about their domestic problems, sends them off on errands, gossips with the neighbors, and has developed no extravagances. She sees no reason why being a Prime Minister's wife should force her to change her character or her habits.

She has never had a full-time maid, although servants are plentiful and inexpensive in this part of the world.

"I am a socialist, like Ben-Gurion," she says, "and I do not believe in exploitation."

She does have a cleaning woman come in occasionally.

One of her few indulgences is to sleep in the summer with an electric fan beside her bed.

Just after the war a nephew in New York wrote that he was coming to Israel and asked her what she would like from America. Of all the wonders she might have chosen she picked:

"Some packages of dehydrated soup."

Paula prides herself on never having interfered in her husband's political affairs, although she admits that many years ago she was bitterly against his idea of a political truce with Jabotinsky. All letters that come to the house that she knows are not personal she sends unopened to the Prime Minister's office.

On the rare occasions when she has given in to minor illnesses and gone to bed, her husband has brought a book and sat beside her, to be within call if needed.

Once when she was in a hospital in Tel Aviv and he was at Sde Boker, in the desert, he wrote her a letter she showed to many people. It was the sort of a love letter a very young man might have written to his sweetheart. It was full of blue clouds, singing birds, poetry, romanticism. It had a great deal to do with Paula's quick recovery.

Half seriously someone once suggested that the State of Israel decorate this unusual woman, without whom the history of the country might have been much different.

The only trouble is that if such a presentation were made, Paula Ben-Gurion would probably turn to the chairman and say:

"What's the matter, have you run out of people to give medals to?"

CHAPTER EIGHTEEN

THE election campaign was over, Dr. Weizmann was President, the frontiers were quiet for the moment, and David Ben-Gurion could turn to the manifold tasks of peace and try to prove to his own people and to the world that he could continue to be as inspiring a leader as he had been during the months of sporadic war.

The measure of his greatness would now be taken.

It was too soon to start beating swords into plowshares. The Army needed to be strengthened, not weakened. But at the same time a nation must be built out of a land and a people almost overwhelmed by problems.

There was no peace with the six enemy countries; just a series of cease-fires, armistices, and temporary truces.

Britain had at last given the new state hesitant diplomatic approval, but the Arab countries still would not even use the word "Israel." ("That group of Jews" was the way Cairo Radio often designated the nation.)

There was no place to put the immigrants who were coming in at the rate of one a minute.

Ben-Gurion had other discouragements.

There had always been a strong Zionist movement in the United States, and he had expected that as soon as there was a state a large number of American Zionists would emigrate; men and women with skills and abilities who would be able to take over positions of responsibility. But by 1949 he realized that the five million American Jews had been so thoroughly integrated that it would be surprising if even a few hundred emigrated and remained in Israel. His disappointment was so great that for years his writings and speeches would be scattered with references to it.

This was the new crisis of his life. Like some of the others, it was not possible finally one day to make a decision and then forget it. There remained a continuous problem of how far to go in being honest and criticizing those whose financial support he needed.

Ben-Gurion knew that the money to bring in several million immigrants, to house them, and to make useful citizens of them would have to be contributed by Jews in the United States. Perhaps also money to keep the state going. If he antagonized American Jewry, the whole dream might collapse in dust.

It was not an easy decision to face. A diplomat, a less honest or less brave man might have found some excuse to temporize. But Ben-Gurion spoke his disappointment boldly, even though he must have known his words would not spark any sudden flow of immigration from New York to Tel Aviv.

There were other problems in 1949.

There was not nearly enough money to finance the conversion into a proud and self-sufficient people of all the sad-faced refugees from the slums of North Africa, the ghettos of the Orient, and the D.P. camps of Europe.

Even with the United Jewish Appeal raising more money per capita among American Jews than any other group in the country had ever given for any unselfish purpose, government funds were so scarce that the most popular joke in 1949 was about the man who approached Ben-Gurion for a job and was told he could be Colonial Secretary."

"But we don't have any colonies yet, do we?"

"No," replied Ben-Gurion, "and we don't have any money either, but we have a Minister of Finance."

Twelve political parties had elected one or more members apiece to the Knesset. Because twelve points of view had to be stated on almost every subject that came up for discussion, the processes of democracy were often slow.

Israel was a country without a capital. Government offices were still at Hakirya, but the Knesset had to meet in a Tel Aviv motion picture theater.

Thousands of men and women were being employed to work in newly organized government bureaus, but it took time to train them, and meanwhile in the cafés of the provisional capital people laughed at the errors of bureaucracy and told stories, like the one about the two lions that escaped from the zoo. One decided it would be safer to go to the Negev. The other remained in Tel Aviv. A week later the Negev lion returned, hungry and tired; there had been few people to eat in the desert. The Tel Aviv lion was plump and happy.

"Every morning at eight I go to Hakirya and stand outside the government offices and have a nice meal of five officials."

"But isn't it dangerous?" asked the Negev lion.

"Not at all," replied the plump lion. "There are so many surplus officials, nobody misses the few I take."

Those in important positions were busy. Ben-Gurion's own day grew longer and longer. It became a saying that he was "harder to see than the Pope."

A "Four-Year Development and Absorption Plan" was one of his creations. He had it printed as a poster, so each government official could tack it on the wall over his desk. He suggested that each official read through the plan every morning and ask himself what contribution he could make during the day to bring it closer to realization.

In those early months of the state Ben-Gurion was the hub of the wheel. All official life revolved around him—or because of him. Ministers had broad powers, but no decree was valid until it had been published in the *Official Gazette*, and nothing could appear in the *Gazette* without passing through the Prime Minister's office. In cabinet meetings the head of the government had only one vote, but he controlled the agenda. More important than that, he dominated the Cabinet with his personality, and they all respected his bright vision of Israel's future.

One of Ben-Gurion's tasks during 1949 was to work out compromises with the religious bloc, whose sixteen votes in the Knesset he needed for a majority.

He agreed to the demand that all cooking in the Army be done in kosher manner, not to avoid a fight but because otherwise there would have been a kosher and a non-kosher mess, and that would have divided the Army along religious lines, which he refused to do.

He also agreed to a law giving the rabbis control over marriage and divorce. Christians, Arabs, and free-thinking Jews who wanted a non-religious wedding would have to get married on a ship at sea or go to some foreign country. Again he acceded in order to avoid splitting the country into two groups whose members would never be able to intermarry.

But Ben-Gurion did resist efforts to make Israel a theocratic state. While buses and trains do not run anywhere in the country on the Sabbath, and cinemas remain closed, and newspapers do not publish, some of the hotels along the sea front in Tel Aviv serve guests ham and eggs for breakfast whether they ask for it or not, and many Israelis smoke cigarettes between sundown Friday and sundown Saturday without anyone bothering them.

Ben-Gurion's greatest fight with the religious bloc was over the draft law, which provided that young women from eighteen to twenty-six, unmarried, should be subject to conscription. The Orthodox parties fought it on many grounds, among them that the Bible forbids women to wear men's clothing. During the debate the Prime Minister was reported to have asked:

"What makes you think that a woman with a machine gun is any less irresistible to a man than a woman with a typewriter?"

Ben-Gurion and the religious parties were, oddly, on the same side in the argument over whether Israel should adopt a written constitution, but for different reasons.

A brilliant Israel authority on constitutional law, who had studied the constitutions of most Western countries, drew up one for Israel.

When Ben-Gurion, reading it, came to the provision for a Supreme Court with power to set aside legislation passed by the Knesset, he turned to an aide and said:

"I will never permit lawyers to tell us how to run the country."

He argued that Great Britain had no written constitution. Eleven years had passed in the United States between the Declaration of Independence and the promulgation of a constitution. Besides, a constitution prevented the people from amending laws easily and therefore was anti-democratic in effect. Even if Israel was to have one, they should wait until more progress had been made with the ingathering of the exiles, so the entire population could have a voice in the matter.

People were worried about a Bill of Rights. Ben-Gurion impatiently replied:

"What we need right now is a Bill of Duties."

When there was discussion about what a Bill of Rights ought to contain, he said:

"It takes many words in English, but just three in Hebrew: *Veahavta re-ekh'a kamoh'a* [Love your fellow human being as yourself]."

And then there was the cold war. If Israel allied herself with the West, which was her natural inclination, how would this affect the 1,800,000 Jews in Russia and the 800,000 in the satellite countries? Some wanted to immigrate to Israel, if they could ever get permission to leave. Nearly three million lives were involved.

Ben-Gurion had a hope. It was worth trying, anyway. After all, Russia had voted for the creation of Israel at Lake Success. Maybe . . .

So he spoke softly, at first.

"It is our policy to promote friendship and reciprocity with every peace-loving country, without prying into its internal affairs."

To Moscow he sent as Minister Golda Myerson, who had been raised in Milwaukee. To Prague he sent Ehud Avriel, a brilliant young socialist. To Bucharest, Reuven Rubin, artist, who had been born in Rumania and had gone to school with Ana Pauker, now Rumania's Foreign Minister.

Mrs. Myerson came home very soon, discouraged.

When word spread among Rumanian Jews that an Israel Consulate had been opened, they flocked to it by the hundreds to beg visas, crowding the streets, causing traffic jams, mobbing the tall, thin artist whenever he came and went. At first Ana Pauker was co-operative, and Rubin was able to start a thin stream of

Rumanian Jews in the direction of Haifa. They were mostly the aged, the ill, the incapacitated; people Ana Pauker and her superiors decided were of no value to Rumania. But they were Jews, going home.

Then suddenly the Jewish Foreign Minister slammed the gates tight, and Rubin was finally forced to give up and return to his paints and canvases in Tel Aviv.

But they came from other directions: the sick, the well; Orientals and Occidentals; tall, thin, short, dark, light, consumptive, some without an arm or a leg, skilled, unskilled, laughing, weeping, pregnant, dying—but Jews, all, cut off for two thousand years from the Land of the Book, welcome now, because the Law of the Return said every Jew in the world had the right to come back, without need of a visa or even a rubber stamp.

They came most dramatically from Yemen, that medieval, sunscorched country on the Red Sea where automobiles were almost unknown and Jews were almost undistinguishable from the non-Jewish tribesmen. These ultra-religious primitive people were transported in five Skymasters that went back and forth, packing in twice the normal number of passengers per plane because they were so undersized, undernourished, and underweight.

To these people and to the immigrants from North Africa, Ben-Gurion was the new David. His title might be "Prime Minister," but to them he was king, the Messiah. He was responsible for the miracle of their coming. When he visited the tents and the shacks in which they were temporarily housed, they brought him their sick to cure and fought to touch his garments.

This ingathering had, even for un-Orthodox Ben-Gurion, a mystic quality. It was much more than just trying to provide a boardinghouse for the homeless, or saving people from oppression, or filling up the open places in a "new" land with pioneers, or putting brave young people along the frontiers to watch the enemy.

For Ben-Gurion this was a turning point that, he kept telling people, occurs only once or twice in the entire historical life of a race. This was the start of the regeneration of the entire Jewish people.

While his associates in the government harassed him with a thousand petty matters—who should be named collector of customs, should there be a law on the maximum height of buildings, and what time should cafés be required to close—Ben-Gurion enlarged his dreams and tried to pass them on; tried to give direction to the change that was occurring so rapidly; tried to communicate the mysticism of it, the greatness of it, the wonder of it.

It was necessary to sign letters, preside at ceremonies, be photographed, consult with ministers, preside over the Cabinet, but most important of all, the philosophy of the nation must be expounded. Somebody must explain that Israel is an experimental station for world knowledge and social equality.

There was the danger of a color bar arising, now that so many dark-skinned Jews were entering. There was the problem of languages and dialects. There had to be revolutionary changes in the habits and occupations of most of these people. Class differences must not be permitted to grow up. Thousands of newcomers must be encouraged to spread out over the land and not settle in overcrowded Tel Aviv and become shopkeepers. There were too many shopkeepers already.

Writing every speech and article himself on his three-by-five cards in longhand, Ben-Gurion during 1949 gave his people the inspiration and guidance they needed, without which they might never have realized the dream.

"If the new immigrant does not choose to go to the land by himself, we shall draw him there by the power of love and brotherhood . . .

"We shall plant our trees in every unsown stretch of the countryside and we shall remove the shame of desolation from all the soil of the homeland. The country will blossom and be beautiful again."

When storms filled their tents with water and the food was bad, he imparted to them his strength and hope—and he set about getting better housing for them. Always he kept pointing the way.

He excited them with reports of what had already been accomplished and with plans that were under way. In the next few weeks twenty-five thousand houses would be completed. A billion trees would be planted on the hills. A two-thousand-man police force had been organized, and all were Jews. Never again in this country would anyone but another Jew arrest a Jew. The graft and corruption of Mandatory days had been almost completely eliminated from the civil service. The currency was stable. An Israel air line was already in operation. It had only one plane, but patience! The railroad was running again. A merchant marine was being organized. Israel was alive. Israel was a nation.

In 1949, as Israel forces began to fan out across the Negev, King Abdullah grew nervous and invoked a treaty he had with London, so British troops were sent to Aqaba, the Jordan port on the northern arm of the Red Sea, just across a wadi from Israel's port of Elath.

The only road to Elath, hardly more than a desert track, ran close to the Israel-Jordan frontier. To secure another route in case the Jordanians blocked this one, Ben-Gurion dispatched reconnaissance scouts into the barren and unfriendly hills on the opposite side of the Negev, bordering Egypt. They worked their way wearily through blocked wadis and over craggy desert mountains, and finally sent back a report:

"Difficult but possible."

This was enough for Ben-Gurion. He authorized Allon, southern commander, to send two brigades to Elath, one by the eastern route, the other by the western. They were to avoid arousing the Arab neighbors. Each brigade tried to reach the Red Sea first. One beat the other by a few hours, but the commander of the first waited for the commander of the second, so they could send a joint signal to the Prime Minister:

"Greetings from Elath."

In his excitement the Prime Minister took a plane to Sodom, and then went over the rough desert road himself until he stood at his country's exit to the Eastern world.

A few weeks later Israel became the fifty-ninth member of the United Nations. The dream was beginning to have substance.

Three days after that the first anniversary of independence was celebrated. Ben-Gurion did no boasting, although he had cause. He mentioned a few of the accomplishments, modestly, (two hundred thousand immigrants had been brought in), but his theme was austerity, a Churchillian call for the tightening of belts.

In July he gave Yadin a new title, Military Adviser to the Prime Minister.

There were many problems in reorganizing the Army. Now that they had ranks, uniforms, insignia, and British-type discipline, some officers thought that they should also have medals, so a design was made and submitted to the Commander-in-Chief. When he saw that it contained the names of such historical avengers as Bar Kochba, Saul, and Simon he said:

"I refuse to sign a bill for a medal which mentions the names of any Jews who lost battles. I do not want my army to carry medals bearing the names of men who went down to defeat. We need to glorify the periods of our history in which we won, not those in which we were unsuccessful."

Despite the press of work, Ben-Gurion took off at least one day a month to visit army installations, frontier settlements, training centers. Once he went for a cruise on an Israel destroyer. A member of the crew said:

"It was nice seeing the Prime Minister with Plato in his hand, sitting in the shadow of an anti-aircraft gun. Rather incongruous though."

He was almost sixty-three now, but his energy was still so great that his aides had difficulty keeping up with him. He always wanted to climb to the top of the highest hill, see the entire defense line, examine every gun, walk around each plane, climb into all the tanks, inspect every soldier in the unit.

The Army became his lasting obsession. He saw it now not primarily as an organization to defend the frontiers, but as the instrument that would bring about the unification, modernization, and education of the country.

Jews from the Yemen, from Morocco, from Iraq, and from Europe were taken by the Army and converted into Israelis. It was the Army that taught them to speak Hebrew, to use knives and forks, to sleep in beds, to brush their teeth. It taught them Jewish history, Middle Eastern geography, civics, hygiene, what soap is for, how to read. Most of all, it taught these diverse people from every corner of the world, with skins of many shades, and with conflicting cultures, to live together as brothers.

The Army was doing the job so well that Ben-Gurion became deeply emotional about it. When he said the words *Tsva Haganah Leyisrael* (the Defense Army of Israel), it was almost as if he were uttering a holy phrase.

His test of the Army was how rapidly it was able to convert the Yemenites. Whenever he talked with a group of officers he would ask:

"How many Yemenites are there among you?"

Then he would question each of them, asking his length of service, rank, background. Always he would say:

"You won't have a good army until you have a Yemenite general." (The highest rank a Yemenite has yet achieved is major.)

Toward the end of 1949, Ben-Gurion and the State of Israel were forced to decide about Jerusalem.

After so many months of siege the New City was a dismal place. There had been death in almost every street, suffering in almost every home.

While the United Nations debated the future of Jerusalem, Ben-Gurion and his ministers tried to pump new life into the half a city in Jewish hands. New housing projects were begun. Ten thousand immigrants were sent there. Financial inducements were given to encourage small industries to move in. Conventions were held there instead of in Tel Aviv.

At Lake Success, Australia introduced a resolution under which all of Jerusalem would be put in charge of a U.N. trusteeship council.

Just before the vote was taken, Ben-Gurion made a declaration that could not possibly be misunderstood:

"Jews will sacrifice themselves for Jerusalem no less than Englishmen for London, Russians for Moscow, or Americans for Washington."

Four days later the General Assembly passed the resolution over the objections of Great Britain, Canada, and the United States.

Ben-Gurion did not equivocate. He proclaimed that the New City of Jerusalem would henceforth be the capital of Israel.

Some people were distressed by this defiance of the very body that had created Israel. Others pointed out that the New City was almost entirely Jewish, contained virtually no Christian or Moslem holy places, that Israel could not be expected to forsake its hundred thousand Jewish inhabitants, and that the spiritual and emotional importance of Jerusalem to Jews ought not to be overlooked.

This was the ancient city of David. Since the dispersal so many centuries ago Jews had been praying for the return.

"If I forget thee, O Jerusalem, let my right hand forget her cunning."

The United States, which opposed internationalization, sent Israel a firm note, warning against any "inflammatory move."

But Ben-Gurion was not to be deterred. During the autumn he had quietly moved several government departments to Jerusalem. Now he climbed into his automobile and drove the forty-five miles from Tel Aviv to the Holy City, leading the way for the rest of the government. He announced that henceforth the Knesset would meet in Jerusalem. All government departments would be housed there except Defense, which would stay in Tel Aviv for strategic reasons, and Foreign Affairs, which would stay in Tel Aviv for another four years to avoid embarrassing the diplomats, some of whom might hesitate to offend the United Nations by moving to Jerusalem themselves.

Nearly two years earlier, when Ben-Gurion left Jerusalem to become a war commander, he had slipped into his pocket the key to his office in the Jewish Agency building, and had said:

"I think I'll keep this. I am sure I will be coming back."

Now the time had come to use the key again.

CHAPTER NINETEEN

On King George V Road in Jerusalem during the days of the mandate the Jewish Agency had erected a massive stone structure to house the offices of all the Jewish institutions. One of the additions built in the late forties was a three-story stone building facing a tree-lined street in the rear that by coincidence bears the same name as the street in Tel Aviv on which the Ben-Gurions live, Keren Kayemet.

Into this building at the start of 1950 moved the Prime Minister, his secretary, his military aide, his office assistants, the typist who copies his speeches from three-by-five cards, and the rest of the staff.

Ben-Gurion's private office on the second floor is a room thirty by forty feet, with maps on each of the four walls. The one at the far end of the room behind his desk is almost six feet square and shows the Arab countries in red, the rest of the world in yellow, and Israel as a dark blue dot, so small that it is hardly noticeable. This prevents the Prime Minister—and his visitors as well—from ever forgetting the geopolitics of Israel's situation.

"It reminds me every day how small we are," Ben-Gurion says simply.

On the opposite wall hangs a map of Jerusalem showing every building in the city. On one side wall there is a seven-foot map of Israel, and beside it a map of the Negev. On the fourth wall hangs a relief map of the Middle East.

The only picture in the room (until 1958) was a photograph of Berl Katzenelson in a leather frame. It stands on the desk to the left. In it the deceased editor looks a little like Einstein, a little like Schweitzer.

On the desk there is also a calendar showing the date, both by Jewish and Christian reckoning; the black iron machine for punching holes; a marble stand holding two fountain pens (Ben-Gurion dislikes ball-point pens); a Bible; a concordance to enable him to find quickly any passage in the Bible to which he wants to refer, and four telephones, three black, one white. The white phone connects with his secretary and is for urgent calls.

The desk is covered with a sheet of glass under which there is a single small piece of paper bearing a two- or three-verse quotation from the Bible. At irregular intervals Ben-Gurion picks out a new quotation.

There are six leather chairs surrounding the desk. An Oriental rug covers part of the floor. At the far end of the room there is a piece of Israel sculpture on a coffee table, two comfortable chairs, and a sofa.

Except for the maps and four small cases of books near the desk, it might be the office of a school superintendent in Atlanta, Georgia, or a bank president in Concord, New Hampshire.

The maps would narrow it down to Israel. The books tell anyone who knows Israel's Prime Minister that this room is his. One shelf contains his own literary works. On the other shelves are volumes in half a dozen languages, mostly philosophy.

It is only a few steps from this office to the cabinet room, where

sixteen dark brown leather chairs surround a massive table. On
the walls are maps, a picture of Herzl, and a copy of the Israel
Declaration of Independence.

The forty-five miles of road between Tel Aviv and Jerusalem
became one of the most heavily traveled thoroughfares in the
Middle East after the Holy City was proclaimed the new capital.
Many government officials retained their homes at the seaside
and commuted back and forth once or twice a week.

It is not an easy drive. At one spot the Jordanian frontier is
less than a mile away. To serve as a constant reminder of the
price that was paid to secure the Jerusalem corridor, the Army
left along either side of the road some of the overturned, bullet-
riddled, fire-gutted trucks that had been shot up while trying to
run the Arab gantlet. They are periodically painted with rust-
proof paint; unique war memorials. As Jerusalem is approached,
the road circles around and around climbing the Judean hills.

Ben-Gurion divides his time between the two cities. Thursday,
Friday, and Saturday are spent in Tel Aviv, following his old
routine, living on Keren Kayemet Boulevard and occupying his
office in the Defense Ministry. On either Saturday evening or
Sunday morning at a very early hour the Prime Minister, his
military aide, and Paula drive to Jerusalem. At 10 A.M. on Sunday the Cabinet goes into session. The meeting often lasts all
day. On Monday, Tuesday, and Wednesday, Ben-Gurion keeps
regular office hours in the stone building just off King George V
Road. On Wednesday in the evening they make the trip back to
Tel Aviv.

At first the Ben-Gurions stayed in a hotel in the capital, but
later the government purchased a house for their use in the Re-
havia residential section at 44 Ben Maimon Avenue, almost across
the street from the Yadins. The owner of the house had been
killed in the King David Hotel bombing.

So Paula, now fifty-eight, suddenly found herself with two
homes to manage. And still she refused to employ a full-time
servant in either place.

The Ben Maimon Avenue house is also two stories, with a large
garden. On the second floor Ben-Gurion established an auxiliary
library, but he continued to keep most of his books in Tel Aviv,

which, therefore, to him is "home." The dominant piece of interior decoration is a five-foot olive grove painting by the former Ambassador to Rumania.

Specific orders from the State Department placed Jerusalem out of bounds for Ambassador McDonald. If he wanted to see Ben-Gurion he had to visit him during the three days a week he was in Tel Aviv serving, technically, as Minister of Defense.

But one sultry day in July, McDonald and his wife decided to drive into the Judean hills to escape the heat. They wound up calling on Paula in her new home. The Ambassador assured his wife that this was not a violation of State Department regulations. The papers said the Prime Minister was in Elath for a military conference, so it was just a pleasant social call and a chance to see the new house.

As they were drinking tea, a man in shirt sleeves and slippers came down the stairs.

"But you're in Elath!" McDonald gasped.

"Not until tomorrow," the Prime Minister replied with a smile.

The war in Korea was only several days old and both men wanted to talk about it, so they ushered the women into the garden and for nearly an hour sat in the living room in earnest conversation.

As soon as the American Ambassador returned to Tel Aviv he cabled the State Department a synopsis of the conversation. A few days later the Israel Foreign Office learned what he had done from its Washington embassy. The next time the Ambassador and the Prime Minister met, McDonald was chided for passing on a personal conversation.

"Besides," Ben-Gurion said, smiling, "your own government says you are not supposed to do business in Jerusalem!"

During 1950, Ben-Gurion was compelled to make one more major decision.

The exiles were still entering at the rate of one every two or three minutes. During the first two years of the state nearly four hundred thousand had come. It would eventually cost twenty-five hundred dollars for each new immigrant, counting transportation, housing, and training.

Israel had already spent the millions of dollars loaned by the

Export-Import Bank and millions more that had been raised by the United Jewish Appeal.

Thousands of immigrants were living in tents. When the rains came, many were flooded out. There was grumbling and impatience. A few actually applied for permission to leave. The economy of the country was creaking and groaning. The public did not know it, but at one time there was grain enough in Israel for only three more days—and a million mouths to feed. If one ship had met with an accident, there would have been a national disaster.

Ben-Gurion began to be barraged with criticism, especially from his financial experts. Immigration *must* be slowed down. The D.P. camps of Europe had all been emptied. The immigrants now were coming from North Africa. There was no crisis in North Africa. Surely a few more months or even years in the shacks and caves of Morocco, Tunisia, and Algeria would not make much difference. They had lived there for centuries already as third-class citizens. Was it right to jeopardize the stability and future of the new young state by this obsession with unlimited immigration?

Ben-Gurion listened to all the arguments and then made his decision. If it wrecked the country, history would never forgive him. But instead of agreeing to close the doors even slightly he began to talk about a population of two million in another three or four years.

He knew that a state of two million would have twice the survival chance of a state of one million. He knew settlements had to be scattered quickly through the Negev or the desert would be lost. He knew the environs of Jerusalem must be populated.

Besides, there was his mystic feeling that the ingathering was even more important than the state itself. What if they did all have to go hungry for a little while?

Jewish leaders from the United States were brought to Jerusalem, and Ben-Gurion spoke to them bluntly.

"During the next three years we will need a billion and a half dollars to do the job. The State of Israel is prepared to give a third."

The American leaders went back and held a conference in

Washington a few weeks later and unanimously adopted a plan to get the billion.

One warm day in 1950, Ben-Gurion assembled his General Staff and commanding officers at Tel Hashomer, a military center not far from Tel Aviv, and gave them a talk he entitled "Mission and Dedication."

It is doubtful whether a Commander-in-Chief of any army in any country in any age ever gave such an address to a group of military men. It lasted for three hours, without a pause. For the first two hours the Army was hardly mentioned. It was not primarily military matters Ben-Gurion wanted to discuss.

He began like a preacher, with a text, from the Book of Deuteronomy:

"'The Lord did not set his love upon you, nor choose you, because ye were more in number than other people; for ye were the fewest of all people: But because God loved you . . .'"

He told them of the strange combination of forces against Israel on the question of Jerusalem: Arabs, Latin-American countries, France (always before a friend), the bloc of Communist states, and those countries in which Catholics predominated.

A few sentences later he was back in Babylonian times, instructing these military men in ancient history; telling them that the Babylonians were the ones who first developed the sciences of astronomy, medicine, and engineering, and refined the art of jurisprudence. Then he escorted them into the Egyptian period, explaining how the ancestors of the enemy they had so recently fought (and might soon have to fight again) had laid the foundations for many branches of science, mathematics, engineering, chemistry, and had been "very good architects, too."

If any officer had dozed off for a few moments he might have awakened to hear his Commander-in-Chief talking now about the Russian and French revolutions. Bar Kochba and the Bolsheviks were mentioned in almost the same sentence.

Then a little story about how, when he went to Moscow in 1923 to represent Histadruth at the World Agricultural Exposition, a group of Jewish Communists ("whose hate of Zion and the sacred tongue exceeded their Communist zeal") had argued with Soviet authorities that he should not be permitted to come.

From the Book of Genesis to 1950. From Einstein to Jonah. From Mohammed to Plato to Lenin to Khmelnitski to Hitler.

Some of the officers must have had the feeling they were in the study of a great scholar, listening to him think out loud.

The abstract and the material were all mixed up.

"Just as we shall eat Argentinian beef and Russian grain, plow with American tractors and smelt Belgian steel, burn Mexican petrol and wear British cloth, and build our homes of Canadian timber, so we shall read the literature of all nations and seek wisdom wherever it may be found."

He was trying to inspire these young military men of whom he was so fond. He wanted to instill in every one of them the excitement of history as he knew it. He wanted them to see the vision, too.

The army men sat for the most part spellbound.

"In a nation as small as ours there are always groups who are attracted by the dazzling appeal of great powers, whose political, economic, and military capacity is tremendous and whose influence in the world is therefore great. They are attracted not only for their private good, although one should not dismiss that prosaic factor, but by the great capabilities, the breadth, the power, the riches of these rulers of the world.

"This weakness, this self-abasement, this obsequious toadying . . . has been called *mayofes* in our modern history, and mayofes Jews may be and are found in circles which lack self-respect or enough faith in their nation. In rightist circles they are called the Council of Judaism, headed by American millionaires; in leftist or revolutionary circles they are called Yevsktzia [the Jewish section of the Bolshevik party], and are headed by writers out of whose mouths their master's voice is always heard."

He traced the vitality of Jews through the ages, their contributions to science, their importance in the field of philosophy, their partnership in intellectual revolutions.

"There is a miraculous vitamin stored in this nation which safeguards its existence and independence and gives it indomitable strength to withstand foreign influences which are hostile to its national and moral being. . . ."

And then there was this challenging thought:

"Liberation from physical exile is easy in our days. It is enough just to settle in Israel. But it is not easy to rid oneself of a spiritual and moral exile. This cannot be done by moving from one land to another. It comes from within, through great spiritual, intellectual, and moral effort, of which not everyone is capable."

At last, late in the afternoon, Ben-Gurion explained his own concept of this new army, which was to be unlike any other in the world.

"Our Army cannot be just a military weapon. It must be a medium of learning and absorption, of settlement and reconstruction . . .

"The conglomeration of humanity, flooding in from foreign lands of exile, will be purified, tempered, and cleansed in the crucible of fraternity and military discipline. Sectarian differences will be wiped out and patriotic unity forged . . .

"The time of fulfillment is now."

Ben-Gurion was becoming more and more a leader of men. Dr. Weizmann told several callers that in his opinion the Prime Minister was guiding the nation in a "magnificent" manner.

Hebrew University awarded him a prize of fifteen hundred dollars "as the person who has done the most for Israel in the past two years." Ben-Gurion endorsed the check back to the university to establish a prize for the student writing the best essay on Plato's influence on Jewish literature and thought.

He was growing in stature month by month, but for newspaper reporters he was still a trial and sometimes a tribulation.

He would often deliver speeches extemporaneously, and even when he had a prepared text copies would sometimes not be available until he had finished speaking. When he was told that in the United States public figures deliver "advances" of their addresses to the press as much as twelve hours before they start to speak, he said:

"I don't understand why."

For years he has had a standing feud with certain Israel papers that he criticized for being sensational and uneducational.

Although he has been writing for newspapers himself for almost half a century, the mechanics of journalism mean nothing to him.

Once he reprimanded a reporter for a minor inaccuracy.

"I'm sorry, but I had to hurry."

"Why didn't you wait another ten minutes and do an accurate job?"

"But, sir, I had a deadline."

"Deadline? What difference? If you'd missed it, the article could have gone in the next day's paper."

American journalism amazes him. When he was told that reporters for an American news magazine had cabled forty thousand words about him and Israel one day at a cost of twelve cents a word, he blinked in astonishment, and when he heard that a correspondent for the same magazine had once cabled twelve thousand words about Israel, of which only two sentences were ever used, he said:

"Didn't he lose his job?"

In recent years his attitude toward the foreign press has mellowed. He has granted hundreds of newspaper, radio, and television interviews, and he no longer gives the impression of finding personal publicity so distasteful, but toward Israel reporters his attitude is still somewhat irreconcilable and he rarely gives them an interview. In order to get the Prime Minister's ideas into their columns some Israel papers buy the reprint rights to interviews he has given to British or American correspondents.

To one Jerusalem reporter who asked for an interview he sent this written reply:

"I do not give interviews to journalists (a) because I am a journalist myself and whatever I say to the public I do so in my own way, and (b) the first reason is sufficient."

Once an Israel paper printed an exposé of a cabinet member whom it accused of selling his apartment to the government at a profit. Ben-Gurion called it an "aesthetic error" and denounced the paper for "besmirching men in public office."

His favorite answer to an Israel reporter who asks him a question is:

"I write for the press myself." Then he will quickly add, "Not for financial reasons, but to be sure I am quoted correctly."

The real reason is that he is a writer at heart.

He is a considerable problem for his own press department. Several years ago he prepared a twenty-minute speech well in advance of the Maccabean athletic festival. The press department translated it into English and distributed copies to all correspondents. But the games lasted longer than had been anticipated. It was growing dark when the time came for the Prime Minister to speak, so he discarded his prepared talk and said:

"I bless you and hope you will remain strong and send some of your young people to Israel."

The same thing occurred with the speech he prepared to welcome the arrival of the first railroad train to Beersheba. A downpour began just before he was to speak, so he said merely:

"I hope to see this railroad reach Elath someday."

Then he sat down.

The opposite happened with an atomic conference.

"I will give just a few words of greeting," he told the press department.

But when he got started, the subject fascinated him and he delivered one of his most important speeches of the year.

During 1950, Ben-Gurion found time to discuss with many people the idea of translating the classics into Hebrew; not just Shakespeare and Plato; not just the conventional classics of English, French, German, and Russian, but the most important books in every one of the Oriental and Occidental languages. There was no money then for such a luxury, but it was a small dream that year by year grew larger in his mind.

Meanwhile Israel was already encouragingly interested in books, perhaps partly due to Ben-Gurion's example. On one street in Tel Aviv (a city at this point with a population between that of Fort Worth and Dallas) someone counted 112 bookshops, far outnumbering the beauty shops or even the cafés.

About this time a new institute of arts and sciences was being created in Tel Aviv and the matter of a name was under discussion. Someone suggested "The Academy of Arts and Sciences."

"I don't like that word 'academy,'" Ben-Gurion said.

"Why not?" an aide asked. "The whole world uses 'academy.'"

The Prime Minister wheeled around on him.

"What do you mean when you say 'the whole world'? There is not one academy in all of Asia."

In October a cabinet crisis occurred, and Ben-Gurion resigned, but President Weizmann induced him to re-form his Cabinet and after two weeks harmony was restored, so he and Paula went off for their first holiday in a long time, perhaps the first holiday they had ever had.

They went to Greece.

One short hop by plane and they were in the ancient city Ben-Gurion knew so well from his reading. He visited archaeological diggings, climbed the Acropolis, and tried to talk to modern Greeks in the tongue of their own ancestors. But neither taxi drivers, nor hotelkeepers, nor even professors understood him. Finally he made a formal suggestion to the Greeks: that they do what the Jews had done, revive their own ancient language.

Eliahu Elath, now Israel Ambassador to Great Britain, was at London Airport shortly before midnight one December evening to meet a Histadruth delegation coming from Tel Aviv. As the passengers streamed from the plane, he was astonished to see the white hair of the Prime Minister.

This was not protocol. And London is a city that lays great stress on protocol.

The Prime Minister explained with a smile that he was traveling incognito. He was just a private Israel citizen.

He was accompanied by Ehud Avriel, former Minister to Prague. They went directly to the home of a friend in Golders Green.

The London press engaged in whipped-up speculation. What crisis had occurred in Israel to bring the Prime Minister himself to London? Whom was he going to see? Where was he staying? Why was he hiding?

A reporter for the weekly *New Statesman and Nation* solved the mystery.

There was no crisis.

Ben-Gurion was not in hiding.

The Israel Prime Minister was in Oxford. He had flown all the way from Athens to spend four days browsing through the stacks of one of the most celebrated bookshops in the world, Blackwell's, because he had heard it had an excellent collection of Platonic scholiasts.

A great many people were skeptical of the story. This was not the way any Prime Minister had ever behaved before.

But the London weekly ended its article:

"In this age of barbarism, it is a pleasant thought that anyone who penetrated to the back rooms of Blackwell's last week and spied a little white-haired man on the top of a stepladder would have seen a Prime Minister indulging his secret vice."

CHAPTER TWENTY

DAVID BEN-GURION started off 1951, which was to be an unforgettable year of his life, in an unusual manner. One of his first public acts was to go to an immigrant camp near the seaside city of Natanya and serve as *sandek* (godfather) for a loudly squalling boy named David Itzaak.

The child was the fourteenth born to a refugee couple from Iraq, who had decided before ever reaching Israel to name their newborn, if a boy, after the Prime Minister.

A photograph of the ceremony was so widely printed that it caused an epidemic of naming boys after the Prime Minister, until his office finally made it clear that he could not serve as sandek for any more babies.

In February a new political crisis occurred. Under a compromise with the religious parties, young women were being exempted from military conscription on grounds of "conscience or religion." Thirty per cent of those called up were claiming exemption. Ben-Gurion was suspicious and wanted a law compelling exempted girls to do non-military work.

But the big issue was education. The Orthodox parties wanted legal control over the religious education of all immigrant children.

"We will never permit anyone but the state to have exclusive discretion in matters of education," Ben-Gurion announced. Then he asked for a vote of confidence. When he failed to receive it he resigned and demanded new national elections. President Weizmann asked him to serve as head of a "caretaker" government until elections could be held in the summer, and he agreed. Then, accompanied by Paula, Argov, and Ted Lurie, managing editor of the Jerusalem *Post*, and several other journalists, he went to America.

Ben-Gurion had been to the United States many times, but on

the other occasions his arrival had hardly been noticed. This time he came as a world figure. He was well known to almost all American Jews and to many others. He was the personification of the fight of the few hundred thousand against the forty million. He was David, and almost every American knew about his battle with Goliath.

He flew in a blue-and-white Constellation, inaugurating the trans-Atlantic service of Israel's own airline, El Al. The plane landed first at Washington, where Ben-Gurion paid his respects to President Truman. Then on to New York.

It was somewhat like the day Lindbergh was welcomed home, or Gertrude Ederle was feted for swimming the Channel.

Few foreigners—and no Jew—had ever received such a reception.

Grover Whalen was on hand to do the greeting. The procession was led by an escort of thirty-six motorcycles, then twenty automobiles full of dignitaries, followed by several thousand members of the United States armed forces, a sixty-piece band, a contingent of Israel sailors, and thousands of members of the police and fire departments. Three thousand policemen were on parade detail.

As Ben-Gurion drove in his open car along Broadway he was showered with ticker tape and torn-up telephone directories.

The police superintendent estimated that a million and a half New Yorkers cheered him, waved at him, or at least got a glimpse of his white hair.

"Why, that's more than the entire population of Israel," one member of the party pointed out when he read the figure that night in the paper.

At City Hall, where he and Paula had been married, there were five thousand seated guests and ninety-five thousand people standing as Mayor Impellitteri welcomed Ben-Gurion, saying:

"The man we honor today has captured the hearts and minds of freedom-loving people everywhere. He has never wavered in his resolve to bring to a realization the two-thousand-year-old dream of the Jewish people . . ."

Then the Mayor proclaimed it Ben-Gurion Day, and shook hands again with Ben-Gurion, who was going to have to forget his dislike of handshaking for the next few weeks.

Although Ben-Gurion before this had never cared for personal acclaim, on May 8, 1951, as he waved to the crowds, he seemed to be enjoying it.

During his visit to the U.N. building a photographer's flash bulb exploded and showered him with glass, but he laughed and said:

"Don't forget, I've been in several wars."

Ben-Gurion, Paula, and Argov stayed in a suite in the Waldorf-Astoria. Another guest in the hotel was General Douglas Mac-Arthur, who had just been relieved of his command in Korea by President Truman.

On the second day they drove up to West Point and placed a wreath on the grave of Colonel David Marcus, which is marked with a stone reading:

"A soldier for all humanity."

That night twenty thousand people packed Madison Square Garden and another seven thousand stood in the streets to hear him open the Bonds for Israel drive.

On the program was a tall young man with horn-rimmed glasses who had presented Israel's case before the United Nations so brilliantly that Ben-Gurion had appointed him Ambassador to the United States. He was only thirty-six, the youngest man to hold such a rank in Washington, but he was already justifying the faith the Prime Minister had placed in him. He was cultured, scholarly, and an orator whose words could be as lethal as a rapier, as dazzlingly brilliant as a fireworks display.

"Their own deeds are the memorial of great men," Abba Eban told the cheering audience. Then he summed up the guest of honor's career:

"In 1943, David Ben-Gurion declared that an independent Jewish state must be established in the Land of Israel. The great powers and the world community at that time had as much intention of supporting the idea of a Jewish state as of organizing a voyage to the moon.

"In the winter of 1947, David Ben-Gurion proclaimed that the Jews in the Land of Israel must be ready to resist and defeat invading armies of all the neighboring states. No military expert who regarded this as a reasonable prospect would have been credited with professional sanity.

"In September 1950, David Ben-Gurion declared that Israel for its strength and survival must have a billion dollars from the United States in three years. This time it was the turn of the economists to greet his suggestion with a tolerant but skeptical smile.

"But the Jewish state was established, the armies were defeated, the billion dollars will be obtained."

By the time the guest of honor rose to speak, the audience was cheering wildly. For the first time that his old associates could remember, he seemed to be seized by emotion. Several times he choked and his voice faltered.

Late in the evening a roll was called of all forty-eight states and an announcement was made of the number of bonds that had been bought. The total amount of money pledged was thirty-five million dollars.

The New York reporters used some of their best adjectives that night about Ben-Gurion, and editorial writers were generous in their praise.

On the fourth day, trailed by a police captain and two plain-clothes men, he went browsing through New York bookshops. He bought altogether nearly thirty volumes, mostly on Chinese philosophy.

At Brentano's on Fifth Avenue a young woman who had waited on him four years earlier said:

"*Baruch haaba* [Blessed are you who have come]."

From her he bought a copy of *The Philosophy of Life*, by Chen Lis Fu, and the manager presented him with a rare edition of excerpts of a Bible printed in 1553 in Hebrew, Latin, and Greek.

Paula had a chance to visit her brother and sister in Brooklyn. Her sister's son, Will Maslow, was now an official of the American Jewish Congress, and Paula invited him to bring his wife and six-year-old daughter to the Waldorf to see Ben-Gurion. That evening Maslow overheard his daughter telling a young friend:

"Yes, and tomorrow my father is going to take me to the Waldorf-Astoria Hotel so we can see the Prime Minister of Israel— he's my uncle—and he's going to fix it up so that we can meet General MacArthur!"

On Sunday the Prime Minister went by motorcar to Princeton,

New Jersey, to visit the best-known Jew in the world, Professor Albert Einstein.

The day was mild, and they sat outdoors in garden chairs, side by side. Ben-Gurion, the man with such disinterest in clothes, was splendidly dressed in a dark, double-breasted suit, white shirt, silk tie of geometric design, and on the lapel of his coat was a small gold emblem that is given to Israel army men when they graduate from the officers' school.

Einstein wore slacks, a cashmere pull-over sweater, and a white shirt open at the neck.

They posed for two or three press photographs, smiling at each other and shaking hands, Einstein, who had just celebrated his seventy-second birthday, and Ben-Gurion, seven years his junior.

In profile they looked alike. Both had a great deal of white hair that almost covered their ears. When they smiled, as they often did during their brief time together, they had the same kind of laugh lines around their eyes.

After the photographers left, the two men sat alone and talked. Except in his journal, which no one has seen, Ben-Gurion has never written about his only meeting with the greatest mathematician of modern times, but he did discuss the interview later with a close friend.

For years he had greatly admired Einstein. Although he himself had no interest in mathematics, he respected the intelligence of a man who could think in coldly abstract terms.

"Do you realize," he said to his friend, "that Einstein is a scientist who needs no laboratory, no equipment, no tools of any kind? He just sits in an empty room with a pencil and a piece of paper, and his brain, thinking."

Ben-Gurion was curious to know Einstein's secret of concentrated thinking and wanted to discuss universal truth with him.

He left Princeton that afternoon still convinced that Einstein had the greatest mind of any living man.

From New York he went on tour of the country.

At Philadelphia when he was shown the Liberty Bell he pointed out that the inscription "Proclaim liberty throughout all the land, to all the inhabitants thereof" is from the Hebrew Bible, the Book of Leviticus, and that the words were spoken by God to Moses.

In Baltimore he was presented with the keys of the city.

In Washington there was a reception attended by a thousand top government officials and diplomats. In a picture taken with Secretary of State Acheson, who seemed to be almost twice his height, the Prime Minister was grinning so broadly that one of his American friends said:

"You look as if Acheson had just given you Long Island, part of Texas, and the American fleet."

In Boston he had his most strenuous day: four major speeches in a few hours. And still he found time to browse in a bookshop or two.

Remembering the large Irish population of Boston, he told the Mayor that the Jews and the Irish had much in common: both had suffered and both had fought for their freedom.

The Mayor replied by telling Ben-Gurion the story of Chaim Solomon, a Jewish merchant who saved the American forces in the Revolution with a gift of two hundred thousand dollars to the Continental Army.

Remembering a little American history himself, the Prime Minister told a Boston Garden rally:

"You had your Boston Tea Party. We had our White Paper.

"You had your Minutemen. We had our Haganah.

"You fought a war for independence. So did we.

"You had to fight one king. We had to fight four.

"You had to fight one army. We had to fight six.

"But we were successful, just as you were."

To the students at Brandeis University he said:

"Come to Israel and help create a new civilization. We can offer you the same thing that was a privilege in this country two hundred years ago. There is nothing to compare with the great happiness that comes when you are creating something. We believe we can show the world how people can live without exploitation or hatred."

At Detroit he predicted that the ancient city of Elath on the Red Sea would someday become Israel's Detroit.

At Cleveland twenty thousand people packed the Mall.

At Chicago he received a twenty-one-gun salute, usually reserved for the heads of important states.

At Tulsa the private plane chartered for the trip had to stop and refuel. It was 2:30 A.M. and raining. Tulsa's Jewish population at that time numbered three hundred families. Yet there was a large delegation at the airport to shout greetings.

At Los Angeles a luncheon was given in his honor by motion picture company executives. There were twenty thousand people in the Hollywood Bowl when Edward G. Robinson read the Israel Declaration of Independence, and Samuel Goldwyn introduced the guest of honor. They laughed when he said California had a climate and scenery almost as good as Israel's, and when he told them that Israel could not afford to leave her desert as unpopulated and unused as the one he had just flown over.

He traveled eight thousand miles on his two-week cross-country trip, made sixteen major addresses in ten cities, listened to the cheers of nearly three million people, was the guest of honor at twenty-five formal breakfasts, luncheons, and dinners, and somehow found time to ply his old trade as a writer by doing a series of articles for the Hearst papers.

Less than a month after their arrival they left. Ben-Gurion had helped sell fifty-five million dollars' worth of bonds for Israel.

As the blue-and-white plane approached the eastern shore of the Mediterranean, six Israel fighters came up to greet it. On the ground there was an honor guard of parachutists, sailors, girl soldiers, the entire Cabinet and General Staff, a large number of Knesset members, the United States Ambassador, and thousands of ordinary citizens.

Paula gave reporters an interview. They wanted to know what it was like visiting what had once been "home." Had she met many old friends?

"Yes, but when we were students together they were all idealists and intellectuals. Now they are married, in business, in the professions and they seem to think of nothing but how to make more money. They can't imagine what austerity means. Our life seems a great deal more real than theirs.

"But, oh, they are so generous! Many bought two, three times as many bonds as they had intended to. Wherever we went they gave me arms full of flowers. Of course I sent them to the hospitals at once.

"My husband is delighted with one gift he received, a large movable globe that lights up from within."

They asked her if she had done any shopping.

She laughed. She had wanted to break away from the official committees and go shopping in a five- and ten-cent store, "to get some little things for the house," but there had never been an opportunity.

While the Ben-Gurions had been away, Bartley Crum, who had written *Behind the Silken Curtain* about his experience as a member of the Anglo-American Committee on Palestine, had arrived. On his way through Paris he had telephoned Jo Davidson, the sculptor, suggesting that he and his wife Florence accompany him. They had agreed. But their visit was now about over.

It was Crum who told the Prime Minister of Davidson's eagerness to meet him.

"He says his fingers are just aching to do a bust of you."

Ben-Gurion told Crum to bring him around that evening.

Both men were tired when they met. Davidson had spent all day doing a head of Moshe Sharett, who stood beside the sculptor's stand dictating to his secretary in Hebrew, talking occasionally to his wife in Russian, and speaking now and then to Davidson in English. Late in the afternoon Davidson, who had recently suffered a heart attack and was not supposed to submit himself to any strain, had gone back to his hotel exhausted, to find Crum there with the invitation. His fatigue seemed to disappear as he said:

"Wonderful!"

Ben-Gurion received the Davidsons in his second-floor library, saying:

"I read in the papers that you came without visas."

Davidson admitted it was true.

"I have an idea that maybe I will keep you here then."

They discussed the matter of a bust. It was Saturday night. The Davidsons had an appointment with Mayor Abba Khoushy in Haifa on Monday and were flying back to Paris that night. Ben-Gurion was going to be busy all day Sunday, starting at 9 A.M.

"I could sit for you early tomorrow morning," the Prime Minister finally said.

"Good," Davidson replied.

"But why not start tonight?" the sixty-four-year-old Prime Minister suddenly said to the sixty-eight-year-old sculptor.

Crum and Florence Davidson went quickly to borrow clay, stand, and armature. For the next four hours Davidson worked with the zest of a young man, while Crum, Ben-Gurion, and Florence Davidson kept up a rapid three-way conversation.

At midnight he stopped, covered the clay with damp cloths, and went to his hotel, exhausted.

At seven-thirty the next morning they were all back in their places again. Ben-Gurion had had his normal quota of sleep, but the other three still were not wide awake.

Davidson jokingly repeated the words of a fellow sculptor:

"I've got to finish this bust before I die."

It was a prophetic remark. This was to be one of the last busts the great American artist would ever do.

When it was time for Ben-Gurion to leave, he looked at the plaster portrait and asked:

"Is it done?"

"Not quite," the sculptor said.

"All right then, I'll give you one more sitting tonight at six-thirty."

At six o'clock that night Ben-Gurion was pacing his library, waiting.

The bust was finally finished at nine.

The next afternoon Israel had one of its worst storms in years. Trees were uprooted, roads were blocked, and buildings damaged. At the height of the storm an automobile stopped in front of the Ben-Gurion house on Keren Kayemet Boulevard. It was Jo Davidson wanting to say good-by. He and his wife had just driven through the storm from Haifa. Ben-Gurion was about to leave by car for Jerusalem. As the two men talked, their wives commiserated with each other about "these violently energetic men" who would not be deterred by storms, falling trees, or anything else put in their way by nature or man.

When they separated, Davidson, as strong a character in his

own way as Ben-Gurion and not one ever to make "polite re-marks," said to the Prime Minister:

"It has been a wonderful experience."

This was high praise, for Davidson had spent most of his adult life in the presence of the great and the near great. He had done the heads of Gandhi and Einstein, Shaw and Whitman, Roose-velt and Rockefeller, Clemenceau and Helen Keller.

But the bust itself expressed his feeling about Ben-Gurion better than his words. The clay became plaster and the plaster became bronze, and anyone who looked could tell that Jo David-son had captured with his sensitive fingers the power and the strength, the longing and the determination of Ben-Gurion. All it lacked was the electricity of the white hair that seemed to stand up on end.

It was good that Ben-Gurion came back from America so full of renewed vitality. He had to plunge almost at once into an election campaign.

His Mapai party had been the dominant force in the govern-ment for more than three years and was being attacked from all sides. It was blamed for everything that anyone thought was wrong with the country: food shortages, the black market, the reluctance of foreign capital to make investments in Israel, and the "pampering of labor." From another quarter it was criticized for kowtowing to American capitalism and permitting private profits at the expense of workers. It was accused of trying to destroy religion and for giving away too much to theocrats. It was blamed for being too belligerent toward the Arabs and for being too docile toward them.

So Ben-Gurion the statesman became Ben-Gurion the politician again and went to the people. They crowded into his meetings. They laughed when, during an attack on politicians who made more pledges than they could keep, he said:

"I will not promise to find a husband and a new dress for every woman in Israel."

The election was held during the first week of August. Hun-dreds of thousands of immigrants cast ballots for the first time. Mapai lost one of its forty-six places in the Knesset. The Ortho-dox parties also lost seats. So did Mapam. The General Zionists, who had accused Ben-Gurion of strangling free enterprise, jumped into second place with twenty seats.

Ben-Gurion continued as Prime Minister, at the head of another coalition government composed of men who were in complete agreement on only one subject: that there was no Israeli better qualified to lead them than the man with the fringe of white hair, an opinion which an overwhelming percentage of the population also held.

Ben-Gurion's contribution to the Israel Year Book in 1951 was entitled "The Call of the Spirit." It concluded:

"Whither is compounded of whence. Nature's 'yea' is never changed to 'nay.' History loses naught. Our past is not behind us, it is in us. Not as blank parchment or dead clay, shapeless and without form, do we march onward to our future, nor with empty hands. We bring to posterity the gift of a great and ancient heritage."

CHAPTER TWENTY-ONE

MONDAY, January 7, 1952, was a cold, gray day in Jerusalem; a day that most Israelis, especially the Prime Minister, wanted to forget as soon as it was over.

Until a proper capitol could be built, the Knesset was holding its sessions in a three-story, slightly curved commercial building on King George V Road in the heart of the business district. On this bleak Monday police had constructed roadblocks in all streets leading to the parliament building, using barbed wire and slabs of concrete. Traffic was diverted, and the area was patrolled by six hundred uniformed policemen with riot equipment: steel helmets, shields, batons, and gas mask kits.

The Knesset had scheduled a debate for Monday on a subject everyone knew was inflammatory: German reparations.

This was another major crisis for Ben-Gurion. First he had to decide how he himself felt about trying to get some compensation from the nation whose leaders so short a time ago had been responsible for the worst pogrom in Jewish history.

Then, having made up his mind that there was nothing morally wrong about it, he had to convince others. He was aware that it was political dynamite. He knew his own people well enough to realize that few would listen with their minds to his reasons. Wounds were still raw. Any discussion of reparations would re-open them, cause new suffering. There was no issue that would unite the political opposition so strongly against him. He knew that. He knew there might even be an attempt at physical violence. That was why he had ordered the barbed wire and chunks of concrete set up around the Knesset.

The parliamentary session began quietly enough. At 4:30 P.M. the Prime Minister delivered the opening statement. He told how Israel had made the first approaches nearly ten months ago. Finally the West German Chancellor had written that he was ready to discuss reparations.

"Let not the murderers of our people be also their inheritors."

As soon as the Prime Minister sat down, the opposition began to fire at his arguments. A General Zionist quoted his small son as having said:

"Daddy, what price will we get for Grandma and Grandpa?"

A Mapam speaker said:

"This is a trick of the Western powers to facilitate the grooming of Western Germany as the spearhead of an attack on the Soviet Union."

He was interrupted by a Herut member who burst into the room, shouting:

"Gas is being used against Jews! Gas against Jews!"

A few city blocks away, from a balcony in Zion Square, Menachem Beigin had been delivering the most demagogic speech of his career to a mass meeting of several thousand people, mostly young men.

Halfway through his talk he paused and pulled a piece of paper from his jacket pocket, held it up dramatically, and said:

"I have not come to inflame you, but this note has just been handed to me. It states that the police have grenades which contain gas made in Germany, the same gas used to kill your fathers and mothers . . .

"We are prepared to suffer anything, torture chambers, concentration camps, and subterranean prisons, so that any decision to deal with Germany will not come to pass."

He ended his speech by addressing a remark to Ben-Gurion, who was a quarter of a mile away, sitting hunched up in his chair at the cabinet table in the Knesset listening to the opposition:

"When you fired on us with your cannon, I gave the order 'No.' Today I gave the order 'Yes.' This will be a war of life or death."

Then at least half the several thousand young men started up Ben Yehuda Street for the Knesset. Many carried knapsacks filled with stones. They broke through the first barrier of police easily. As they approached the Knesset, guards stationed on the roofs of surrounding buildings lobbed down a few tear gas bombs. But the wind was from the wrong direction and the fumes blew into the faces of the police rather than the rioters.

The defending force fell back to positions close to the Knesset. Some fired over the heads of the crowd. Stones were raining down on them. When Star of David ambulances arrived to care for the wounded they were attacked. Doctors were prevented from giving first aid.

During the first assault thirteen policemen were wounded, including the assistant and deputy superintendents of police.

After an hour of fighting, an automobile was turned over. As gasoline began to leak from the tank, someone tossed a small bomb and the car was suddenly in flames. Then other automobiles were attacked.

Inside, a Communist member jumped up and shouted:

"We sit here and argue while people are being murdered outside. Listen!"

Just then a volley of stones crashed through the Knesset windows. Several members were hit in the head. Others were showered with glass. They fled to shelter. More stones, and then through the broken windows came the fumes of tear gas. Ministers and legislators were choking and crying.

At the cabinet table one figure had moved hardly a muscle all this time. He was in complete control of himself, a perfect soldier. His jaw was hard-set as he sat waiting for the hysteria to die down.

Paula, who as usual had come to watch over her husband and see that he got his tea, although he had told her there might be trouble, was behaving just as admirably as he was. She helped establish an impromptu first aid station and worked with the only doctor in the building, dressing wounds.

More stones came through the windows, along with the noises of battle: revolver shots, the crash of breaking glass, the sound of small explosions, the sirens of ambulances and fire-fighting apparatus, the shouts of angry demonstrators. After the tear gas fumes there was the acrid smell of burning rubber.

The Knesset was a place besieged.

When a woman member sitting in the General Zionists section fainted, Ben-Gurion helped carry her from the room, saying angrily:

"This wrath has all been staged."

Now Begin stepped to the podium and began reading a list of rabbis, scholars, poets, and other literary and religious people who had signed a petition against German reparations.

Ben-Gurion, who had returned to his place, pointed to the windows and said:

"The people you mention are not connected with your hooligans."

"You are the hooligan!" Begin shouted.

Uglier words than this had already been used. Begin had called the Prime Minister a "murderer," and someone had called Begin a "madman," but the previous remarks had been from the floor.

The Speaker demanded that Begin apologize. He refused. The Speaker ordered him to leave the platform. Again he refused, saying:

"If I am not permitted to speak, no one will speak."

The Speaker banged his gavel and declared a three-hour recess.

When the Knesset reassembled, the Herut leader, who had just returned from semi-retirement after the setback of his party in the last election, apologized for his castigation of the Prime Minister, but then announced that this would be his last Knesset appearance.

"If an attempt is made to negotiate with the Germans, my party will go underground. There are some things dearer than life, some things worse than death . . . People went to the barricades for lesser things than this. I know we will be dragged to concentration camps, but we will die together."

By late evening order had finally been restored in the streets. Seventy rioters were under arrest. Well over a hundred policemen and civilians had been treated for injuries, some serious. At least a hundred demonstrators were also thought to have been wounded, but all had been smuggled out of the battle area and then out of the city, to avoid arrest.

During the night the broken Knesset windows were refitted with glass and covered with wire netting.

The next day the streets of Jerusalem were deserted. An occasional shot was heard. The city was nervous. The whole country was disturbed. If civil war broke out, the dream would surely collapse. Again a strong, clear voice was needed.

That night the strong, clear voice spoke to all Israel by radio.

"Yesterday the hand of evil was raised against the sovereignty of the Knesset and the first steps were taken in the destruction of democracy in Israel.

"A wild mob composed of Irgun and the Communists stormed the Knesset . . .

"I consider it my duty to tell the nation of the gravity of the criminal and treacherous plot, and to assure the nation that we have taken all the appropriate measures to safeguard . . . the security and peace of Israel . . .

"I do not underestimate the declaration of Menachem Beigin that he is preparing for a war of life or death, nor have I any illusions against whom these threats are directed. I know that it is not difficult to carry out acts of murder against members of the government . . . Nor am I ignorant as to who is the principal target of Mr. Beigin's plans . . .

"But do not panic or be afraid . . . Israel will not be turned into a Spain or a Syria."

The next day snow fell on the ancient city of Jerusalem as Minister of Education Zalman Shazar made an impassioned speech in favor of the reparations resolution.

"For two thousand years we were chased from pillar to post, but we were never able to claim compensation for the evil done to us."

When the time to vote came, Beigin's party brought in on a

stretcher a member who had suffered a heart attack. Ben-Gurion had ordered David Hacohen, who was in Paris attending a U.N. meeting, to fly back in time for the balloting. The extremists voted en masse, but the Prime Minister's resolution was passed, 61 to 50, paving the way for the eventual arrival of $715,000,000 worth of reparations in the form of rolling stock, machinery, and raw materials.

Some people never forgave Ben-Gurion, and when railroad trains arrived from Germany as part of the reparations they refused to ride in them.

But Ben-Gurion had once more followed the dictates of his conscience, had championed an unpopular cause, and had given his people strong, democratic leadership in a moment of crisis.

Lieutenant Colonel Nehemiah Argov, aide-de-camp to the Commander-in-Chief, was not in Jerusalem during the rioting. When he heard about it at the army camp where he was taking a refresher course, he said to one of his associates:

"If anything had happened to B.G., I would have committed suicide."

In February, Ben-Gurion had a reunion in Jerusalem with a man he had known slightly thirty-three years earlier. He and Sam Hamburg had served together in the Jewish Legion in World War I. In those days Hamburg had been only seventeen, a raw-boned Jewish boy with ideals. After the war he left Palestine for America, where he borrowed money to study agronomy at the University of California, and became a legendary figure among desert farmers, with five million dollars' worth of enterprises and a ranch almost as large as Manhattan Island, the outgrowth of his successful fight against the California desert.

Now this square-shouldered, sun-scorched, rugged individualist was visiting his old homeland.

Ben-Gurion knew all about his career: his wheat crop had been wiped out by rust; his wells had run dry; he had made a river run forty miles uphill, and every time a fresh disaster struck he doubled the size of his holdings, just to show fate that he refused to give in. It was Jews like this one that Israel needed. So the Prime Minister sent for him.

"Your farming here is no good," Hamburg said bluntly.

"Why not?"

"Your farming has no horizons. Your people plant tiny fields with tiny plants, the way they used to do in Europe."

"What should we do?"

"Mr. Prime Minister, you have vision but you're afraid of your own land. You don't know what you've got here. This is the best soil in the world. You have a uniform climate. You could grow fine cotton here, and sugar, tobacco, peanuts, irrigated grains, winter vegetables."

Ben-Gurion raised his bushy eyebrows.

"You could export. Do a big business. Bring in lots of foreign capital."

"Our scientists tell me we can't raise cotton because of a bad insect."

Hamburg waved the idea aside with one of his massive hands.

"There is no insect in the world that can't be controlled, and economically, too, if you raise large enough crops."

The conversation went on for hours. Finally the Prime Minister hit his desk with his hand and said:

"How about coming to the Negev with me next week?"

"Impossible," Hamburg answered. "It's spring back in California already. I have crops to put in. But I'll tell you what I'll do. I'll return later if you want me to."

"When?"

Hamburg pulled out a pocket diary.

"I'll meet you in front of your office on March 6—that's a Thursday—at eight o'clock in the morning."

Ben-Gurion grinned. This was the sort of precision he liked.

"You'll surely be here?"

"Certainly!"

On Thursday, March 6, 1952, at 7:45 A.M., Ben-Gurion and about fifty other men were in front of the Ministry of Defense in Tel Aviv. A convoy of cars stood at the curbing. Chief of Staff Yadin was there, several cabinet members, and a large assortment of agricultural experts and scientists.

They kept looking at their watches. There had been a number of bets that the bluff, blunt American would not appear.

At exactly 8 A.M, he arrived, and they started for the Negev and toured the desert the whole day, guarded by jeeps mounting machine guns. They surveyed tens of thousands of acres of land that looked as if it could never be productive. Finally they stopped at Beersheba.

"Well, Hamburg, what do you think?" the Prime Minister asked.

"Master—— You don't mind my calling you Master, do you? All my life I've been fighting deserts, battling nature, doing it in order to have financial independence and to be really free. The last thing in the world I have ever wanted was a boss. But I'm willing for you to be my boss now. You know, B.G., you remind me of a poem I once used to like. It was called *The Prophet*. But now, about the desert——"

Ben-Gurion smiled.

"Yes, about the desert."

"That last place we visited. I can tell you that when you get water there, you can produce some of the finest cotton and sugar in the world."

This advice from Sam Hamburg was the start of cotton growing in the Negev. There would be other chapters in which the large-featured, largehearted man from California would also have a part. There would be disappointments and near disasters. But this was the start.

Before he left Israel that first time, Hamburg asked Ben-Gurion for a piece of what he called "desolation," some acreage that the specialists all agreed was worthless, a place that would be a challenge to him, and on which he could build a model farm.

They gave him six hundred acres in the Beit Shean Valley of Galilee, two hundred feet above the level of the Jordan River; yellow, parched land covered with weeds and wild pigs.

"How are you going to get water up to this level?" they asked him.

"I have a love affair with rivers," he said. "God and me—we'll do it together."

In the spring the British fleet made a series of courtesy calls on the Mediterranean countries. The Israel Government was informed that on a certain day at a certain hour the Prime Minister would receive a ceremonial visit from the Admiral of the Mediteranean Fleet, Lord Louis Mountbatten, former Viceroy and Governor-General of India, Privy Councillor, Grand Cross of the Star of India, Knight of the Garter, Grand Cross of the Indian Empire, D.S.O., Grand Cross of the Victorian Order, and holder of several dozen other honors and decorations bestowed upon him by Britain, by various members of the Commonwealth, and by numerous foreign countries.

This was a delicate moment. Relations between Britain and Israel were still a little strained. Where would the meeting be held? Ben-Gurion wanted it in Jerusalem, but the Foreign Office had still not dared move out of Tel Aviv, and no one expected that the British Admiral would risk violating protocol by coming to Jerusalem.

The first surprise was a message that Jerusalem was satisfactory.

On the day of the visit the Prime Minister came to the office without a necktie. His secretary finally said to him:

"Don't you really think that in the case of the Admiral of the British Mediterranean Fleet you ought to wear a tie?"

The Prime Minister contemplated the matter a moment, then said:

"I suppose so."

But no one had an extra tie in the office, so a messenger was dispatched to 44 Ben Maimon for one.

Just as the sirens of Lord Mountbatten's motorcycle escort were heard in the street, the messenger came through the door. Ben-Gurion was still adjusting the tie when his visitor appeared.

Even the Prime Minister blinked a little as Mountbatten entered the room. He was well over six feet tall, as handsome as a matinee idol, dressed in a fleckless white uniform, with gold epaulets, a gold shoulder cord, fourteen medals hanging from ribbons pinned onto the left breast of his jacket, and below them the large medal of the Order of the Garter and two other major decorations. He carried a ceremonial sword, elaborately festooned.

There was no particular reason for these two men to like each other, and there were many reasons why they should not, but almost from the moment they met they were *en rapport*.

Ben-Gurion brushed aside protocol and asked almost immediately about Mountbatten's years in India.

A quarter of an hour later the Admiral was still talking about his experiences with a wisdom and a sensitivity that pleased the Old Man. They talked of refugees in India and refugees in Israel, of illegal immigration, of a great variety of subjects, all informally and without strain.

As Mountbatten was leaving he said:

"I hear you once served in the British Army. What was your rank?"

The smallish Prime Minister looked up at the towering Admiral and said:

"I was a corporal, but then I was busted."

Mountbatten laughed, put his hand on Ben-Gurion's shoulder, and said:

"I'm not at all surprised!"

A few weeks later a package came, covered with official-looking seals. It contained a book from Mountbatten to his "good friend" Ben-Gurion, to serve as a reminder of a very pleasant visit.

Late in 1951 Jo Davidson had published his autobiography, *Between Sittings*. Just before it went to press he was able to add a few pages about his visit to Israel, the last of the many excitements of his rich life. He sent a copy to Ben-Gurion. Several weeks later he died of a heart attack.

But there was some unfinished business in Israel, and his widow came, months later, to take care of it. On her first night in Tel Aviv someone took her to the theater. It was one of the rare occasions on which the Prime Minister was taking an evening off from work and books. He happened to be sitting directly in front of Florence Davidson, so she spoke to him before the curtain went up. He had received Jo's book and wanted to talk about it. He had liked it very much.

As he sat with his back to the stage talking, the curtain went up and an actor began to speak his lines. There was not a sound in the theater except the voice of the actor and the voice of the Prime Minister telling what he thought of the great sculptor's book.

Florence Davidson wondered what to do—how long it would

last—whether one had the right to interrupt a Prime Minister.

At last Ben-Gurion sensed that something was wrong, turned around, and permitted the rest of the audience to turn its attention to the stage.

The Prime Minister's secretary at this time was Ephraim Evron (now representative of Histadruth in the United States). He had previously been secretary to Sharett, who had permitted him to go to Ben-Gurion in the hope that he might be a link to bind the Foreign Office and the Prime Minister's office closer together. He was young, about the height of his new chief, a former Haganah intelligence officer. He had only one handicap for his post: he was married and had two small children.

Evron's favorite story was of receiving a telephone call at Jerusalem from Ben-Gurion, who was taking the cure at Tiberias. The Prime Minister wanted a certain book on Greek philosophy. Eppie (the only name by which he ever called Evron) was to drive the forty-five miles to Tel Aviv, go to the largest of the three second-story libraries on Keren Kayemet Boulevard, turn to the right on entering the room, count the third shelf down from the top; the fifth book in from the left would be the one he wanted. He even gave Evron a brief description of the contents, which were in Greek.

The next day when Evron arrived at Tiberias he handed his chief a file of important cables.

"But the book?"

"I have it here."

As Ben-Gurion took it and looked at the title, his face turned red.

"This is the sixth book in from the left. Not the fifth. I told you to bring the fifth."

Evron tried to explain that the sixth seemed to answer the description Ben-Gurion had given him better than the fifth.

The Prime Minister soon got over his anger, but for months he would tease Evron for not knowing which book was fifth and which was sixth on that particular shelf.

There was another story illustrating Ben-Gurion's memory. At the National Airport in Washington one day Congressman Cel-

ler's secretary saw Ben-Gurion about to board a plane for New
York and ran up to him, saying:

"Mr. Ben-Gurion, I am supposed to be on your plane, but
there is no room so I must wait for the next one. I have a friend
meeting me at the New York airport. There is no way I can get
word to her. If you see her at the gate waiting for me, explain
what has happened, please."

Ben-Gurion agreed, and the Congressman's secretary gave him
a full description of her friend.

Years later Celler went to Israel and took his secretary with
him. As they entered the Prime Minister's office and before any
introductions had been made, Ben-Gurion said to the secretary:

"By the way, I never did find your friend at the New York
airport."

One day Ben-Gurion called Evron to his desk and pointed to a
package he had just received from Argentina. It contained a four-
volume work in Spanish by Professor Leon Dujovne of Buenos
Aires on the life, works, and influence of Spinoza.

"Eppie, I want to read those books. Where can you find someone to teach me Spanish?"

Evron's first thought was of Yitzhak Navon, who had succeeded him as Sharett's secretary, after serving in the legations
in Uruguay and Argentina.

Ben-Gurion knew Navon. They had met years ago when
Navon was chief of intelligence of the Arab division of Haganah.
In that capacity one year before independence he had concocted
what he always referred to as "a secret piece of monkey business
with the Arabs," for which he urgently needed four thousand
dollars. Only one Haganah officer had any idea where such a
sum could be raised.

"Go see Ben-Gurion," he said. "This is the sort of a crazy idea
that will appeal to him."

Navon had timidly approached the Jewish Agency chairman.
Ben-Gurion had listened and then had asked:

"How about two thousand dollars?"

Navon accepted, the money was immediately forthcoming, and
"the monkey business" was carried out.

The two men had liked each other from the start. Navon was

not only a sabra, but his family had lived in Jerusalem for three hundred years. Now he became Ben-Gurion's Spanish teacher.

"I have no desire to speak Spanish," the pupil explained. "Just teach me to read."

Navon found that Ben-Gurion, despite his polyglottism, had no special talent for languages and did not have a good ear for foreign sounds. He had mastered ancient Greek, Turkish, and so many other tongues all through the eye.

Two or three times a week Navon would go to the house on Keren Kayemet Boulevard in the evening, and he and the Prime Minister would spend several hours together. The teacher would teach the pupil the meaning of words, and then the pupil, having grasped the words, would teach the teacher the meaning of the sentence, explaining its philosophical import.

One day Ben-Gurion called Evron in and said:

"I'm going to have ten minutes between two meetings this afternoon. Get Yitzhak to come and give me a Spanish lesson."

That was the shortest. The longest lasted five hours.

After several months Ben-Gurion was actually teaching himself, working every night with grammars and dictionaries. Anything he did not understand he would write on a slip of paper. When he had a pile of slips he would send for Navon to clear up his doubts.

He was interested in the origin of words. He was excited one night when he and Navon found that many Spanish words have Arabic roots. He would give his teacher long discourses on the attitude of Jews to Spinoza. Often linguistics were forgotten while they talked pure philosophy.

About this time an office crisis occurred. Mrs. Evron issued an ultimatum to her husband.

"Either you are married to me or to the Prime Minister's office. You must decide."

Evron went to his chief and explained his predicament. He would like to remain a loyal servant, as devoted as Nehemiah Argov, but his wife had spoken.

"Send her to me," the Prime Minister commanded with a smile.

Mrs. Evron came, but her mind had been made up before her arrival. After a short discussion the Prime Minister admitted defeat, patted her on the shoulder, and said:

"All right, I'll give your husband back to you."

So late in 1952, Evron was transferred to Washington, Navon moved into his place, and Foreign Minister Sharett once more had to look for a new secretary for himself.

The day Evron left, Ben-Gurion gave him a book to commemorate their several years of happy association. As he autographed it he said:

"I'm sorry but I've got to make it just 'Eppie' because honestly I don't know your last name."

In the autumn Paula and Ben-Gurion went to Tiberias for a brief holiday and took Navon with them. The Prime Minister had already asked his new secretary what Spanish literature he ought to read, now that he knew the language, and Navon had suggested Cervantes' *Don Quixote,* so Ben-Gurion sent for a two-volume edition, which he took on the trip.

He finished the first volume in record time and turned it over to his secretary. The margins were full of penciled questions about grammar, syntax, and vocabulary.

"Write out the answers for me while I read the other book."

Each morning he would spend the breakfast hour telling Paula and Navon what he had read during the night. Paula was not pleased with some of the Cervantes jokes.

After Navon had answered all his questions, Ben-Gurion went back and read both volumes again.

His favorite passage was Don Quixote's soliloquy to the goatherds standing in front of their campfire, beginning:

"Happy the age and happy those centuries to which the ancients gave the name of golden, and not because gold, which is so esteemed in this age of ours, was then to be had without toil, but because those who lived in that time did not know the meaning of the words 'thine' and 'mine.'"

Now that Navon was in the outer office, Ben-Gurion often sent for him between meetings to discuss Spanish and even general literary and philosophical matters.

The new secretary soon learned that it was always permissible to interrupt his chief when he was working on cables with a philosophical remark but dangerous to interrupt a philosophical discussion with cables.

The Prime Minister talked with Navon about studying Italian

as he had Spanish, so he could read Dante and Machiavelli, but events occurred in the middle fifties that made it impossible.

Navon had a good influence on Ben-Gurion. Like Argov, he had been married for a short time and then divorced, and had no family to interfere with his singleness of purpose. Unlike Argov, he did not hesitate to criticize his chief. He found subtle ways of letting him know when he was making errors.

During the summer Arthur Lourie, now Israel's Ambassador to Canada but then Consul General in New York, returned on leave. During his last evening in the country he called on the Prime Minister at his home to say good-by. The Ben-Gurions were about to have supper, and invited him to join them around the kitchen table. As they sat down, the Old Man produced a book on Spinoza in Spanish and began translating passages aloud into Hebrew for his guest. He almost ignored the food Paula had prepared, as well as Lourie's desire for some political directions before leaving for America. Toward the end of the meal his wife said to him:

"Don't forget, it's your turn tonight."

Ben-Gurion looked at her with a wry smile.

"I know."

A few minutes later the Prime Minister was busy at the kitchen sink. He refused to allow Lourie to help him. He kept up a running complaint about the lack of hot water. After he had finished and had wandered upstairs to his library, Paula inspected his work and found it highly unsatisfactory. She was about to call him down to do most of the dishes over again when Lourie persuaded her not to. The Consul General left for New York without the political advice he had wanted.

Late in the year a rupture in relations occurred between the Prime Minister and Yadin. The archaeologist had been made Chief of Staff, with instructions to reorganize the Army. The break came over finances. Late in 1952 the Prime Minister decided that there was not going to be a war in the Middle East for at least several years and that the defense budget could accordingly be severely cut.

"I know your economic problems," Yadin told him, "but you must let me have the same budget for one more year, otherwise you will have to find another commander."

Neither would compromise, so Yadin resigned. At the ceremony of changing commanders Ben-Gurion recounted, in what was extremely sentimental language for him, his years of association with Yadin. There were tears in his eyes before he finished. He gave the retiring commander one of his favorite books, *Archaiologia Bios*, by Flavius Josephus, with a warm inscription.

About this same time Dr. Chaim Weizmann died. He slipped gradually away. He had been ill for years, but that did not lessen the grief of Israel and of Jews everywhere in the world. The Prime Minister walked in the funeral procession with deeply bowed head.

When the question arose of a successor, Ben-Gurion proposed Einstein.

"I am almost certain he will not accept," he told an associate in the government, "but it would be wrong not to offer the position to the greatest living Jew."

When Einstein rejected it, Ben-Gurion turned to Itzhak Ben-Zvi, who had been his friend for almost forty-five years and who was elected on the third ballot.

In the 1952 Israel Year Book the Prime Minister wrote on "The Vision of the People":

"When there is no vision, the people perish."

Of Ben-Gurion's own vision one of his office assistants said:

"His strength is that when he believes in something he can instill his enthusiasm into others. The first time he says it, it sounds crazy, like establishing the capital in Jerusalem or making Elath a great seaport. But after a few weeks or a few months it isn't crazy any more, and people begin to say, 'Why, yes, why not?'

"I guess that's what it means to be a prophet and have visions."

CHAPTER TWENTY-TWO

THE YEAR 1953 started off with a practical joke.

Months earlier Ben-Gurion and his Foreign Office had exchanged secret communications with the Kremlin in an effort to win permission for Russian Jews to immigrate to Israel. In one note Israel had offered not to join any non-aggression pact against Russia in return for free emigration. But Moscow had ignored the suggestion.

Then came the Communist purge in Czechoslovakia, which all Israel followed with interest because of the accent on anti-Semitism and because an Israeli (a member of Mapam), who was in Czechoslovakia at the time, was one of the defendants. This was almost an announcement that Israel could give up hoping for consideration from Moscow or any other Communist capital.

Ben-Gurion had hesitated at forming a government with the conservative General Zionists out of fear that he would drive the more left-wing members of his own party over into Mapam, but when the eleven principal defendants at Prague were found guilty and executed late in 1952, he went into conference with the General Zionists, who agreed to enter a new coalition on the understanding that he would eliminate some of the government controls over business, take steps to encourage private enterprise, and create conditions more attractive for the investment of private capital from abroad.

Next, Mapai's newspaper carried an article caustically attacking Mapam for trying to ride two horses at the same time: for wanting to be part of the Communist world and still collect money for the support of their kubbutzim from capitalist sources.

The article was written with boldness and vigor. It was not in the style of any politico-literary figure anyone knew. It was signed "Saba Shel Yariv [Grandfather of Yariv]," obviously a synonym.

While many people were trying to figure out who this new, devastating writer could be, a second article appeared, discussing the purge in Prague and suggesting that Mapam had better decide which it considered more important, Communism or Zionism.

Then came a third, describing the Soviet Union as a "house of slavery" and Stalin (then still alive) as one of the worst "butchers" of history. A fourth discussed family quarrels within Mapam.

The mystery was settled to the general public's satisfaction when someone remembered that Ben-Gurion's daughter Geula had a son named Yariv.

This was obviously the Old Man's way of speaking out without jeopardizing his position as head of the government or risking

international complications. He never formally admitted author-
ship, but months later during an address before the Knesset he
said:

"I now wish to quote something from an article signed Saba
Shel Yariv."

The room echoed with laughter.

"You may be surprised when I tell you that I agree with almost
everything this man writes."

At 10:10 P.M. on Monday, February 9, three days after publication of the article attacking the Soviet Union, a bomb was
thrown into the courtyard of the Soviet Legation in Tel Aviv.
There were many injuries. The wife of the Soviet Minister, the
wife of a member of the staff, and a chauffeur were taken to a
hospital.

On Tuesday morning Ben-Gurion, gravely concerned over the
possible international complications, went before the Knesset
and made a statement that began:

"It is with deep regret that I have to report on an abomination
committed in Israel last night."

He used the word that had angered Beigin on another occasion:

"The hooligans who have committed this dastardly crime are
more the enemies of Israel than haters of a foreign state. If their
intention was to fight for the honor of Israel, let me say that it is
they themselves who have profaned by this senseless crime the
honor of Israel."

On Wednesday there were pro-Communist demonstrations,
sponsored by the Israel-Soviet Friendship League. Twenty men
and women were treated for injuries.

On Thursday the Soviet Union broke diplomatic relations with
Israel, and Golda Myerson, who had been Minister to Moscow
for a short time, declared, "This is a black day for Israel, for
the Jewish people, and especially for the Jews of the Soviet
Union."

Rebecca Sieff, president of the Women's International Zionist
Organization, and mother of Marcus Sieff, invited Ben-Gurion
and his wife to spend a weekend relaxing on her estate at Tel

Mond, north of Tel Aviv. Ben-Gurion in turn asked an English-woman, Mrs. B., to go with them.

On the way by automobile Mrs. B. said:

"Ben-Gurion, why did you want me to come along?"

The Prime Minister smiled.

"I know you to be a resolute woman and I am counting on you to keep our hostess, Paula, and anyone else who may be there absolutely quiet the entire time."

Mrs. B. worked diligently to carry out her commission. No one saw the Prime Minister except at meals. Late Saturday he came from his room and invited Mrs. B. to go for a stroll in the garden. Two policemen walked close behind them. (Tel Mond is in the narrowest part of Israel, with the sea only five miles to the west, the Jordanian frontier only two miles to the east.)

Mrs. B. waited for Ben-Gurion to begin a conversation. He walked in silence. Not a word was spoken during the promenade.

The next morning the Prime Minister read the newspapers and then went back to his room and worked all day in solitude.

On the way back to Tel Aviv that night the Prime Minister said to the Englishwoman:

"I'm now going to tell you why I wanted peace and quiet. I had a very important decision to make. The Tubiansky case. But now I have made up my mind, so we can talk."

Almost everyone in Israel knew about the Tubiansky case. Meir Tubiansky had been a young Haganah officer. During the War of Liberation he was accused of treason, tried before a court-martial, found guilty, and executed.

For several years his widow spent much of her time and most of her energy as a detective, lawyer, and investigator, trying to clear her husband's name. She was motivated largely by her son's unhappiness. He often came home from school and reported that his classmates had taunted him because of his father's crime.

Just before the weekend at Tel Mond, Mrs. Tubiansky had completed her work and had placed on Ben-Gurion's desk a mass of documents that she said definitely proved her husband's innocence. As Prime Minister and Commander-in-Chief of the Army, Ben-Gurion had to make the final decision.

As soon as he mentioned the case, Paula asked:

"Well, what have you decided?"

It was almost possible to see the answer in his relaxed face and quiet manner.

"I am convinced that he was not guilty."

The next day he sent a letter to Mrs. Tubiansky that might have been written by Abraham Lincoln.

"I cannot adequately express my profound regret . . . The judges who were present at the time of his death said he behaved bravely, without his hands or his eyes being bound, and he asked that his son be well educated . . . A special parade will be held in his son's school, where it will be announced that the Army made a tragic mistake. Thus his classmates and his friends will know that his father fell as the result of an error, and your son may be proud . . ."

In June, Sam Hamburg was back in Israel. He had planted ten acres of his model farm to cotton, and now he had come to inspect the crop. One day he appeared at the Prime Minister's office with an entire plant in his hand. He greeted Ben-Gurion by holding out the stalk and saying:

"Master, look! I think someday we're going to be a most important factor in the world cotton-production picture. Look at that plant! I have never seen such luxuriant cotton in June, and I've been raising it for thirty years."

The Prime Minister took the plant, felt the cotton with his fingers, then smiled.

"Israel thanks you."

Hamburg fumbled with his hat.

"No, Mr. Prime Minister, I must thank you. I never thought cotton could be so spiritually important. I never imagined that a little ten-acre field could give me a greater feeling of purpose, of continuity, of belonging, than anything else on earth."

On a summer day when the Negev seemed like the inside of a cauldron and the sand was burning-hot to the touch, Ben-Gurion made a trip with a large military escort to Elath. About fifty miles south of Beersheba they stopped at Avdat, a place marked on maps with an inverted pyramid, indicating that it is an ancient historical site.

On top of a five-hundred-foot hill there are traces of Byzantine ruins and the remains of old cisterns, indicating that here a flourishing civilization once existed.

Ben-Gurion was so excited he climbed to the top of the hill. He led the way himself, sometimes going so rapidly that his entourage had to run to keep up with him. It was a severe physical effort for even the younger men, but the white-haired commander was so exhilarated that neither heat, exhaustion, thirst, sand in the eyes nor sun on the bald spot on top of his head seemed to bother him.

Close to Avdat the military party met some young men who said they were from a nearby kibbutz called Sde Boker (Field of the Cattlemen). They were prospecting for a place suitable for the raising of sheep.

Sde Boker was only a few hundred yards off the main road, so Ben-Gurion and his party stopped there on the way home.

It had been founded just the previous year by two girls and twelve young men who had done military service in the Negev during the war and had enough archaeological knowledge to be sure that this had once been the site of an ancient town. They had borrowed money from the Jewish Agency on a twenty-year promissory note, and were now trying to prove that the desert could sustain human life. The Prime Minister asked them many searching questions about their experience and what motivated them.

Sde Boker so far was only a few wooden buildings and one scraggly tree, surrounded by barbed wire.

Life was primitive, often unpleasant, and occasionally dangerous.

When strong winds blew across the desert, it was sometimes impossible to see the hand before the eye. The Arabs call the southwind the *khamsin*. (In Hebrew, *sharav*.) It is so hot that it seems to blister the face. Desert people say it can drive a man out of his mind. Other winds lift the sand and mix it with the air, and then drive it into ears, eyes, wagon axles, the working parts of motors; through crevices in a house that seem not to be crevices at all; down the throat and into the soul of every desert dweller.

There was danger from Arab nomads, and from Egyptians, whose frontier was not far away. One of the two girl founders had been herding sheep one day not long ago. When she failed to return, they sent out a searching party. No trace of the sheep was ever found, but they brought back the girl's dead body.

Another danger was from the Egyptian cobra, which injects its poison into the nervous system, paralyzing the victim's entire body and causing death in twenty minutes. The Sde Boker pioneers caught two or three every month.

The kibbutzniks had dug a well and at a great depth struck water, but it was salty and therefore worthless.

Seven months a year they suffered a drought during which the sun baked the earth as hard and dry as a sheet of steel. During the other five months there would be three deluges, with water running down the desert hills as though the sand were glazed cement. It accumulated in wadis. As Jews had done in ancient times, these young settlers built dams of earth to form small lakes, from which they would distribute the water to their fields as it was needed.

Water for humans and animals had to be brought in by tanker trucks, for as yet no pipeline had been extended this far.

The temperature changed rapidly. There were times in the year when the water would remain frozen until 8 A.M.

When Ben-Gurion got back to his office he gathered his staff around him and told them of all he had seen. Of the Sde Boker settlers he said:

"I am jealous of those young people. What a wonderful experience!"

From time to time in the days that followed, he made other remarks.

"No one is indispensable."

That was something he had often said. But now he added:

"None of us should hold on too long, just trying to prove that we are vitally needed."

Again he said:

"Old people ought to give younger people a chance."

Finally he asked Paula:

"How would you like to live in the desert?"

Then one day he began to write a letter to Mapai on three-by-five cards for his typist to copy.

Still, those in the office could not really believe it.

Ben-Gurion was present at the meeting of the Mapai Central Committee at which his letter was read.

"I can no longer continue . . . I cannot bear up any more under the mental strain that I suffer in the government . . . For six years I have been working in a state of high tension . . . Mine is no ordinary tiredness . . ."

Then he told of his decision to resign as Prime Minister and Minister of Defense (he would continue to hold his seat in Parliament) and move to Sde Boker.

At first the party leaders reacted as if some great disaster had paralyzed their minds and their tongues. Then, one by one, they made speeches insisting that the Prime Minister reconsider.

Ben-Gurion sat hunched in his chair, silent.

A woman member who had lost two sons in the War of Liberation addressed him directly.

"If I gave my sons to the nation, how can you consider abandoning it?"

The meeting adjourned without the Prime Minister adding to his letter—or subtracting anything.

When the news was published, Ben-Gurion's decision became the only subject discussed for days.

In Haifa some of his socialist followers threatened to strike until he reconsidered. Paula was kept busy answering the phone and telling people she was sorry but she could not let them speak to her husband. Letters, telegrams, and cables piled up.

Paula's own reaction was that of a devoted wife who seldom questioned any decision her husband made. She was past sixty and he was sixty-seven. She knew that life is not easy in any kibbutz. In the desert it might be more than either of them could bear. But Ben-Gurion had made his decision and there was nothing to do but start packing.

Even those who knew him best disagreed on what the real reason was. One member of his staff was sure he wanted to find out if the mind grows old as the body does, or whether, free of routine problems, a mind at sixty-seven could forge out into new fields, have fresh adventures, remain as agile as ever.

The more conventional answer was that he wanted to be free of petty government chores so he could catch up on his reading, have more time to write, and lead an unhurried intellectual existence.

Others thought that in the peace of the Negev he wanted to concentrate on possible solutions of Israel's most pressing problems.

Another theory was that he was disappointed in the younger generation of Israel. He felt something had happened to the pioneering instinct. Israel had frontiers but few frontiersmen. This was the age of chewing gum, lipstick, comic books, movies, and other "cultural refinements" that seemed to interest young people more than trying to revive ancient desert cities that had been dead a thousand years or two.

And then there was his rebellion against so many immigrants settling in Tel Aviv, cluttering up the city's cafés, trying to open small shops, refusing to go onto the land.

The best explanation seemed to be that Ben-Gurion was going to try to inspire by example rather than preach with words.

Some few scoffers said it was a theatrical gesture; others, that he was trying to show conflicting elements in the government he was indispensable. Still others saw in it his rebellion at having to sacrifice so many of the principles of labor socialism in order to assure the flow of financial contributions from America.

Most Israel kibbutzim are connected with political or religious groups. Sde Boker has no such affiliations. This was an indication that, whatever his purpose, he wanted his adventure to be above and beyond political considerations.

Nothing else that had happened in the five years of Israel's existence had caused such a flutter abroad, for it was not every day that a Prime Minister resigned at the height of his popularity and went off to live in a shack on a desert.

In several capitals professional writers expressed sympathy and understanding. They knew why he had done it. It was those four telephones on his desk jangling constantly, and too many visitors, too many interviews, too much stupid office routine. It was because of the organizational treadmill, which eventually drove all executives a little crazy with an occupational disease of the nerves and which frustrated creative people.

A few publications congratulated Ben-Gurion for having the

strength of character to flee from the noise, the hurry, the commotion of Jerusalem and Tel Aviv.

Without giving names, they wrote of other statesmen with duodenal ulcers and various occupational diseases who, they said, ought to move to at least figurative deserts and let younger, healthier men take over. To such men Ben-Gurion had set an example, even though few of them might follow it.

At a farewell luncheon given by the government, Ben-Gurion leaned across the table to Paula, who was not looking very happy, and said in a quiet voice, quoting from the Book of the Prophet Jeremiah:

"'I remember thee, the kindness of thy youth, the love of thine espousals, when thou wentest after me in the desert, in a land that was not sown.'"

December 5 was the day of the Ben-Gurions' thirty-sixth wedding anniversary. Paula celebrated it by talking to a Jerusalem reporter about the past and the future.

During these thirty-six years Ben-Gurion had been "a good husband, a kind and considerate man." He had helped her wash the dishes all these years and he had promised that at Sde Boker he would also help scrub the floors, but she was not going to permit it.

"He is going to be very productive. He is going to write most of the time."

On the morning of December 7, Ben-Gurion submitted his resignation to President Ben-Zvi:

"No one man is indispensable to a state, and certainly I am not . . . Israel is not leaderless. The fate of the nation does not depend on who is Prime Minister . . . A Prime Minister goes and a Prime Minister comes, but government by law is maintained . . . I hope my departure will cause no crisis. My friend Moshe Sharett will be acting Prime Minister . . . I am confident that . . . a new government will be formed and approved by the Knesset without any undue delay or upheavals."

In the evening the retiring Prime Minister made a farewell broadcast to the nation. It was not meant to be a sentimental speech, but his voice quavered several times and many who listened were deeply moved.

"I have endeavored to fulfill my mission as far as it lay in my power, with devotion and in all humility. But I do not claim to have been free from fault and error. With complete sincerity I can repeat literally the words of the Psalmist in the first verse of Chapter 131:

" 'Lord, my heart is not haughty, nor my eyes lofty: neither do I exercise myself in things too high or in matters too wonderful for me.' "

He concluded with a paraphrase of the words of the prophet Habakkuk, which perhaps gave the best description of his reason for going:

"Righteous man lives by his faith. He will not preach to others, will not act the saint by calling on others to live justly, will not look for fault in his neighbor, but he will practice his faith in his daily life; he will live it."

On Sunday, December 13, Paula and her husband got up earlier than usual. There was still some last-minute packing to do. Before they had even finished breakfast, callers began to arrive, mostly government officials and old friends who wanted to say good-by.

The household goods were put in a Ministry of Defense truck. Jeeps filled with soldiers were waiting to escort the trekkers.

As they were leaving the house for the last time, Ben-Gurion turned to Paula and said:

"Did you pack that cotton plant Sam Hamburg gave me?"

Paula assured him she had.

Breaking his custom, the retired Prime Minister shook hands with the policemen who for years had stood guard outside 17 Keren Kayemet Boulevard, and his wife gave each of them an autographed photograph of her husband.

As they entered the car, Ben-Gurion looked at the crowd that had gathered. Some were daubing their eyes with handkerchiefs. He waved his hand toward them and said:

"Do not weep. Follow me."

CHAPTER TWENTY-THREE

THERE is nothing immense about the Negev, by American standards. In Texas there are four counties larger than this badlands area of Israel. Yet for Paula Ben-Gurion, who had lived all her life in cities, Sde Boker, hours across billowing, forsaken sand from even a grocery store, seemed frighteningly remote.

She was leaving children, grandchildren, neighbors, friends, modern conveniences, civilization. At Sde Boker there would be a few young women, the oldest not half her age, several dozen young men, and Ben-Gurion. He would be busier than ever with his books and papers. There would not even be anyone with whom she could gossip. But in her devotion she made no mention of these things.

A rapidly advancing swirl of brown dust announced to the pioneers of Sde Boker the approach of the convoy. Paula was the first to step to the ground. Her arms were full of bouquets that had been given to her in Beersheba.

As the secretary of the kibbutz (appointed by an elected committee) came up to say "Welcome," Paula thrust the flowers into his hands.

"If there's anyone sick, give them these. But they'd better be put in water right away."

There were no formalities. Everyone helped unload the truck. Military police, on the order of the former Prime Minister, told the photographers they could take one shot apiece and then they must go. It was not fair to these hard-working settlers to disturb the routine of their life and make a Roman holiday.

The reporters wanted to ask a few questions.

"What will your job be here?"

"I have no idea," he answered crisply. "This is a kibbutz. There is a secretary to arrange such matters as the distribution of work. I shall do what he gives me to do."

He waved aside other questions, saying:

"When I have been here a few years I will be able to make a statement about what is happening and the chances of the future."

By late afternoon reporters, photographers, friends, and aides had all left.

Paula had on a simple cotton dress. Ben-Gurion had worn a suit and a necktie because it was an occasion, but now he got into khaki shorts and shirt.

"Welcome to Sde Boker," he said to his wife, smiling.

"I hope you will be happy here," she answered warmly.

Then she started to set the house in order, while he began arranging his books.

Their first visitor was a four-and-a-half-year-old boy, Chemi Cohen, the youngest inhabitant. He wandered through the open front door, saying in Hebrew:

"Who are you?"

The former Prime Minister smiled at him and answered:

"I am the newest *chalutz* [pioneer]."

Actually the Ben-Gurions were the nineteenth and twentieth volunteers to become members of the kibbutz.

The first time Paula saw the house they were to occupy she said to her husband nostalgically:

"This reminds me of the bungalow at Coney Island some girl friends and I rented one summer when I lived in New York."

It was mustard color, one story high, forty-five by eighteen feet, with three rooms: a bedroom for each of them, and a library-study-workroom for him. It had been prefabricated in Sweden. A screened porch across the front of the house faced the settlement's modest office building, its air raid shelter, and its community house. Nearby stood a radio tower, which also supported some meteorological instruments. On the roof of the Ben-Gurion house there was a device that the new occupant liked to show to visitors.

"It's the cheapest water heater in the world," he would explain.

It was all done by mirrors. They caught the rays of the desert sun and focused them onto a small metal reservoir, giving the Ben-Gurions a moderate supply of water as hot as most hotels provide.

The rising hour at Sde Boker was 5:45 A.M. Ben-Gurion's first job of the morning was to record the readings of the several meteorological instruments.

Breakfast was eight to eight-thirty; lunch, twelve-thirty to one;

supper at seven. Work hours were from six to eight, eight-thirty to twelve-thirty, and one to four. Evenings were spent mostly in self-education, planning, and emergency work.

Everyone ate in a community dining room. Some of the men wore khaki shorts, some long trousers. Few ever wore shirts. The girls dressed in shorts or slacks and a shirtwaist. The only ones who wore shoes were newcomers whose feet were not yet inured to the heat of the sand.

Paula was assigned to work in the kitchen and the nursery. She would also put her medical training into use when injured or wounded people were brought in from the road, victims of automobile accidents or shootings. (At first there was no doctor. Later a law was passed that no graduate of a medical college could begin practicing in any city until he had given a year of his time to a settlement. After that Sde Boker had a young doctor.)

Gazelles often passed by on the desert. At night jackals and foxes could be heard.

Sde Boker had almost thirty acres planted to peach trees, grapes, and vegetables, but the principal part of its acreage was for grazing.

The kibbutz had several hundred sheep, two cows, a dozen Arabian and Yugoslav horses, and several thousand chickens. The settlers sheered the sheep, carded the wool, dyed it, and used it to make rugs.

A truck went once a month to Tel Aviv for supplies.

They could get Cairo and Tel Aviv on their radios.

The irrigating of the fields could be done only between midnight and dawn. The rest of the time the winds were so strong they blew the water away.

Electricity was available six hours a day. Water was strictly rationed.

The settlement's big gift to Paula was a refrigerator operated by kerosene.

At least one of the settlers armed with a machine gun was always on guard, day and night. In addition to the girl, one other kibbutznik had been killed.

Ben-Gurion followed the settlement's work schedule until lunch, but he devoted the afternoon work period to writing.

After the evening meal he went back to his writing and then read an hour or two before he went to sleep.

His first work assignment was to labor in the fields. Later he became a shepherd.

In addition to her community chores, Paula kept her own house in order, made the beds, dusted, scrubbed, and ironed all the linen and clothes that came back from the community laundry.

Those who came to Sde Boker for visits observed a new relationship between Ben-Gurion and his wife. One of his oldest associates said:

"Before the desert experience he seemed to take Paula for granted. He never questioned that she was always at hand to care for him. But at Sde Boker, being almost always under the same roof with her, he observed for the first time how hard she worked and he realized how much of a sacrifice it had been for her to leave Tel Aviv and Jerusalem. He reacted by becoming more considerate and attentive than he had ever been before."

Desert life began to have another effect on him. He became warmer and friendlier toward those around him. Ideas were still more important than people, but in this small community in the middle of a desert he was closer to more people than he had been since the days of his youth, as a pioneer in Galilee, and he seemed to enjoy the human contacts.

In January a new settler arrived, Ruth Alexandrovski Gil'adi, twenty-four years old, dark-haired, sparkling-eyed, and a sabra. She and Ben-Gurion often worked together, and they became immediate friends. She represented his idea of what Israel's youth ought to be like. She was strong, physically attractive, intelligent, and fearless.

She never spoke to him unless he began the conversation. Often there would be long periods of silence while they worked and he seemed to be thinking of distant matters. But then suddenly he would turn to her and ask:

"What is the trouble with the young people of Israel? Why aren't there thousands like you in the Negev?"

Several times she tried to explain. Once she said:

"We had our glorious hours during the war, didn't we? After that we lost something. I don't really know what it was. Maybe it was that we no longer had anything to be afraid of. Maybe we got lazy. Maybe we wanted a soft life. Maybe we thought too much about inconsequential things."

During their conversations Ben-Gurion discovered that she had spent nearly a year visiting farms in Ohio and Georgia, and that he knew her father, who had come to Palestine in the second aliyah, from Kishinev.

Paula and Ruth often talked English together, one with a Brooklyn accent and the other with a cross between a Georgia drawl and an Ohio intonation.

The arrival of the Ben-Gurions caused many problems for the kibbutz. In good weather, despite the isolation of Sde Boker, tourists, government people, visiting dignitaries, reporters, photographers, and other outlanders would come, sometimes several parties of them in a single day. They had to be fed and sometimes housed for the night.

There was also the problem of how to address the new members. The settlers had always called each other by their first names, but now . . . ?"

It was not difficult to address Mrs. Ben-Gurion as "Paula," but there was general agreement that they could not call the former Prime Minister anything more familiar than "Ben-Gurion."

Toward the end of February, Ben-Gurion agreed to receive the press. The reporters found him bronzed, fit, and jovial. There were too many of them for the small house, so he invited them to sit around on the ground outside.

"It's good earth, and no dishonor to sit on it."

He refused to answer questions about current political matters, but otherwise he was friendlier and more communicative than he had ever been to Israel reporters. He even injected a little humor into the interview.

"I am not a member of the government any more. I am just a member of the Knesset who is working in a stable."

They asked what his work was, and he replied:

"At the moment I'm looking after the kids and the goats in the barn."

He refused to discuss his own future, but of the Negev's future he said:

"One day this area may develop into the main center of population of Israel. The only problem is water."

Then he glanced affectionately toward the Sde Boker settlers standing around and added:

"The people here in the Negev are a little crazy, but I happen to like crazy people."

In March, Ben-Gurion wrote an article for the New York *Times* on "Why I Retired to the Desert." In it he said:

"If power is not the end but only the vehicle for service to the nation and its people, any responsible statesman must eventually ask himself: Has he perhaps become a victim of routine? Is his capacity to come to grips with reality still fully alive? Has he a sufficient awareness of the simple citizen in the nation—on whom, after all, everything depends? . . .

"A statesman who sees himself as the determining factor in the fate of his country is harmful and dangerous. And when constant strain and long service have perhaps deprived him, or may deprive him, of the freshness of his outlook, the earnestness which must accompany his every decision will be weakened; he will tend increasingly to deal lightly and in routine fashion with grave matters . . . When this happens it is better that he should retire . . ."

The last half of the article was about his two loves: working on the land and reading.

"To my mind the surroundings most worthy of human beings are natural surroundings. The more a man is able to remove himself from the artificial life of modern civilization . . . and stand face to face with wild and primary nature as it was fashioned by the Creator—and in this sense the desert is ideal—the more he is able to get at the truth of existence and of his mission on earth."

It was no accident, he said, that the Torah (the law of Israel) was given in the desert and that Israel's greatest teacher, Moses, led his people into the wilderness.

He concluded with this explanation of the step he had taken:

"After all, there is room for only one Prime Minister, but for those who make the desert bloom there is room for hundreds, thousands and even millions. And the destiny of the state is in the hands of the many rather than of a single individual. There are times when an individual feels he should do those things which only can and should be done by the many."

In May the sheep-shearing season began. By this time Ben-

Gurion felt in excellent physical condition. He and Ruth were working together. He would lift hundred-and-twenty-pound lambs with apparently no difficulty and put them on the table, and then he and the young sabra would clip the wool. But he was forgetting that he was sixty-seven and that his back had troubled him for years. Eventually he had to go to bed, and then, because there was no doctor at Sde Boker, to a hospital near Tel Aviv. It was three weeks before he was pronounced improved enough for the rugged life of a pioneer again.

During the sheep-shearing season Ruth had confided a secret to him. She and a tall young settler, Zeev Steinhardt, were going to be married in June. She wanted him to be one of the first to know.

"The desert is a good place to fall in love," she said.

About this same time Paula had acute trouble with arthritis and went to the Hadassah Hospital in Jerusalem for treatment.

After she and her husband returned to Sde Boker, they were inundated with visitors.

Sam Hamburg arrived with an unusual gift: a small bale of cotton, the first ever ginned in Israel. As he placed it on the table in front of Ben-Gurion, Paula came into the room and asked:

"What on earth is that?"

Before Hamburg could explain, her husband said:

"This, Paula, is the most important thing in Israel right now."

Ben-Gurion had a faraway look in his eyes as he stared at the produce of soil that experts had said was worthless. Hamburg had talked to him often enough to be able to guess what he was thinking.

Reverence for work. Pride in the accomplishments of labor. Understanding of the importance of a field of cotton, an almond orchard, an orange grove, a sugar field. This was what Ben-Gurion wanted to teach his people.

Hamburg went with him to the barn and watched the white-haired, retired Prime Minister feeding barley to the lambs.

"Looking at him, I thought of Gandhi and his spinning wheel," Hamburg told friends later. "I thought of Biblical prophets. In that sheep barn at Sde Boker that night I seemed to experience communion with the spirit of man in its highest manifestation."

Another visitor was U Nu, Premier of Burma. His country and

Israel both had been under British influence, Burma for more than three hundred years, Israel for thirty years. One month before the United Nations voted the partition plan that led to Israel's independence, a treaty was signed in London providing for Burma's independence. Burma achieved full statehood four months before Israel. She was the fifty-eighth state admitted to the United Nations; Israel was the fifty-ninth. The powers of Burma's President are limited, as are those of Israel's President. In both countries the Prime Minister is the real leader. U Nu had been Premier during the same period as Ben-Gurion.

The two men talked about these matters as they walked around the desert settlement.

A few small eucalyptus trees had just been planted, and Ben-Gurion showed them off proudly to his guest.

U Nu laughed and said:

"In Burma we have too many trees. Too many can be worse than too few. Mr. Prime Minister, I suggest that you pull up these trees right now, while there is still a chance."

Ben-Gurion took him to see the dams that had been built to hold back the rain water.

U Nu shook his head.

"In my country our worry is about too much water. We have to fight to get rid of it. Here you fight to try to get enough of it."

Then they went back to the mustard-colored cottage and discussed more profound matters.

Ben-Gurion wanted to talk religion and philosophy with this man from a country where Buddha is worshiped. He wanted to expound his theory that Israel, India, and Greece were the three nations of antiquity that had bequeathed eternal values to the human race.

"I have always considered Buddha one of the ten greatest figures of history," he told his visitor.

They discussed the similarity between Buddha's ethical precepts and the Ten Commandments of Moses.

They talked of ancient days and then of the modern world. During their discussion of the importance of scientific research Ben-Gurion said:

"While science aspires to reveal the secrets of nature, it cannot tell man what path to follow."

Premier Nu urged his host to read the Nikayas, which are the discourses on doctrine that form part of the Tripitaka or canon of the older schools of Buddhism.

They discussed U Nu's belief in reincarnation and his idea that a man progresses from one life to the next until he finally becomes holy enough to be a saint and eventually a Buddha.

U Nu's visit to Sde Boker began an era of close economic cooperation between the two far-distant countries, and it encouraged Ben-Gurion to make a much deeper study of Eastern religions and philosophies. It was a meeting Ben-Gurion always remembered with pleasure. On Burma's eighth anniversary he sent U Nu a message:

"Your unforgettable visit, during which I had the privilege of getting to know you . . . remains forever alive in my memory . . . I cherish the personal lesson you gave me in the teaching of Buddha and I continue with deep spiritual satisfaction to read the Nikayas."

At Sde Boker, Ben-Gurion turned out hundreds of thousands of words. He wrote for several Israel papers and for publications in the United States, Canada, South Africa, and other parts of the world. His principal literary work was editing *The Rebirth and Destiny of Israel,* a collection of essays and speeches he had delivered or written between 1915 and 1952, which was published that year in both the United States and England in a 539-page volume.

His writing ranged over wide fields. He wrote of the future:

"We are going to enter the period of solar power. We have an endless supply in the Negev. We will desalt sea water and pump it into the Negev, which will become something quite different from what it is today."

He wrote a message to Israel schoolteachers, telling them that each of them ought to spend a few days of each year with the Army, a few more days in a border village, and then a few days in some isolated Negev settlement.

He wrote an essay on Plato for a periodical on classical studies.

In one article he became the fighting socialist again.

"There are among us not a few who think that private initiative (i.e., the love of money) will do all the work, and they want to build our whole future on the basis of private enterprise. These people are guilty of endangering the state and the nation. By virtue of mere love of money you can establish at best a Hebrew Carthage which would not exist even as long as the Canaanite Carthage existed.

"Carthage was defeated and wiped off the face of the earth because behind Hannibal was only a great city of traders and money-makers whose god was private enterprise, and his opponents were a people of peasants, with roots in their soil.

"Private enterprise will not unite the Diaspora, it will not make the desert bloom, it will not create a Hebrew culture worthy of the people of the Book, and it will certainly not found a new society."

But several weeks later he took a more catholic position, arguing that in every area of Israel there should be collective farms, co-operative farms, and private farms, with each settler free to choose the economic system under which he wished to live.

He gave youth the slogan "On to Elath!" but as he looked toward the horizon he could see that there was little traffic on the road leading from Beersheba past Sde Boker to the south. There had been no dramatic exodus from the cities, no swarms of young people following in his trail, no substantial increase in the population of kibbutzim and frontier settlements, no great trek to the south.

But it was not the failure it seemed. Ben-Gurion during 1954 had made everyone in Israel acutely aware of the desert, of its potentialities, of its inevitable place in Israel's future.

In Tel Aviv a simple shoemaker of Polish origin stopped Baruch Tal, one of Ben-Gurion's associates in Mapai, as he was passing by and asked:

"Can you get me the measurements of the Old Man's feet?"

When Tal asked why, he explained:

"I've been thinking a lot about him being down there in the desert. They tell me it gets cold at night this time of the year. I think of him down there, suffering, maybe. He's not a young man. He's older than I am. So he's down there suffering in the desert and here I am, just an ordinary *chaver* [comrade], living in comfort in Tel Aviv. So I think I'd like to make him a pair of shoes. It would help my conscience to feel better."

CHAPTER TWENTY-FOUR

ONE DAY early in 1955, Minister of Labor Golda Myerson traveled to Sde Boker to tell Ben-Gurion the troubles his old colleagues were having in keeping the coalition together, and to extend an invitation from Prime Minister Sharett to come out of retirement, return to his post as Minister of Defense, and thus help prevent a government crisis until elections could be held in the summer.

Three days later Sharett made the acceptance public. A few days after that the white-haired man from the desert arrived in Jerusalem in battle dress and an army overcoat and was sworn in.

His abdication had been abrupt and complete. His return to power was gradual.

There were almost as many reasons for his leaving Sde Boker as there had been for leaving Jerusalem and Tel Aviv fourteen months earlier.

Life on the desert had been difficult physically for him and for his wife. Once his lumbago had been so bad that Paula sent a radio message for an ambulance. By the time it arrived he was feeling better, so it went back empty. But his back and Paula's arthritis caused them frequent pain, making it hard for them to carry out their work assignments, yet neither wanted to be regarded as a weakling.

At Sde Boker he had not found as much time to read as he had anticipated. Somehow in Tel Aviv and Jerusalem, even with all his official work, he had been able to give more time to his books.

Besides, he had already accomplished much of what he had set out to do. He had focused attention on the Negev, had had a chance to do a great deal of self-appraising, and had had more than a year's rest from government routine.

But he did not really move away from Sde Boker. He arranged with the committee to keep the mustard-colored house with the water heater on the roof. He left many of his books there, and he and Paula promised that they would return often.

As a token of the value he placed on the fourteen months he gave the kibbutz a present of two camels, for herding sheep.

In one of his first speeches after his return he admitted that during his time on the desert he had not "discovered any new truths," but he said he now saw many things in a clearer light.

"Let me tell you briefly what I saw:

"Too much concentration and crowding in the cities; not enough population in border areas.

"Too much chasing after comforts and wealth; not enough productivity and pioneer initiative.

"Too many splits and quarrels; not enough joint effort and common responsibility.

"Too much empty talk about brotherhood and Jewish unity; not enough practical aid to new *olim* [immigrants].

"Too many middlemen and servants; not enough productive workers.

"Too much demanding from the government; not enough demanding from oneself.

"Too much asking for privileges; not enough fulfillment of obligations."

With the state almost seven years old, he gave his people a new goal.

"With time we will acquire the habits of sovereign responsibility. We will learn to work properly. We will raise our standard of living through productivity and efficiency, and not be dependent on outside help. We will provide for the younger generation a proper free education, not only in elementary schools, but in high schools and vocational schools as well.

"We will develop centers of science and research, and attract the finest Jewish scientists in the world to us.

"We will bring water to the desert. We will exploit every drop of water from the skies and from the ground. We will make the wasteland fruitful and turn it into a Garden of Eden. We will raze the slums and assure every citizen of a reasonable level of education, income, housing, and economic security throughout his life.

"We will build here an example to the world, and we will be truly a chosen people, without classes, without exploitation or discrimination, fulfilling the dreams of our prophets of old . . ."

Among Ben-Gurion's many visitors from abroad during the summer was Mrs. Franklin Delano Roosevelt, whom he entertained at 17 Keren Kayemet Boulevard. They talked earnestly of world affairs and Middle Eastern problems. They seemed to be equally impressed with each other. Mrs. Roosevelt later in her writings and addresses referred to him as "a wonderful man, whom I greatly admire," and Ben-Gurion spoke enthusiastically of her.

During their conversation he told her about Sde Boker, and said his fourteen months there had been one of the happiest periods of his life.

"My husband thought that the bare rocks in parts of Israel did not serve as a great encouragement to agriculture," Mrs. Roosevelt remarked.

Ben-Gurion smiled and replied:

"It is true that the Lord did not put soil on all the rocks, but that was only because He wanted us to have the satisfaction of putting it there ourselves."

For Mrs. Roosevelt the remark symbolized this dedicated man.

During the summer Ben-Gurion, Paula, and Argov went by automobile to Tiberias for a short holiday. As they passed the base of Mount Tabor, the Defense Minister said:

"Nehemiah, while we're here this time, I want you to get me a horse so I can ride to the top and see the monastery up there."

Paula raised immediate objections.

There was a perfectly good automobile road. Besides, he was too old for horseback riding.

"Nonsense, Paula," her husband replied. "Forty years ago I went on horseback all the way from Mount Tabor to Jerusalem, and you know how far that is!"

"Yes," Paula replied quickly, "that was forty years ago, and you were just a youngster of twenty-eight. Now you are sixty-eight, don't forget!"

Her husband ignored her and asked Argov to make the arrangements.

"Don't you dare!" Paula warned him.

Argov decided to say nothing for a few days in the hope that his chief would forget it. But two days later Ben-Gurion demanded:

"What have you done about the horse?"

There was now no way to avoid the issue, but Argov decided at least to see that Ben-Gurion had the tamest horse in all Israel.

On the appointed day, husband, wife, and military aide drove to the foot of the mountain. There by pre-arrangement a police unit met him.

Paula was still arguing against the adventure.

One of the police officers led forward a horse. The Defense Minister looked at it and said:

"Not that one! I'm not riding any old Rosinante."

After inspecting the other horses he picked the one that seemed the most aggressive.

"That's the one for me!"

The party mounted and were soon on their way up the mountain.

"But we fooled the Old Man," Argov explained later. "I had anticipated his taste for gallantry, and so, with the co-operation of the police, I played a trick on him. The horse he finally picked was the one we had chosen for him. It was the tamest of the lot. An attendant, without Ben-Gurion being able to see, had provoked it into restlessness, hoping that that would impress the Old Man, which it did."

In July candidates for nineteen parties began to campaign for seats in the third Knesset. Ben-Gurion made many speeches. The opposition used the mounting cost of living as a major campaign issue. Three bombs were thrown at General Zionist buildings.

The result of the balloting was a shock to many. Mapai dropped from forty-five to forty seats, the conservative General Zionists from twenty to thirteen. Beigin's Herut party nearly doubled its parliamentary strength, becoming second only to Mapai, with fifteen seats. The Communists tripled their representation to six. Nine parties won seats.

President Ben-Zvi asked his old friend to form a government, but Ben-Gurion indicated that he was not going to hurry about it. Meanwhile Prime Minister Sharett's Cabinet would continue in office.

In the autumn the Defense Minister was put to bed with a strange malady. He had disturbing noises in one ear and acute vertigo. False reports were circulated that he had had a slight stroke. Actually it was a mild attack of Ménière's disease, an ailment of the inner ear, the cause of which is uncertain and for which medical science knows no definite cure.

For days he lay in bed in a Jerusalem hotel, often with walls and ceilings whirling.

Late in September the world suddenly learned of the Czechoslovak-Egyptian arms transaction. Ambassador Eban sent a long cable to Jerusalem about the "enormity of the danger" to Israel's existence. Emergency cabinet meetings were held.

So security once again became Israel's chief concern, and the Minister of Defense the most important member of the Cabinet. His job was to get weapons.

"We tried in America, in Britain, France, and Italy, and our efforts were almost fruitless. Yet we did not despair, nor did we take up arms, although many people believed that time was working against us."

On a chilly Wednesday in November, Ben-Gurion made his first speech to the Knesset as the new Prime Minister. He was still weak from his illness and tired from his new labors.

To get a majority he had given two ministerial posts to the left-wing Mapam, and two to Achdut Avoda, a group that had split from Mapam.

He made a bold speech:

"It is my duty to tell all the powers that rule the world—all of them without exception—with all the modesty becoming the emissary of a small nation, but with all moral force, that the people of Israel will not be led like cattle to the slaughter."

"I am prepared to meet with the Prime Minister of Egypt and with every other Arab ruler as soon as possible in order to achieve a mutual settlement without prior conditions."

That night a thousand Israel soldiers, on Ben-Gurion's orders, went off by truck on a grave military venture.

Forty miles southwest of Beersheba, on the Negev-Sinai frontier, there was a demilitarized zone set up by the U. N. Armistice Commission, near El 'Auja. For weeks the U.N. commissioner had been ordering Egypt, without success, to cease military activities within the zone.

That night the Israel soldiers, their faces blackened because of the bright moonlight, made an attack on Egyptian trenches and gun emplacements inside the zone. After several hours of fighting they dislodged the Egyptians and retired, with five of their own men dead and a few wounded, and with nearly fifty prisoners.

They also brought out with them, as proof of what their neighbors had been doing in the "demilitarized zone," a heavy loot of Egyptian mortars, six-pounders, anti-aircraft guns, and machine guns that had been bought from Sweden, Spain, and Belgium.

The year ended with another military action in the opposite corner of the country.

Lake Tiberias had been given entirely to Israel under the armistice agreement, but for years the Syrians had been firing on Israel fishermen who ventured out onto the lake. Many had been killed. The raid of December 11-12 was in retaliation. The Israel force came back with twenty-nine Syrian prisoners, two pieces of Syrian artillery, and six of their own dead. They left behind fifty-five dead Syrians.

The raid had been the idea and complete responsibility of Ben-Gurion. He was not only Prime Minister and Defense Minister, but was directing foreign affairs as well, for Sharett was on a trip abroad.

Nothing Israel had done during her seven and a half years of existence caused such an international furor. There were resolutions in the U.N., threats of retaliation, a demand for sanctions, and even a suggestion that the Jewish state should be expelled from the United Nations.

Sharett, always conscious of world opinion, came back disturbed.

Ben-Gurion faced his critics, at home and abroad, without flinching.

If no one was going to guarantee Israel's frontiers, if there was no legal way of punishing those who killed innocent Israel fishermen, then the state must be permitted to take such actions as this one and the raid near El 'Auja, otherwise her neighbors before long would be emboldened to march in from all sides again, as they had done in 1948.

In a world that still seemed to respect force more than reason, no one must expect Israel to be the first to adopt a policy of pacifism; her back was too close to the sea.

CHAPTER TWENTY-FIVE

EARLY in 1956 it was apparent to most of the world that a great crisis was evolving in the Middle East. At first it was not clear, probably not even to Ben-Gurion himself, what form it would take. But any sensitive person could *feel* the tension, the nervousness, the speeded-up quality of life.

The basis of the trouble was the unceasing flow of weapons to Egypt from Communist countries. They flew past Israel on their way to Cairo. They sailed past Israel on their way to Alexandria.

Egypt had already received from England great Centurion tanks, Archers (the latest in tank destroyers), Vampire and Meteor jet planes, heavy bombers, destroyers, and even a plant for the production of fighter planes.

She had received from the United States two frigates, six hundred military vehicles, and much other matériel. Italy had sent thirty jets.

Other Arab countries had received almost as much.

But Czechoslovakia was sending Stalin heavy tanks by the dozens, destroyers, mine sweepers, submarines, hundreds of troop carriers, self-propelled guns, jet bombers, tank destroyers, transport planes, anti-tank guns, five-ton trucks, scout cars, radar equipment, the latest in automatic mines—everything but atom bombs.

Israel still had found no one to sell her anything, not even discarded war matériel.

Describing the problems of this period, Ben-Gurion said:

"Arms are not the type of merchandise you can go into a shop, pick out whatever you want and take it home with you, if only you have the money or credit. We knocked at many doors and found them closed. The British Government, which sold the Egyptian dictator heavy tanks knowing they were intended to strike at Israel, obstinately refused to sell them to us. . . . The United States, to whom we owe thanks for much political and financial assistance from the day the state was founded . . . encouraged their allies to supply us with defensive arms. But we cannot be content with this encouragement alone."

Violent clashes on the frontiers were growing in number. All the Arab neighbors sent Fedayeen into Israel at night to penetrate as deeply as they could before using their bombs, grenades, and rifles indiscriminately on Jewish men, women, and children.

Eric Johnston, U.S. negotiator, had worked out a plan for the division of Jordan's water, which Washington was urging both sides to accept, but the former Mufti of Jerusalem said:

"If the Johnston Plan gave 99 per cent of the Jordan water to the Arabs and helped Israel by only as much as one gallon, I would still say no."

In January, Ben-Gurion, who had been harshly criticized in some quarters for the retaliatory Syrian raid, was now being heckled for not striking out in a full-scale preventive war. He defended his policies by saying:

"We believe the maintenance of peace is preferable even to victory in war. War is legitimate only in absolute self-defense. It is not legitimate if one's aim is the securing of peace or the destruction of an evil regime."

At that moment such a policy, commendable as it was on moral grounds, was not popular in Israel. The leader of the General Zionists was one of many who flatly demanded that a war be initiated before it was too late.

In February, Edward R. Murrow and a large television crew met Ben-Gurion at Sde Boker to record an interview that would become part of the Israel half of a *See It Now* program to be broadcast by CBS in March. Howard K. Smith was in Cairo filming the other half.

When Michael Arnon, director of the Government Press Office (now Israel counselor in Washington) told the Prime Minister the subjects that Murrow proposed to discuss, Ben-Gurion said:

"These are all elemental questions that other people can answer as well as I. Why don't you answer them yourself? That's what you get paid for."

But finally he agreed.

The two men sat side by side on the veranda during the interview. At first the Prime Minister was a little formal, but the

longer the conversation continued the more animated he became,
until at the end he was pounding the arm of his chair with the
palm of his hand to emphasize his words, causing great distress
to the sound engineers.

Although he talked extemporaneously for forty-seven minutes
in a language not his own, and often used complicated gram-
matical construction, he made only a few slight errors, such as
calling statesmen *statesmens.*

Once he used an Arabic expression and then went back and
translated it for the audience. When he used *kibbutzim* he explained how Hebrew plurals are formed.

Murrow began one question:

"You came here in 1909——"

"No, 1906," the Prime Minister interjected.

It was a warm, friendly interview. Once the Prime Minister
glanced in Paula's direction and said into the microphone:

"This is the first time in these countries that a woman becomes
an equal partner with man, to share his liabilities, his hardships,
and the joy which is derived from this creative work."

"Was there ever a time in all these years when you were
tempted to give up?" Murrow asked.

Ben-Gurion repeated the question in surprise, as if he had not
heard it correctly. Then he laughed and said:

"Oh no. Oh no. Never. Never."

Then he laughed again.

Of Zionism he said:

"Real Zionism means creating a home and a life for yourself.
By your own creative physical and intellectual effort. Not to buy
something. Not to get what is already made. But to make it yourself."

Each time he spoke of the desert he pronounced the word
softly, almost reverently.

He told of a gifted young contemporary Israel writer, a sabra.
When he came back from his first trip to Europe, Ben-Gurion
asked him what his strongest impression was, and the young man
replied:

"In Europe everything has already been done. It's finished,
with little chance for pioneering. Agriculture is finished. Industry

is finished. Language is finished. Literature is finished. Civiliza-
ton is finished. How can people live there?"

Ben-Gurion added:

"Here we are making everything from the beginning. Here you
have to start making even the earth, not only cultivating it but
making it, because it was made by the Almighty as a desert, but
we can turn it into cultivated land."

"At heart you are a frontiersman, aren't you?" Murrow asked.

Ben-Gurion hesitated.

"Well—it is—perhaps—I would say a desert man."

One of his aides had made a bet that the Old Man would find
a way to work Buddha in. Toward the end of the interview, in
answer to a question about the relationship between Israel and
Asia, he said Asia had produced great moral teachers.

"There was Buddha. It will be twenty-five hundred years since
he was born. He left his impress on hundreds of millions of people. For instance, one of them which I met, the Prime Minister
of Burma, U Nu. I think he is one of the great moral figures of
our time. This is the result of Buddhist teachings."

Murrow's last point was:

"You have said before that you are quite prepared to sit down
and talk with Arab leaders at any time."

"Yes, any time."

Then the Prime Minister went on, striking the arm of the chair
to emphasize particular words.

"All the Arab countries need is not *war*, not *tanks*, but *education, sanitation, development*. We can help them with that. And
they need peace in order to develop their countries, to *educate
their people*, to do away with *diseases* . . .

"When they will have real representatives, for whom the welfare of the people will be the main concern, they will realize the
best thing is to *live in peace* . . . to *co-operate with Israel* . . .
Until then you must be prepared to defend yourself when you
are attacked."

Murrow said "Thank you" and the engineers were about to
flick off the buttons, but Ben-Gurion wanted to say "Thank you,"
too.

"It is a very nice thing that you came over here. Of course it
is a pity you did not come thirty-three hundred years ago, when

Moses not far from here stood on Mount Sinai and received the Ten Commandments from the Almighty. What a television that would have been for humanity!"

After they had packed up their equipment, Murrow went to say good-by to the Prime Minister, who had returned to his quarters after the interview. He knocked twice on the door, and when he received no answer he pushed it open.

"I wanted to call the cameraman right away," he told Pearlman later, "but then I knew no viewers in America would ever believe that we hadn't staged it."

What he had seen was the Prime Minister of Israel washing cups and saucers at the sink.

March was a busy month.

In the Knesset, after Ben-Gurion one day had defended his policy of not provoking a war with Egypt, Beigin introduced a no-confidence motion and delivered a withering attack on the Prime Minister.

"I agree with the speaker about one thing," Ben-Gurion retorted. "Our fighters will fight. But he himself did not fight in the last war and he will not fight in the next."

As the Herut members jeered, Beigin jumped to his feet.

"You were a traitor to Israel. Traitor! Traitor!"

Benjamin Arditi, another Herut member, over the din that now filled the chamber, shouted at the Prime Minister:

"Provocateur!"

Demands were made that the Deputy Speaker expel the offending members. He found a technical loophole.

"I did not hear the remarks, and therefore cannot take action, and of course I cannot ask that the remarks be repeated for my benefit."

The Murrow show was televised in March, and in the next few days CBS received several thousand letters. A majority of those who wrote in had been more impressed by the man in the open-necked khaki shirt sitting on a veranda in the desert than by the sartorially splendid Egyptian dictator. A woman in Indiana wrote:

"That dear white-haired man looked like a character out of the pages of the New Testament. I longed to put my hand out to touch his wind-blown hair."

In March each member of the Israel armed forces gave one day of work to help fortify outlying settlements. To dramatize the day Ben-Gurion drove from Jerusalem to Mivtahim near the Gaza frontier and, with a cold morning wind from the desert blowing uncomfortably, he helped string barbed wire. When Nehemiah Argov handed him a pair of gloves, he threw them to the ground.

"A man is given hands to work with," he said.

A few days later on the lawn outside the Ministry of Defense he met forty members of the U. S. Society of Editors and Commentators who had just come from a tour of Arab countries. He greeted them by saying:

"I was a pressman once myself."

They had a barrage of questions ready for him. One of the first was about a map the Arabs had described to them, showing the size Israel eventually would be; proof of Israel's desire to expand from the Euphrates to the Nile. It hung in the Knesset and many other public buildings.

Ben-Gurion bent his head back and laughed.

"Sheer nonsense. You are free to look anywhere in Israel. I will be asking my friends to lead you to any place you like and have a look yourselves and see that the maps are not there. I do not want you to rely on my word. You are welcome to go anywhere. These people are ignorant. They do not know that when we were called out of bondage in Egypt we were under injunction never to return to Egypt, and the Nile is in Egypt. We prefer to stay here. It is sheer nonsense."

Then his eyes twinkled as he added:

"Of course, there are certàin promises in the Bible, but these were made by the Almighty, and if you can visit Him you can ask Him yourself."

Then he laughed and told them a story.

"I met once a man who came from America. President Roosevelt sent him as an emissary. He was a general. On one occasion when we had finished our business we talked about history. I said his history went back only three hundred years but ours went back three thousand years. He said:

" 'What? I'm an Irishman. My history goes back eight thousand years!' "

It was also in March that the Ben-Gurions gave their first really elaborate reception, attended by the diplomatic corps, the Cabinet, members of the Knesset, and many other notables. It was in honor of Renana, who had just been married to a young engineer.

A few days later Paula received a degree of Doctor of Philosophy from Hebrew University. It belonged to Renana, but she was on her honeymoon and asked her mother to accept it for her.

In April a young man presented himself at the Israel Consulate in London, introduced himself as Ibrahim Izzat, a correspondent for the Egyptian weekly paper *Rose el Youssef*, and politely asked for a visa to visit Israel.

This had never happened before. After recovering a little from the shock the consular official asked the purpose of the visit. With stark simplicity the Egyptian replied:

"To gather information for a series of newspaper articles."

London communicated with Jerusalem, and finally Mr. Izzat was offered a visa on one condition:

For his own safety he must pose as a South American merchant.

He would be given freedom to go anywhere, interview anybody, in the hope that he would write exactly what he saw and heard.

The young journalist accepted the condition and traveled all over Israel. Interviews were arranged for him with most of the Cabinet, except the Prime Minister. When he left he was given a message from Ben-Gurion:

"When you go back to Egypt and if you should see Abdel Nasser, tell him I am ready to meet him at any time, at any place he chooses, to discuss any problem or question he wishes: refugees, border questions, political matters, economic problems, or military affairs, without mediation and without announcing anything publicly about such a meeting or its results. Tell him I am ready to meet him even in Cairo."

This was a bold offer, but no reply was ever forthcoming.

In his first article Izzat said he had "outwitted the stupid Israelis" by posing as a South American businessman and that he had tricked them into letting him interview not only the rest of the Cabinet but Ben-Gurion as well. Apart from this harmless braggadocio, his first article was objective, although the subsequent ones gave evidence of outside pressure.

In June, Ben-Gurion completed and sent to the printer his contribution to the 1956 Yearbook, which would not be published for months. In the light of the developments that would be taking place before the end of the year, the title was prophetic: "Southward." It was headed by a quotation from Ezekiel:

Son of man, set thy face toward the South and drop thy word toward the South.

It was written at a time when the annihilation of Israel seemed to many people an imminent possibility. There was trouble on all the frontiers. Israel had not a single friend in the world who would even sell her the arms she needed. Many of the hundreds of thousands of immigrants who had poured in were still in tents. A quarter of the cotton crop had been lost. Internal political enemies were creating constant dissension.

It was written by a man who would be seventy years old in a few months and who was not well. He had no leisure, for he was Prime Minister, Minister of Defense, and head of eighty-four departments, and he had offices in two cities more than an hour's drive apart.

Yet it was a document that informed, instructed, educated, preached, and prophesied.

He wrote of the prophets who had not been reconciled to the desolation of the Negev; of Isaiah, who predicted that the desert would someday "rejoice, and bloom as the rose"; of Solomon, Jehoshaphat, and Uzziah, three kings of the house of David, who attempted to make Elath into a magnificent Jewish port.

"King Uzziah was a great commander, successful in conquering and in settling the desert and making it flourish. In his days the Jewish army increased its strength; settlement and irrigation were fostered; a port was built at Elath and, simultaneous with political and economic progress, there was a remarkable development in spiritual and moral values."

If David Ben-Gurion could guide his small nation successfully through the crisis of 1956, all these same words could someday be written as his own epitaph.

In "Southward" he tried to excite his people with stories of the hidden wealth in the Negev. He even told them how many billions of tons of each chemical were estimated to be there for the taking; of how uranium required for atomic research was already being processed from phosphates by a cheap method discovered by Israel scientists.

But he warned:

"If the state does not put an end to the desert, the desert is liable to put an end to the state."

"Southward" was a long message; almost a book; a book in the scriptures of the modern Jewish state.

In June two men who had worked together politically for decades reached the end of their collaboration.

Moshe Sharett, slender, wiry, and soft-spoken, is the antithesis of Ben-Gurion in many ways. He has had much more formal education and is a naturally brilliant linguist.

He is erudite and urbane, friendly and warm. He likes people and most people like him. He would sit on the floor of a New York apartment until dawn exchanging stories or engaging in fast repartee. He would remember the name of a man's wife and ask about the health of his children.

During the five months he was imprisoned by the British at Latrun he gave his fellow prisoners lessons in Arabic, economics, and Hebrew grammar.

A favorite story in government circles years ago was about the foreign diplomat who after a few months in Israel boasted that he knew how to say "Your Excellency" in Hebrew: "*Shma, Moshe.*"

"Shma, Moshe," is Hebrew for "Listen, Moshe."

When the diplomat was asked how he had picked up the idea that these words meant "Your Excellency," he said:

"I notice that every time any of his own people talk to Foreign Minister Sharett they always begin by saying, 'Shma, Moshe.'"

He is by nature a diplomat, with a quick, penetrating mind, is nimble in debate, and follows a set of principles from which he never budges. He can occasionally be deeply human and moving, at other times quite cautious and legalistic. Even the most minute details are important to him. He is never a pragmatist.

His deprecators call him "Count-the-Costs-Sharett" and say that he is pedantic.

In cabinet meetings the split was generally between those who sided with Sharett's point of view and those who supported Ben-Gurion.

The Prime Minister's friends said that he recognized facts and faced them; that Sharett tried to argue them away. Sharett's friends said Ben-Gurion often in his impetuosity disregarded elemental facts.

Ben-Gurion is inclined to be impulsive and audacious, and applies to every action, every plan, every proposal the test of whether it will further the goal. Sharett is deliberate in judgment, cautious in action, and deeply concerned about reactions.

Sharett always served as a brake on Ben-Gurion, who was probably aware of his need for such a brake, so he insisted that Sharett be in every Cabinet he formed.

As Foreign Minister the younger man always considered the possible consequences of a line of action before approving any of Ben-Gurion's plans. Often he would have more than half the Cabinet with him, so Ben-Gurion, a firm believer in majority rule, would have to abandon the plan.

The relationship became more strained after the Syrian retaliation, which Ben-Gurion ordered while Sharett was in Washington, where he had gone expressly to obtain Dulles' answer to a request for jet planes to match the Soviet MIGs Egypt had just received.

The Foreign Minister upon his return did not hesitate to point out how disastrous the consequences in Washington had been, and how unfavorable the world reaction.

In announcing the divorce of convenience Ben-Gurion told the Knesset that he had insisted on having Sharett in the Cabinet not in spite of their differences, but because of them. Lately, however, with the security of the state threatened, and the matter of foreign policy more important than ever before, he had decided that complete harmony was necessary between the Defense Minister and the Foreign Minister.

In his statement Sharett said that after the last elections he had asked Ben-Gurion not to include him in the new Cabinet, having well-founded reasons for doubting whether they could co-operate successfully any longer, but Ben-Gurion had rejected the idea. Sharett added:

"In recent weeks it has been clear to me that my resignation was unavoidable. This situation did not arise in connection with any pending political issue or current event or incident. Nevertheless, in a frank conversation which I had with the Prime Minister on the evening of last Sunday, I reached the absolute conviction that it was impossible to remain in the government of which he is the head."

After his resignation Sharett became more active in Mapai affairs, directing its educational work.

At a Mapai dinner Ben-Gurion, in the course of paying a tribute to his former Foreign Minister, said:

"Sharett and I have gone through forty-three years of history together."

Sharett smiled.

"Forty-four and a half, to be exact."

After the divorce Sharett seemed younger, fresher, and less harassed. He has never been remiss in acknowledging the outstanding merit of Ben-Gurion in forging Israel's destiny.

An official of Mapai, speaking for at least a segment of the party membership, said:

"Our attitude toward B.G. is compounded of faith and fear; faith in his uncanny powers; fear of him and fear to lose him. Moshe we love and trust. We don't feel safe without him. We have always had confidence in his judgment and sense of fairness and decency."

Late in June another "Israel miracle" occurred. Ben-Gurion, telling about it, said:

"A great thing has happened, one of the greatest that has happened since the war of independence. In an out-of-the-ordinary way we succeeded at last in acquiring the bare minimum that we needed for our defense."

It was almost a year before the public was told any more. The arms came from France. The arrangements were made with a minimum of diplomatic formality. Orders for millions of dollars' worth of equipment were handled by a small group of men on each side who decided to trust each other.

In four months forty thousand tons of military equipment reached Israel without accident. Although the eyes of the world were on the Middle East, the secret was kept. The shipments arrived and were unloaded and distributed without the enemy ever knowing.

Meanwhile, under Ben-Gurion's direction, Israel's own arms industry had increased its output by 50 per cent and was turning out mines, anti-tank grenades, and bazookas, as well as ammunition and spare parts.

In July an agricultural crisis occurred. Cotton had become a vital part of Israel's economy. But the boll weevil seemed to be immune to all insecticides and the entire eight-million-dollar crop was in danger of being destroyed.

Ben-Gurion sent a cable to Sam Hamburg. It reached California one morning. That afternoon Hamburg was in a plane heading for Israel. It was his sixteenth trip to the Holy Land. He found two million dollars' worth of the crop hopelessly eaten up, but he directed a salvage operation that saved the rest.

In July, Nasser seized the canal and nationalized it.

In August, Ben-Gurion told a congress of young people from eighteen countries that Jews abroad had the choice of a luxurious existence where they were or a life in Israel full of dangers and privations, but a life of Jewish dignity and freedom.

"This is something you can't buy at Macy's," he added.

By mid-October the tension had almost reached the cracking point. Nasser said publicly that he was "fighting not only against Israel, but also against international Jewry and Jewish capital." It reminded some people of the speeches of a now deceased German.

On October 15, Ben-Gurion quietly stood up in the Knesset and began to talk. His speech ran to 15,200 words, but no one went to sleep. He talked bluntly about war, not as a Minister of Defense but as a philosopher and humanitarian. To the surprise of those who knew how little he normally cared for poetry, he read a long contemporary poem. One line said:

This is the night that was or yet will be.

Finally he faced the situation of the moment.

"The enormous arms superiority at their disposal [the Arab leaders'] may intoxicate them and upset their mental balance, since they never cease to proclaim to their masses that there is war between them and Israel which can end only with our destruction."

He listed what had been happening on the frontiers: a man killed here, a two-story house blown up at Azuz, a police vehicle attacked the same day somewhere else, a tractor driver ambushed, two civilians murdered, an Israel truck blown up by a mine, a civilian vehicle fired on and two passengers killed, booby traps planted in a field near Jerusalem, a grenade thrown into a children's home, four civilians murdered in another part of the country, six Israel soldiers killed, an archaeological gathering fired upon by Arab Legion soldiers, Yemenite women picking olives killed at their work.

Just yesterday a group of Feyadeen sent into Israel by Egyptian commanders were captured near Sde Boker, his own desert home.

With brilliance and skill he was paving the way for what he knew would soon happen, because it would be done on his order. Its success would depend on secrecy. Few other men in his position would have spoken at all. But Ben-Gurion was a master at what he was doing this afternoon. He was talking for publication. Foreign reporters were present. In an hour a summary of his address would be in New York and London, and a half hour after that in Cairo, Damascus, Baghdad, and Amman. Yet he was a believer in democracy, even in emergencies, so he was trying to take the Knesset members into his confidence and still give no secrets away.

"According to the U.N. charter, every member of the United Nations has the right to self-defense . . ."

"I cannot imagine that there is a single country in the world which would leave its people defenseless against murderers organized by neighboring governments . . .

"We have proposed a peace meeting with the Arab rulers, but our voice has been the voice of one that crieth in the wilderness."

Then he deviated from today and tomorrow.

"Some countries easily acquire friends because they are great and powerful, control rich and extensive territories, and have populations of scores or even hundreds of millions.

"Some countries acquire friends as a result of a common religion or language, like some of the Arab countries, the countries of Latin America, or the countries of Scandinavia.

"Some countries enter into alliances because they have a common enemy or object of fear.

"Israel does not possess great power, tremendous wealth, or broad territories; she has no common language, religion, or race with any other state; and the peoples who are closest to us from the point of view of language and race are the Arab peoples, which, for historical and I believe temporary reasons, are at present our bitterest enemies."

This was the genius of the man; that on this afternoon just fourteen days before Israel would take one of the boldest, most hazardous steps any small group of people had ever taken, their leader could stand talking by the hour, quietly and calmly, about such subjects as how a people acquire friends.

He concluded:

"We may be facing fateful decisions and events. Let us stand ready and united, and the Rock of Israel will not fail us."

CHAPTER TWENTY-SIX

THOUSANDS of people all over Israel disappeared on Thursday, October 25, 1956.

A bank manager's secretary went out for lunch and failed to return.

An Ambassador complained that his chauffeur had apparently quit without giving notice.

Shops apologized for their poor service, saying:

"We're sorry, but we've lost some of our help."

Twenty-four hours earlier a tripartite military alliance had been signed by Egypt, Jordan, and Syria, placing the armies of the three countries under Nasser's command.

This created a crisis that forced Ben-Gurion to make the eleventh grave decision of his life. In his own words the alternatives were:

"Either to be destroyed and serve as a subject for funeral

orations and expressions of grief on the part of our friends and sympathizers" or to take military action.

Gradually during the next five days he took at first two or three people, then more, then a few more into his confidence, but it remained one of the best-kept military secrets in history, which was one reason the plan succeeded so well.

On Thursday, as the mobilization of the Israel Army was taking place by what is technically called "the silent method"—word-of-mouth orders from officers to N.C.O.s and finally to the troops themselves—Ambassador Abba Eban was addressing the United Nations in New York.

"Israel will start no war. It will initiate no violence."

Ambassador Eban had not yet been told of Ben-Gurion's decision.

Later in his speech he said:

"War is the last resort in defense. But sometimes claims of self-defense cannot be set aside."

It was not until Friday that officers of the Southern Command, who would be in charge of what was about to happen, were told the plan. They had just seventy-two hours to make all preparations.

On Saturday the United Nations gave a cocktail party in Tel Aviv at which the mobilization was the chief topic of talk. Most of the diplomats present seemed to agree that the situation in Jordan was the cause.

By this time the men who had been called up had assembled at their mobilization centers and were on their way to the Negev.

On Saturday, Chief of Staff Dayan, who had become one of Ben-Gurion's favorites, approved the General Staff's final plans for the campaign, then went home and spent the evening as an amateur archaeologist piecing together bits of a Byzantine vase he had recently dug up.

On Saturday the Prime Minister began to feel ill. His body was hot and he had a severe headache, but he remained at his desk all day. In the evening he summoned the Mapai members of the Cabinet to his home and told them briefly that he was planning a large-scale military operation with three objectives:

"1. To destroy Egyptian aggression bases in Sinai.

"2. To expel the Egyptian invader from the Gaza strip.

"3. To safeguard freedom of navigation for Israel and international shipping in the Straits of Elath."

He also told them that the operation would be based on three considerations: surprise, speed, and keeping casualties at a minimum.

His own party's ministers gave him their approval. He was now over the first hurdle.

He went to sleep that night satisfied that everything was going according to plan.

But he felt as if he were burning up with fever.

He left his bed Sunday morning with some effort, but he continued to take personal charge of the vast operation he had begun to put into motion. He even insisted that he would handle all the public relations problems himself.

Israel diplomats abroad were not to be given any advance notice, even though this might put some of them in embarrassing positions.

On Sunday at a full cabinet meeting the non-Mapai members heard the news for the first time. Hurdle number two. Still no opposition. A public announcement of the mobilization was authorized. It stated that a number of reservists had been called up because of recent events in neighboring Arab states. It was designed as a smoke screen, so it stressed the situation in Jordan.

Throughout the cabinet meeting Ben-Gurion took periodic doses of medicine, but it did not seem to be doing him any good. The color of his face indicated that the fever had not abated. He complained of severe pains in his head and stiffness of the body. He reported the Cabinet's decision to President Ben-Zvi and then got into an automobile with Paula and Argov to drive over the twisting road to Tel Aviv.

When they arrived, Paula urged him to go to bed immediately, but his day was far from over. First he had to receive a delegation from each of the parties represented in the Knesset, except the Communists, who were excluded at his own insistence. He gave each group the complete explanation he already had made to the General Staff, the Cabinet, and the President. Fortunately there was no disapproval. He had now cleared hurdle number three.

Between the arrivals of the various delegations four Tel Aviv

physicians called. They diagnosed his trouble as a virus infection.
His temperature was 103.5. They ordered him to bed at once.
Paula said there was no need for a nurse; she would put her New
York training to use.

Ben-Gurion spent the afternoon propped up in bed giving final
instructions to the military and civilian officials who paraded up
the stairs, through the library, and into the bedroom.

At 8 P.M., American Ambassador Edward Lawson arrived with
a cable from President Eisenhower addressed to Ben-Gurion asking that Israel exercise restraint in whatever she was planning
to do.

Ben-Gurion sent at once for Yaakov Herzog, son of Israel's
Chief Rabbi, a brilliant scholar and an Orthodox rabbi himself,
who at one time had been liaison officer between the government
and the Christian communities in Israel. Now he headed the
American desk in the Foreign Office. During the next few weeks
he was to become one of the Prime Minister's most intimate
advisers, and later would be named Minister to Washington.

"We must answer this quickly," Herzog was told. "The reply
must contain no commitments."

As the young rabbi went off to work on the text, one of the
doctors arrived and discovered that the patient's temperature
had gone up nearly two more degrees.

On Monday at 5 A.M. the counselor of the American Embassy
appeared at the Ministry of Defense in Hakirya looking for someone to accept a letter from President Eisenhower. A watchman
finally took it. The envelope read:

> *Personal to the Prime Minister*
> *of Israel, Mr. David Ben-Gurion*

Herzog arrived at 7 A.M., took the letter, and drove at once to
17 Keren Kayemet Boulevard.

Ben-Gurion was already awake. He had not had a good night.
His temperature was still high. He read the second Eisenhower
communication, which again expressed American concern and
urged "no forcible action which would endanger peace," and
suggested the reply.

After Herzog had left, he said to his wife:

"You look pale. Are you ill, too?"

Paula had been sick for days, but was trying not to let him know. She shook her head and left the room.

Navon arrived with a sheaf of cables. The Prime Minister shuffled quickly through them. Apparently it was still a secret. Everyone was speculating about the mobilization, but nothing more.

At eleven-thirty Herzog returned with the draft of his reply to the President of the United States. Ben-Gurion read it carefully, made a few revisions, and then approved it.

During the rest of the day the invalid half sat up in bed. His face was bright red with fever. He dictated a "briefing" to be cabled to Israel embassies after the event had taken place.

But he was too exhausted to go on, and he lay back and fell asleep. An urgent telephone call from the Foreign Office woke him up a short time later.

All day the street in front of No. 17 was lined with parked cars. Navon stood downstairs screening those who wanted to see the Prime Minister. One of those he admitted was the French Ambassador. Ben-Gurion was exceedingly polite to him but told him nothing. (Despite stories that were later circulated about "collusion," the French, although they had made the enterprise possible with forty thousand tons of war matériel, were not advised in advance.)

During the afternoon the second-floor library and the bedroom began to fill up with military men, political advisers, aides, cabinet members.

One of them described Ben-Gurion's condition as "sang-froid with high temperature."

Despite the medicine the doctors had given him, the fever had not gone down. His face was puffy and his eyes seemed partly closed.

About 4 P.M. he looked at his watch and turned to General Dayan.

"What time do they jump?"

"Seventeen-fifteen."

"Why so early?"

"Because if they jump after it's dark many will get injured on the rocks."

At five-fifteen they all glanced at their watches, then looked silently at each other.

The next fifty-five minutes, until messages began to arrive from the front, seemed like hours.

At six-ten Navon brought in the first report. One of the doctors had just taken Ben-Gurion's temperature. It was up another one tenth of a degree centigrade.

The message read:

"Our Dakotas have dropped the men on target and have returned unharmed."

The target was Mitla Pass in Sinai, only twenty-five or thirty miles from the Suez Canal.

"I am worried about what will happen to this battalion," said the Old Man, propped up in bed.

Fifteen minutes later Navon brought in the second report.

"The drop has been successful. No enemy forces are to be seen within a radius of fifty kilometers. No Egyptian aircraft has tried to interfere with our operation."

The Prime Minister gave a sigh of relief and picked up one of the books on his bedside table and began to read. The words on the cover were: *"The Intellect of Pre-Historic Man."*

From then on a constant stream of battle-front messages, field reports, and diplomatic cables streamed in.

At 9 P.M. a call came from Jerusalem that there had been machine-gun fire directed into the Musrara quarter of the Holy City from an Arab Legion post. There were no casualties. After this one outburst it was quiet again on the Jordan side of the line.

That night, because of the possibility of retaliatory air raids on Tel Aviv, Paula insisted that Ben-Gurion be moved downstairs so he could be near their improvised air raid shelter.

Israel's intelligence officers had learned that Egypt's Air Force now included more than a hundred MIG-15s, fifty Ilyushin fighter-bombers capable of carrying two tons each, sixty Vampires, and twenty Meteors. If this force or any large part of it were sent against Tel Aviv, nothing could prevent the virtual obliteration of the city. Yet Ben-Gurion agreed very reluctantly to move downstairs.

On Tuesday, he awoke early, feeling a little better. But the doctors ordered that he remain in bed.

At 9 A.M. he authorized the issuance of the first communiqué. "Israel forces have struck into the heart of Sinai and are more than halfway to Suez."

Now at last cables could be sent to Israel embassies and legations telling them the secret.

There had already been some embarrassing incidents. Ambassador Eban had been in conference at the State Department when news of the Sinai operation reached Washington from Egyptian sources.

Sharett, now on a "peace tour" of the Far East, had been on his way to keep an appointment with Prime Minister Nehru when he learned from newspaper headlines what had happened.

After the first communiqué was issued, it was possible to order a blackout. Israelis spent most of Tuesday putting up blackout curtains and pasting strips of paper over plate glass windows.

This was a mad operation and everyone knew it. Ben-Gurion was aware from intelligence reports that a large percentage of the modern weapons Egypt had been obtaining from Czechoslovakia were in Sinai. If Egypt were half ready she might use this as an excuse to sweep in and overrun Israel. The bases for her jet bombers were only a few minutes' flying time from the most remote corner of Israel. And Cairo now had the power to command Syrian and Jordanian troops as well as her own.

It was a big gamble for a Commander-in-Chief to take. It was no wonder that, despite his illness, the seventy-year-old Prime Minister read the battle-front reports as nervously as a bettor at Monte Carlo watches the ball on the roulette table.

On Tuesday morning Ben-Gurion was handed a report that Egyptian aircraft had attacked his ground forces. This would require a reassessment of plans. He had given orders that Israel's Air Force was not to reconnoiter across the Suez, attack enemy ground troops, fire on enemy aircraft, or bomb enemy cities. This was because of his fear that aerial warfare would lead quickly to total warfare, which might even set off World War III. His plan was to keep it a localized ground action. But now that enemy planes were strafing his troops, he ordered the Israel Air Force to support them.

All day Tuesday, No. 17 was G.H.Q. at the height of a hazardous military operation. Army men of high rank came and went.

Messengers rushed in and out with brief cases full of reports. The Commander-in-Chief spent hours holding conferences with his Chief of Staff, and the commanders of the Air Force, the Navy, the Armored Corps, and the Paratroopers. He received the Foreign Minister at least four times during the day. Cables were flowing in from all the forty countries with which Israel had diplomatic relations.

It was like any other G.H.Q. except that the Commander-in-Chief lay propped up in bed and the books in a mound on the table beside him were not on military strategy but on Greek and Oriental philosophy.

Walking through the three library rooms and then into this inner sanctuary was almost like wandering through the British Museum and finally coming to a small reading room where a white-haired scholar was consulting old manuscripts.

Ben-Gurion gave some of the officers the impression that he wanted them to leave as soon as possible so he could get back to his books. While they were there he dealt with each problem logically, calmly, and rapidly. But as soon as they turned to leave, he would pick up the book he had been reading when they arrived and shuttle back to that other world of his own creation.

On Tuesday evening he received radio news that Britain was sending an ultimatum to both Israel and Egypt to keep their troops from approaching closer than ten miles to the canal. This called for a cabinet meeting. It was almost midnight before a cable came from the London embassy giving the exact terms. Then a reply had to be drafted.

The invalid had very little sleep that night.

The first piece of news he received when he woke up on Wednesday was that an Egyptian warship six to eight miles at sea had attempted to shell Haifa. In ten minutes and eleven seconds she had fired a hundred and sixty shells. All had exploded in the water just a little short of land.

Throughout the morning other reports poured in. She was the *Ibrahim el Awal* and had been in many British actions in World War II, then was loaned to the Chinese Government, and finally was sold to the Egyptians. She was now being chased by an Israel destroyer of the identical type, also obtained from Britain.

Next report: a sea battle was taking place between the two vessels. The Egyptian ship had received several direct hits. Israel planes were overhead. The *Ibrahim el Awal* was on fire.

Now the Egyptian crew had surrendered and the *Ibrahim el Awal* was being towed in to Haifa. An attempt had been made to scuttle her, but the Egyptian sailors had not been able to find keys to fit most of the sea cocks and the valves were so rusty they could not be turned.

Ben-Gurion's mind roamed back over history trying to figure out how many centuries it had been since the last Jewish naval victory.

But bigger news came later that day. Britain and France suddenly turned Ben-Gurion's bold but limited action into a major world event by their attack on Egyptian airfields and on the canal itself.

The destruction of a large part of the enemy air force on the ground ended any worry about the bombing of Israel's cities, but a diplomatic storm broke almost immediately.

Most Israelis, including the Prime Minister, went to bed that night quite happy. The Egyptians' Air Force had been greatly damaged; British and French troops were on the canal, and in Haifa Harbor there was an Egyptian destroyer, a little old, a little damaged now, but a neat prize of war.

On Thursday good news poured in from all fronts. But there was one unhappy note.

Kfar Kasim was an Arab village near the Jordan frontier. When the Sinai campaign began, security precautions were taken in all parts of the country and a 5 P.M. curfew was imposed on Kfar Kasim by the commander of that area.

A crowd of villagers who knew nothing about the emergency regulations because they had been working in distant fields came home after the curfew hour and were fired upon by Israel police officers. There were women and children among the victims. Twenty-five were killed.

Ben-Gurion was indignant. He appointed a civilian committee to make an immediate investigation.

On Thursday a stream of prisoners and captured Egyptian war matériel began to flow back from the front; enough equipment to supply a small army; enough prisoners to create problems.

On Friday, Gaza surrendered, and at 10:15 P.M., Navon received a telephone message:

"The entire Sinai Peninsula is in our hands."

He ran to Ben-Gurion's bedside to tell him. But the Prime Minister was deep in thought. A political upheaval had occurred at the U.N. The vote had been 64 to 5 in favor of a resolution demanding an immediate British-French-Israel withdrawal. Almost the whole world was condemning the Sinai operation. Russia and the United States had voted together for the creation of a Jewish state. Since then they had not voted together on any major issue. Now they were united in their condemnation of Israel.

On Monday, just one week after the paratroopers made their jump into Mitla Pass, a message came from the brigade commander: the island of Tiran had been occupied and, in his opinion, the entire campaign could now be considered concluded.

The results:

Israel's losses: 174 dead, one captured.

Egypt's losses: 1,000 dead; 6,000 prisoners (including 202 officers); one destroyer lost; hundreds of tanks, artillery pieces, and other major items of war equipment left behind for the Israelis.

Every time Ben-Gurion would quote these figures he would add:

"The one captured Israeli did not surrender; he parachuted out of his plane when it was shot down over enemy territory."

It was Ben-Gurion who conceived the idea of taking the captured Egyptian officers on a tour of Haifa and Tel Aviv by motorbus before they were repatriated, so they would have something to talk about after they reached home.

On Monday he received a letter from Premier Bulganin of Russia. Its wording was blunt, its spirit unfriendly. It called the Sinai campaign "armed aggression" and a "senseless adventure." It said Israel was acting as a tool of "foreign imperialistic forces." The Soviet Union was recalling its Ambassador as a warning.

At first Ben-Gurion did not take the note or the possibility of Soviet intervention, directly or through the use of "volunteers," very seriously. He decided it was a propagandic rather than a diplomatic move.

On Tuesday, after nine days in bed, he got up, dressed, and worked for hours on his address to the Knesset.

That day Israel was left as the sole "aggressor" when Britain and France acceded to United Nations pressure and agreed to a cease-fire.

Among the documents Navon brought to Ben-Gurion on Tuesday was a report of the Kfar Kasim investigation. The story was entirely true.

With Israel already being criticized from Boston to Bombay because of the Sinai campaign, there might have been a temptation to suppress the news, but Ben-Gurion did just the opposite. He made certain that it would be published in almost every newspaper in the world by issuing an official statement giving the essential facts, with no attempt at making excuses. This took intellectual integrity and political courage.

"There are no people in the world who hold life more dear than the Jewish people, and this means the life of every human being, without distinction of sex, race, religion, nationality."

Then he made a solemn promise that "nothing like this will ever happen again in Israel."

The officers responsible would be placed on trial, and each family that had suffered casualties would receive compensation up to $2,750 if the head of the family had been killed.

The next day he arose even earlier than usual and drove to Jerusalem. His doctors had suggested that one of them accompany him, that he make his address sitting down, and that he rest for a full hour upon arrival in Jerusalem. He agreed to only the third. He stood at the podium for forty-five minutes. Paula was close by with a thermos of strong coffee in case a stimulant was needed.

In the eyes of most Israelis this was a time for rejoicing. Once more their armed forces had done the "impossible." Jews occupied Sinai. Gaza was theirs. No one could block the Gulf of Elath any more.

But Ben-Gurion gave them solemn warnings to temper their joy.

"It may be that in the near future we shall have to face a difficult political struggle, and perhaps something even graver. We shall not give way to the futile arrogance of the Arab rulers, but on the other hand, we shall not humble ourselves before the powerful forces of the world when justice is not on their side."

He was obviously thinking of the Bulganin note in his pocket, which had not yet been made public.

On Thursday, despite his exhaustion, he started work at 7 A.M. The newspapers and cables from Israel diplomats painted a picture of international hysteria unprecedented since the days of the Korean War. An emergency cabinet meeting was called for 10 A.M. Foreign Minister Golda Meir had been on her way to New York to appear before the United Nations, but she was recalled. Because her plane from Paris was delayed, the meeting was postponed until eleven o'clock.

The cabinet meeting lasted two hours. It approved an uncompromising reply to Bulganin. Ben-Gurion went home. He was relaxed because he had decided to be firm and his ministers had approved.

He was having lunch when a note from President Eisenhower arrived. It had been written the day before, but because of a breakdown in communications between Washington and the American Embassy in Tel Aviv it had just arrived.

It was more like a personal letter than a diplomatic message, yet it was stern and unequivocal. If Israel did not withdraw she would be seriously undermining urgent U.N. efforts to restore peace in the Middle East, and Israel would be condemned as violating the principles as well as the directives of the U.N. Sanctions were threatened.

With the written note had come some verbal "clarifications," which implied that none of the great powers would be able to assist Israel if the Soviet Union intervened with "volunteers."

This changed the entire situation and forced Ben-Gurion to make perhaps the most difficult decision of his life. As soon as he finished reading the Eisenhower letter a second time he knew that he would probably have to give in.

It had been more than ten years since he had met the man who then was Chief of Staff of the American Army during his tour of German refugee camps, but he felt now as if he were in personal conversation with him. He had liked the open honesty of the General then; he felt now that he could trust him.

But it was going to take a special kind of courage to stand up before the Cabinet and ask permission to say "yes" after arguing just a few hours ago for permission to say "no."

Then there was the Army. Its morale had been its greatest strength, but it had never been forced to withdraw before. An army going backward is hard to control. There would be bitterness among officers and men who might not understand that something had been accomplished, even if they had to give up Sinai. The thought of hurting the army for which he had such affection was one of his main considerations.

There was also the public. The Sinai campaign had given the people an emotional release, after eight years of fear and tension. There had been no hysteria at the thought of Soviet bombers with Egyptian markings trying to obliterate the cities of Israel. Nor had there been any panic over the prospect of sanctions. Israel would tighten her belt and go hungry if necessary. Ben-Gurion knew it would be much easier to sell austerity to his people than what he was now going to have to persuade them to accept. They might even feel he had betrayed them.

In his "victory speech" the day before he had fortunately made no statement about the future of Sinai, but he *had* said that Israel's armed forces would not give way to any international body. Yet for Israel to live cut off from all official and unofficial American aid, from the contributions of Jewish individuals and groups as well as help from Washington, would be impossible. Besides, Eisenhower surely could be trusted not to betray the Jewish state.

A second emergency cabinet meeting was held. After hours of discussion the ministers unanimously approved Ben-Gurion's proposal to tell President Eisenhower that Israel would evacuate Sinai under reasonable arrangements for the entry of U.N. forces. The Cabinet also approved his idea of telling the nation in a broadcast that same night.

Representatives of all the opposition parties (except the Communists) were called into conference. It was 9:30 P.M. when he finished this consultation. He had a light meal in his office and then started to write his radio speech.

There were frequent interruptions. The Foreign Office had been working since midafternoon on drafting a reply to Eisenhower. It took more than six hours. Every word, every letter, every comma was the subject of consultation between Jerusalem, Washington, and New York. Telephone lines between the three cities were kept open almost continuously.

During the evening someone suggested that because the letter from the American President had been a personal communication permission would have to be obtained from Washington before it could be made public. An urgent call was put in for the Washington embassy. Because of the difference in time it was still midafternoon there. The permission was promptly received.

For hours Ben-Gurion sat at his desk covering three-by-five cards with the text of his speech. His aides took them one by one to his typist. Both the Eisenhower and Bulganin letters had already been translated into Hebrew, but the Prime Minister copied them onto his cards, perhaps feeling he could read them better over the air if he actually wrote them down himself, word for word.

During the evening an extra secretary was needed, so one was requisitioned from the Government Press Office. When she arrived and Ben-Gurion saw her, he said:

"What is your name?"

"Shifra Rabinovitch."

"Why don't you have a Hebrew name?" the Prime Minister asked, not unkindly.

She blushed and said:

"I hope to change my name by marriage someday."

Ben-Gurion smiled.

"I wish you a nice husband—and a nice Hebrew name."

The speech was tape-recorded shortly before midnight at Kol Israel studios in Jerusalem. It would be broadcast at 12:30 A.M. Frequent announcements had been made urging everyone to remain awake for it.

Ben-Gurion went back to his office. Navon had a small radio. Chairs were drawn into a semi-circle. Someone made Turkish coffee. Foreign Minister Meir, Minister of Labor Namir, and Minister of Education Aran were there, as well as the aides.

Just before air time Ben-Gurion picked up one of the four telephones on his desk, dialed a number, and when a voice answered said:

"Paula, I promised to wake you up in time. The broadcast will begin in five minutes."

It lasted a full half hour. As Ben-Gurion sat back listening to himself he seemed thoroughly relaxed. The strain was over. One more momentous decision had been made by this man whose main task during nearly a generation of strife had been to make decisions. With the attitude of a surgeon after he has performed a delicate operation, he would go home now, read a little about *The Intellect of Pre-Historic Man*, and then have a sound night's sleep.

On Friday a warmly phrased letter arrived from President Eisenhower thanking Ben-Gurion for his withdrawal decision.

One of the greatest disappointments of the Prime Minister's life was that illness had prevented him from touring Sinai during the fighting. A week after leaving his bed, as soon as his doctors would permit, he made a two-day air and ground tour of the entire occupied area. (Israel forces had not yet begun to retire.)

The next day he faced angry extremists in the Knesset. The Communists, following the Moscow line, were indignant that he had ordered the attack. Herut was indignant that he had promised a withdrawal. The motions of both groups were overwhelmingly voted down. Before the session was over, the Prime Minister gave the Knesset a new definition:

"Courage is a special kind of knowledge: the knowledge of how to fear what ought to be feared and how not to fear what ought not to be feared."

There was another aspect of courage he did not mention, the courage to make unpopular decisions. This was not the first time Ben-Gurion had displayed such courage, nor would it be the last.

Toward the end of December a recent immigrant living in Beersheba wrote that he had worn out his only pair of shoes on military service during the Sinai campaign and had neglected to pick up one of the thousands of pairs the retreating Egyptians had discarded in the desert.

Ben-Gurion out of his own pocket sent him money for a new pair.

CHAPTER TWENTY-SEVEN

ONE WEEK during 1957 newspapers and magazines from Paris to Brisbane carried pictures of Israel's Prime Minister standing on his head on a sandy beach near Tel Aviv.

Some people assumed it was a hoax. Even when the photographs were greatly enlarged, the features were not distinct. It might have been *any* short, stocky, white-haired man. Besides, those who knew David Ben-Gurion best were aware that he had never been interested in gymnastics, calisthenics, or any other form of physical exercise. Furthermore, he was past seventy and for several years had not been well.

But it *was* David Ben-Gurion, and behind the photographs there was a story that was never completely disclosed.

Soon after the War of Liberation, Israel's Ministry of Defense invited Moshe Feldenkrais, who had spent ten years in Palestine as a boy and then had gone to France and England and become a scientist, to return and head its electronics department.

Feldenkrais is a man of many interests. For years he worked with the Curie family on radium. At the same time he became a personal pupil of Jigoro Kano, the judo expert, was awarded the first judo black belt in Europe, and founded the Jiu Jitsu Club of France. When the Germans approached Paris, he moved to England. There he served in a scientific capacity with a submarine detection unit. When Britain was beleaguered and her Home Guards were protecting the island, armed in some cases with nothing more lethal than wooden clubs, Feldenkrais wrote a small book, *Practical Unarmed Combat,* which showed the Home Guardsmen how to disarm an attacker with their hands.

Feldenkrais described judo as "the art of the highest and most efficient use of mental as well as physical energy directed to the accomplishment of a definite purpose." He then went into deeper studies of how to train the body to submit to the personality, and how to deal with an immediate task without being handicapped by old habits of thought or attitude.

One of his nine books, *Body and Mature Behaviour,* is a study of anxiety, sex, gravitation, and learning, in which he asserts that emotional instability and behavior disorders are connected with indigestion, faulty breathing, crooked toes, unsatisfactory sexual experiences, postural rigidity, and muscular tension, and that the solution is physical re-education.

In England he worked with people who had both physical and emotional difficulties, and found he could help them. But he had the opposition of a conventional and well-organized medical profession.

In Israel, a young country that still believed in "the impossible," physicians were suspicious but not antagonistic. Before long he had so many patients that he had to abandon his work in electronics.

It was Professor Aaron Katchalski of the Weizmann Institute who brought Feldenkrais to the attention of the Prime Minister.

To Ben-Gurion, Feldenkrais' ideas were provocative and stimulating.

"The average brain is like the sky," he told the Prime Minister, "practically empty. A normal brain can absorb up to seventy languages, and an experienced conductor may know by heart dozens of operas and as many symphonies. There is room in the conductor's head for sixty-eight or sixty-nine more languages and in the linguist's for all the operas and symphonies.

"The man we call a genius uses only 5 per cent of the human being's innate mental capacity."

About man's misuse of his body he said to Ben-Gurion:

"We walk like badly made puppets instead of like kings of creation."

Ben-Gurion knew, from his reading, about Yoga exercises and the theory that man can make intellectual and spiritual progress through control of the body. Still, he was somewhat skeptical.

"I want proof," he told his visitor.

Feldenkrais offered him either a list of his patients, copies of his books, testimonial letters, or a few sample lessons.

"I'll read one of your books," the Prime Minister decided.

A few days later he sent for Feldenkrais.

"How many lessons will it take?"

"Ordinarily one lesson a week for a year is enough," Feldenkrais said. "But I have never had a pupil over seventy before. You may be too old to change your ways."

But Ben-Gurion wanted to try, so they agreed on a one-hour lesson at the end of his office routine each day.

During the first exercise Ben-Gurion was instructed in how to lie on his back on the floor with his eyes closed, raise one leg and turn it slowly in half circles, concentrating intently on the movements he was making.

As Feldenkrais studied his new pupil he realized that, despite the pains in his back, he made certain movements with the perfection of a tightrope walker, indicating a high degree of integration already.

After the second lesson the Prime Minister said:

"Maybe you have something. For months I have had such pain in my hip joints that I wake up every fifteen minutes during the night. But last night I slept for several hours."

This did not change Paula's opinion. She had been unimpressed from the start, and had nicknamed the teacher "Mr. Hokus-Pokus." She told him bluntly that she thought he was wasting a lot of her husband's valuable time with "all this monkey business of yours."

Just when Ben-Gurion seemed to be making progress in the control of his body he went on a military inspection trip by motorboat on the Gulf of Aqaba and came back with a severe cold. Then he went to Jerusalem, where the temperature was below freezing, to address an emergency cabinet meeting, and his condition grew worse.

One evening when Feldenkrais arrived at No. 17, Paula greeted him more caustically than usual.

"*Shalom*, Mr. Hokus-Pokus. You can't see him tonight. The doctor says he has pneumonia."

Ben-Gurion, hearing them, called from his room:

"If that's Feldenkrais, I want to talk to him."

Instead of the usual work, the teacher proposed some exercises in proper breathing.

Paula stood by protectingly.

"You mustn't make him work tonight. He's sick."

"I am sure I can bring down his temperature."

Paula laughed.

"I used to be a nurse and I don't believe it."

So they made a wager. Paula took the patient's temperature, and then Feldenkrais began the exercises.

After ten minutes they took his temperature again. It had dropped a full degree Fahrenheit. But by this time he was annoyed.

"Go away and leave me alone."

After several weeks he was well enough to return to his routine of daily lessons.

The first three months of 1957 were a time of continuous crisis. As more and more pressure was put on Israel to withdraw from the Gaza strip and the Gulf of Aqaba, "emergency" cabinet meetings became routine, nearly all cables were marked "urgent," and everyone was under strain. Yet Ben-Gurion issued instructions that nothing was to interfere with his daily engagement with Feldenkrais.

Once, halfway through a critical cabinet meeting, he looked at his watch and realized it was time for his exercise.

"I am sorry," he said, "but we will have to take a recess. I will be back in exactly an hour."

The only time an exercise was interrupted was one day when Argov knocked at the door and said:

"Excuse me, but an important message has just arrived from President Eisenhower."

Sometimes the Prime Minister and his instructor would talk about psychology and ethics. One day Feldenkrais said:

"The well-integrated man never acts without the ability to reverse himself. No decision is important unless the person making it has been thinking all the time of the possibility of making exactly the opposite decision."

This started a long discussion, for Ben-Gurion was faced at this time with the necessity of making one more grave decision: whether to give in to international pressure and withdraw his troops from Gaza and the Gulf of Aqaba.

Feldenkrais would never know what strange new subject the Prime Minister was going to introduce. One evening he said:

"You are a specialist in electronics, so tell me, can an electronic machine ever be built which will perform all the functions of the human brain? Is the brain really a machine? Or is there a value of some sort which can never be mechanically reproduced?"

Paula had many objections to the exercises.

"I don't like people who are too much interested in themselves. You are making my husband too conscious of how he stands, how he walks, how he sits."

But gradually, as she saw that it was improving his health, she dropped her objections, and eventually sent a number of patients to "Mr. Hokus-Pokus."

For months President Ben-Zvi, who came in by chance during an exercise, was the only one besides Paula, Professor Katchalski, and personal secretaries who knew exactly what was happening during the mysterious hourly visits of the electronics expert.

The secret might never have leaked out had it not been that Feldenkrais made a trip abroad. Just before he left Israel he had been working with Ben-Gurion on how to drive fear out of the body by more acute awareness. One of the exercises was a headstand. The Prime Minister was able to do it on a bed, but did not yet have the control to do it in the middle of a floor.

Several weeks later Feldenkrais opened a London newspaper and saw a photograph of his pupil executing a perfect headstand. He put in a telephone call for Tel Aviv and learned that Ben-Gurion had been at the Sharon Hotel at Herzlia on the sea and had decided that a secluded sandy beach would be a good place to practice his exercises.

"I thought the beach would be soft like a bed, but extensive like the floor of a room. And it worked. I had no idea anyone ever saw me."

The photographer was unobserved because he was working with a telephoto lens. He sold the two photographs he took to magazines and papers all over the world, and they were more widely printed than any of the hundreds of other photographs taken during the years of Ben-Gurion's prominence.

The wisdom of standing on the head became a subject of cocktail conversation, although many people misunderstood the purpose of the exercise.

"Standing on the head," Feldenkrais explained, "is not an aim in itself. It is merely one of a hundred ways of getting to know oneself thoroughly; a road to greater awareness. After it has served that purpose, there is no use in continuing to do it."

An Indian doctor visiting in Israel was asked whether it was a healthful exercise.

"I do not know whether it is healthful, but I know that only a very healthy man can do it."

This was the first year since Ben-Gurion's youth that he had had no physical troubles of any kind, except having some teeth and some assassin's bullets extracted.

He stopped wearing his "corset," no longer had trouble getting in and out of automobiles, lost surplus weight, and could get up from a prone position on the floor with the agility of a young man.

Once when he was tying a shoelace standing on one foot, he laughed and said:

"It has been thirty years since I've been able to do that."

One day, accompanied by several aides, he went to call at the Tel Aviv offices of the committee planning the tenth anniversary celebration.

"What floor are the offices on?" he asked.

"The fourth."

"The rest of you ride in the elevator. I'll walk."

When they all reached the fourth floor, an aide told him that he had disappointed the elevator operator, who had wanted the honor of serving him.

"All right. I'll ride down with him then."

Few statesmen in the world have been under such pressure as Ben-Gurion was during the first nine weeks of 1957.

In defiance of the Soviet Union, the United States, the United Nations, and the Communist party of Israel, he was refusing to withdraw troops from either the Gaza strip or the Straits. He was playing a game with no diplomatic weapons, no allies (except perhaps France), nothing to threaten, no chance to bluff.

He was the leader of fewer than two million people, facing the spokesmen for most of the other 273,000,000. He was even defying the United Nations, which had created Israel. But except for a handful of local Communists, his own people were united behind him, and he was certain that he had justice on his side.

Perhaps he might eventually have to back down, but he felt that the longer he drew out the war of nerves the better his

chance of convincing the world that Israel, the only nation
denied the use of the Suez Canal, at least should have the right
to send her ships in and out of her own Red Sea port of Elath,
and that she should be permitted to keep the Egyptians from
using Gaza as a launching site for more deadly Fedayeen raids.

The United Nations passed six resolutions calling on Israel to
withdraw from the occupied territory.

President Eisenhower sent six strong letters. He cut short a
holiday and rushed back to Washington to make a broadcast,
warning Israel of what might happen to her if she failed to co-
operate.

Eban and Mrs. Meir were shuttling back and forth between
Jerusalem, Tel Aviv, New York, and Washington.

Sometimes as many as three cabinet meetings were held in a
single day.

For the first time since the Sinai invasion there was disagreement among the ministers when a vote was taken.

A break in the international deadlock finally came in February
when Eban had a three-hour talk with Dulles, who said the
United States agreed with Israel about a United Nations administration in Gaza and freedom of shipping in the Gulf of Aqaba.

The Ambassador cabled Jerusalem, and Ben-Gurion ordered
the Cabinet rounded up at once. Motorcycle policemen were
sent racing down highways after the ministers. One was summoned by a message flashed on a Jerusalem movie screen.

"There comes a time," he told them, "when you can get the
maximum in your struggle, but if you miss that moment the
opportunity may not come again."

The Cabinet debated until 2 A.M. At last a vote was taken.
There were four against him, but he decided to proceed anyway.

The ministers went home. Ben-Gurion stayed at his desk for
another hour drafting instructions to Eban and Mrs. Meir.

Mrs. Meir spent the day in conferences in Washington. Then
she wrote the announcement she would make to the U.N. and
cabled it back home for approval.

On Friday the Cabinet met at 3 P.M. The arguing went on
until after the rise of the evening star, which signaled the start
of the Sabbath. This disturbed the two ministers representing the

religious parties. Four others were antagonistic toward Ben-Gurion's new policy.

It was a difficult decision for him to make, because it would probably embitter the three groups of Israelis for whom he had the most affection: the Army, the immigrants, and the Negev settlers.

First he must try to explain to the Army, so he called a conference of the Chief of Staff and seven generals. They were waiting for him when he came from the cabinet meeting. He explained briefly the situation, the pressures, the decision.

Then he asked each what he would do if he were Prime Minister. There was disappointment but no disagreement.

That night he made a plan to tour border settlements to explain to those who had had a few months' respite from Fedayeen attacks. (In places like Sde Boker they at last had been able to stop carrying rifles to work.)

Ben-Gurion went to bed extremely tired, but satisfied that he had made the right move.

At eight-thirty the next morning he flicked on his bedside radio to listen to Kol Israel's broadcast of the previous day's U.N. proceedings. Mrs. Meir announced in a calm, undramatic manner Israel's willingness to withdraw on the three "assumptions" (Dulles had rejected the use of the word "conditions") agreed upon.

But a few moments later U. S. Delegate Henry Cabot Lodge made a speech that seemed to repudiate the "assumption" that the Gaza strip would be administered by the U.N.

The Prime Minister bounced out of bed. The crisis was on again. He called the Foreign Office, his secretary, and his military aide.

It was the Sabbath, but the Cabinet must be convened anyway. Messengers were sent to the homes of the two Orthodox members, who by religious custom could not make use of a mechanical instrument on this day. The other ministers were summoned by telephone. The meeting lasted three hours.

This anti-climax came to an end with the receipt of a letter from President Eisenhower saying that the hopes and expectations expressed by Mrs. Meir in her speech were "reasonable."

So on Monday, Ben-Gurion ordered General Dayan to meet

with the Commander of the United Nations Emergency Force to work out withdrawal arrangements.

The Sinai campaign was over at last.

Israel had emerged the winner of a great quantity of Soviet war material, with the prestige of having beaten the Egyptian Army a second time, and now with the assurance that her ships could sail untroubled up to Elath, and that no Fedayeen would harass her settlements from the Gaza strip.

Ben-Gurion himself emerged with many new critics at home who felt he had given in when he should have continued to resist. Yet in the eyes of the world he had proved himself a master statesman, wise enough to say "yes" at precisely the right moment.

In the United States a public opinion poll listed him as one of the ten best-known and most respected world figures, "more admired" than even Nehru, Lodge, Dulles, or Eden.

CHAPTER TWENTY-EIGHT

It was a chilly, gray day in Jerusalem.

Because it was the first anniversary of the start of the Sinai campaign, and also of the killings at Kfar Kasim, the Inspector General of Police had assigned extra officers to the Knesset.

The parliamentary debate that was going on inside the slightly curved building on King George V Road was a routine discussion of foreign policy. At 6:15 P.M. a minority party member had the floor. Five years earlier he had been speaking when stones and gas fumes broke up the Knesset debate on reparations. As he talked this time, many members drifted toward the canteen.

The Knesset is arranged like an operating theater in a medical school, with a long table in the "pit," surrounded by circular tiers of seats for members, and then a circular balcony for spectators and the press. The chairs around the long table are normally occupied by the Prime Minister and his thirteen ministers. A few feet away there is a desk for distinguished visitors.

On this Tuesday afternoon two ministers were attending a reception, a third was on government business in America, a fourth was absent for personal reasons, and a fifth had gone out for a cup of tea. Ambassador Elath had just vacated the distinguished visitors' desk.

The Prime Minister was hunched down in his chair, thinking. His military secretary had gone to Tel Aviv for the day.

In the balcony there were a few students, about a dozen soldiers, several tourists, and an unemployed waiter who, tired of walking the streets, had decided to come in and watch the proceedings.

The speaker was mentioning the peril all Israel had faced just a year ago to——

Suddenly a short young man with dark brown hair, a sharply pointed nose, and a fanatical look in his eyes jumped up from his seat in the back row of the balcony and threw something in the direction of the Cabinet. It whizzed past the head of the Prime Minister, missed the table by a few inches, and fell between the chair occupied by Moshe Shapiro, Minister for Religious Affairs and Social Welfare, and the distinguished visitors' desk.

The speaker stopped in the middle of a word. There was a moment of complete silence. Then a voice in the balcony said:

"What nerve! Throwing a stone."

Minister Shapiro turned to look at the object at his feet.

There was a loud, dull explosion. Shapiro fell back in his chair. Blood was streaming from his head and stomach.

Foreign Minister Meir gave a gasp and clutched one leg with her hands.

The Prime Minister, who had ducked his head when the object flew past him, shouted in the voice of a military commander:

"Sit down! Don't leave your seats."

Blood was turning one leg of his trousers dark red and there was blood running down one arm.

An acrid smell of powder filled the room.

In the balcony guards grabbed the brown-haired young man as he was running toward an exit.

Two members of the Knesset who are physicians made their way down an aisle to the sides of the injured.

Several minutes later the siren of an ambulance sounded in King George V Road. Shapiro was carried out and taken to Hadassah Hospital.

Mrs. Meir's foot wounds were bandaged with handkerchiefs. Moshe Carmel, Minister of Transport, had a broken arm. The Minister of Health and a woman Knesset member had slight injuries.

Although a number of small pieces of steel had lodged themselves in Ben-Gurion's right arm and right leg, he insisted on walking from the building to an automobile that took him to the hospital.

Two crews of Hadassah surgeons began two separate operations on Shapiro. Splinters were removed from Mrs. Meir's leg, which was then put in a cast. The broken arm of the Transport Minister was set. Ben-Gurion, because of his age and the possibility of shock, was given sedatives and was not operated on at once.

Back in the Knesset, police began to investigate. The object had been a Mills grenade. If it had landed on the table it probably would have killed the Prime Minister and all the cabinet members present. A deep hole had been blown in the floor. The ceiling, three stories up, was pock-marked. One man in the balcony had been injured.

The assassin was Moshe Ben Yaakov Dueg, twenty-five years old, born in Aleppo, Syria, where in his childhood he had suffered an accident that made him mentally unbalanced. He had had another accident in a youth camp after coming to Palestine just before the founding of the state. This led him to sue the Jewish Agency for sixty-six thousand dollars. When he lost the case he wrote threatening letters to the judge. He was arrested, but a court psychiatrist said he was mentally unfit to stand trial. He was placed in an institution and was only recently discharged. Two years ago he had tried to stow away on a plane for New York. He had no political party affiliations.

As the facts came out, all Israel sighed with relief. It was an ordinary, common, non-Middle Eastern type assassination attempt, with no political implications, no connection with terrorism, nothing to spark a renewal of the Arab-Jewish war or an internal conflict.

In its congested, temporary quarters Hadassah had no private rooms, but the doctors' second-floor rest room (endowed in memory of Fannie Goodman of Los Angeles) was converted into a bedroom for the Prime Minister.

Argov, distraught at not having been present when his commander was in danger, arrived quickly from Tel Aviv. He and Paula set up a watch over the Prime Minister, admitting only his children, the President, an immigrant girl named Mazal who took care of the Jerusalem house in the Ben-Gurions' absence, and a Druse physician to whom the Prime Minister said:

"It is to my great regret that we do not yet have a Yemenite physician."

The next day Ben-Gurion insisted that Argov bring him all the cables and mail he normally would have handled in the office.

The first letter he wrote was to the parents of the man who had tried to kill him. It was not easy to do, for it was his right hand and arm that had been injured. Yet in careful longhand on a piece of Hadassah stationery he wrote:

> To the Parents of Moshe Dueg:
>
> I know that you regret, as do all the people of Israel, the abominable and senseless crime which your son committed yesterday. You are not to blame. You are living in Israel, where justice reigns, and I hope that nothing untoward happens to you or your sons. Would that you succeed in educating the rest of your children to good deeds and to love Israel.
>
> (signed) David Ben-Gurion

In many Arab countries the entire family would have been arrested. That was probably why the parents, who had arrived seven years earlier from Syria, were cringing in a corner of their hut in a village near Tel Aviv when the courier arrived to deliver the letter.

Because they spoke only Arabic, the courier translated the letter to them, reading it by the light of a kerosene lamp.

That afternoon the Minister of Industry and Commerce came to call. As he approached the door of the Prime Minister's room, Paula barred the way.

"You can't go in. I'm not admitting anyone but doctors."

As the Minister stammered his regrets, she added:

"It's easy to get past those policemen downstairs, but nobody's getting by me!"

That week a hundred American Jewish leaders were in Israel on a United Jewish Appeal Study Mission. The Prime Minister was to have been the principal speaker at a banquet the final evening. Instead his wife appeared for him.

After a long introduction she arose, smiled, acknowledged the applause with a bow, and said:

"You've done a good job. Continue."

Then she sat down.

Nehemiah Argov was in constant attendance during the first four days. By Saturday the Prime Minister was in good spirits, and the doctors said he would be able to leave the hospital the first of the week. Argov had urgent military matters to deal with at the Defense Ministry, so he drove to Tel Aviv. On the return trip, near Ramle, a wasp flew in the window and stung him on the eyelid. During the instant he took his attention from the road, the car struck a cyclist.

Argov stopped, picked up the unconscious man, put him in the back seat, and drove to a hospital in Rehovoth. There doctors said his condition was grave; he had only a slight chance of recovering.

After learning that the victim was a forty-four-year-old Moroccan immigrant who had a wife and four children, Argov drove back to Tel Aviv.

On Sunday officers of the Defense Ministry broke down the door of the Argov apartment and found him sitting at his desk, dead. He had fired a bullet from his service pistol through his temple.

He left two notes. One was to Ben-Gurion. The other was addressed to "My dear friends." In the second he said:

"Today I knocked down a cyclist . . . I fear he will not live . . . I cannot forgive myself for the suffering I have caused this family . . . I beg his forgiveness and that of his family."

Then he asked that all the money he had in the bank and $1,512 owed to him by two friends be paid to the victim or his widow.

"My dear friends . . . I cannot bear living in the circumstances which have occurred, and beg the forgiveness of those to whom I might have been of some service . . . I believe it is not customary to eulogize those who die by their own hand. If I am wrong I request that there shall be no eulogies at my funeral, and no sorrow for my action . . . I am not worthy to be mourned."

When the news was received in Jerusalem, a conference was
held with Hadassah doctors. The Prime Minister had a slight
post-operational fever. The doctors wanted to avoid any form of
shock. So a plot was conceived to deceive him. Kol Israel was
instructed not to use the suicide on its news broadcasts, to which
Ben-Gurion always listened. Then all the morning and evening
papers were called. Each was asked to print one copy making no
mention of the Argov case. A messenger would pick up this paper
right after press time and bring it to the hospital.

That evening a reporter called the Rehovoth hospital. The injured cyclist was now out of danger.

In New York on Saturday at about the hour of the suicide
Evron, with whom Argov had once lived, was discussing personalities with a young woman in the Israel Consulate who also had
once been on Ben-Gurion's staff. When Argov's name was mentioned, Evron told of the military secretary once saying to him:

"I had been worrying about what I would do if an attempt
were ever made on the life of the Old Man. For a few days I
was not at peace with myself, but now I have made my decision
and I feel better. If anything like that should happen, I would
kill myself [and he tapped his service revolver]. Having decided
this, I now feel serene."

Twenty-four hours after hearing that story from Evron the
young woman from the Consulate telephoned him:

"Did you hear the news? The radio has just said that Nehemiah has killed himself."

In Israel several of the military secretary's friends said they
could imagine his thoughts. He had been absent when Ben-
Gurion was in danger in the Knesset in 1952. This time he had
also been away. He felt he not only had failed in his duty but
had missed what might have been the supremely satisfying
moment in his life. Had he been in the Knesset that Tuesday
afternoon he could have thrown himself on top of the grenade,
clutched it to his body, and died gloriously, blown to bits by the
explosive that was meant to kill the man he worshiped.

On Monday, Argov was buried with full military honors. Six
colonels bore the coffin to the grave. His death wish was not
violated. Chief of Staff Dayan merely stood beside the hole in
the earth and said:

"Death is no stranger to us. But not this kind of death. I do not understand the death of Nehemiah Argov."

After a moment's silence he added:

"The man closest to him is not here."

Paula was among the several hundred distinguished mourners. Her husband was reading quietly in his bed at Hadassah Hospital, unaware.

Finally, on Tuesday, it was decided to tell him. Dayan was chosen for the task. He was accompanied by several Hadassah doctors, and by Kollek, Paula, S. Peress, director general of the Ministry of Defense, and Navon, who had been in South America on an Israel bonds mission and had been ordered back quickly after the suicide.

The Prime Minister was in a cheerful mood. He was soon to leave the hospital. He talked eagerly with his personal secretary, whom he had not seen for six weeks. Finally Dayan spoke.

"We have bad news for you. Nehemiah is dead."

Ben-Gurion turned pale, sat upright in bed, and demanded: "What did you say?"

His voice was trembling.

Dayan described briefly what had happened, then handed Ben-Gurion the sealed letter Nehemiah had left.

He opened it slowly. As he read his eyes clouded. There was not a sound in the room. Finally, as he came to the last page and the signature, the man with the wispy halo of white hair turned painfully in bed until his back was to those in the hospital room.

Someone said later that the silence was broken once by a single word:

"Nehemiah."

Others said that he spoke not at all.

After a few moments a low sobbing began to fill the room. They looked at each other, embarrassed. Most of them had never seem him display such emotion before, although one or two remembered that he had cried also the day the Teacher was buried, years ago.

Quietly they made their way, one by one, to the door.

At last he was entirely alone with his heavy grief.

The wounds in his arm and leg, from which the surgeons had dug small pieces of steel, suddenly began to pain again. But the hurt in his heart was the greater, for he knew there was probably no man in the world to take Nehemiah's place. Everyone else knew it. Nehemiah had known it, too. That was why it was difficult to understand what Nehemiah had done.

Days later Ben-Gurion showed the letter to a few people. It threw no light on the reasons. It made no mention of the road accident. The five closely written pages were filled mostly with expressions of the love and admiration the younger man had had for the older. He thanked Ben-Gurion for his exceptional friendship and said he never felt he deserved the honor. The past ten years had been the happiest in his life. The three greatest men of all time, in his opinion, were Moses, King David, and David Ben-Gurion.

"I know my action will cause you pain, but I cannot do otherwise."

He admitted it was not the deed of a strong man. Ben-Gurion himself was a strong man and he needed strong men around him. He, Nehemiah, was no longer a strong man.

He begged his chief to go on leading "the stiff-necked people" who needed him and whom he alone could guide.

Because Ben-Gurion lay so quiet and refused to eat or sleep or talk with visitors, the doctors decided it would be better if someone could persuade him to discuss the suicide and thus work some of the unhappiness out of his system. Paula and the children agreed that Yadin was the man to try.

Renana was there when he was admitted to the room. Her father had his face to the wall. Suddenly he turned, saw Yadin, shook off his morbidity for a moment, and asked:

"Have you finished your excavations at Hazor?"

"Yes."

"Tell me about them."

Yadin talked a long time about this ancient place he had been unearthing, which had been the largest city in the Holy Land in the days of Joshua. Then he stopped. This was not the reason he had come. He looked straight into Ben-Gurion's sad eyes.

"Let's talk about Nehemiah."

The Prime Minister shook his head.

Yadin insisted.

Ben-Gurion began reluctantly. He wanted more details. They

had told him only the bare facts of the suicide. Why had he done it?

They talked a full hour about it.

But that cathartic did not eliminate the hurt. For weeks Ben-Gurion was a different man. For the first time in decades he no longer made entries in his journal.

In the hospital there was great competition among the nurses over who would attend the Prime Minister. A dark-haired young woman, Edna, was his day nurse when Navon returned from abroad. He told her:

"You must get over the idea that you are taking care of a Prime Minister. You must not let him order you around. You order him. Treat him like an ordinary sick man."

Ben-Gurion had been listening.

"But I am not a sick man," he said.

"All right," Navon said to Nurse Edna, "then you treat him like an ordinary well man."

About this time Paula became a victim of Asian influenza. At first she refused to go to bed. She must make her morning and afternoon calls on her husband or he would be worried. As her condition grew worse, the Hadassah doctors agreed to a compromise. They put her to bed in a room directly over his. Then, every midmorning and midafternoon, she would get up, dress completely, put on her hat, take her shopping bag and a magazine or a newspaper, and go down one flight to call on the invalid, just as if she had come directly from the house on Ben Maimon Avenue.

Upstairs the nurses would be waiting to help her undress and put her quickly to bed again. This extraordinary routine made her illness last much longer than it normally would have, but it kept the Prime Minister from worrying.

The relapse he suffered after hearing about Nehemiah delayed his departure from the hospital. It was two weeks before he was permitted to leave. In the meantime he had many visitors, among them Marcus Sieff of London, who had been of such help in the early days of the state, and his wife. As they were leaving, an energetic young man in an open-necked shirt came bouncing up the stairs and was admitted to Ben-Gurion's room.

Outside in the street there was a crowd of excited Israelis. Sieff turned to his wife and said:

"B.G. surely is popular with his people, isn't he?"

Then as an afterthought he added:

"By the way, have you any idea who that kibbutznik was with the open shirt who just went up?"

"Yes, dear," said Mrs. Sieff patiently. "That was Danny Kaye. He and B.G. are old friends."

Ben-Gurion was a man of many moods after Argov's death. There was one day when he lay for hours with his face to the wall, refusing even to eat. Early in the evening the nurse put some mail on his bedside table. He glanced at it with little interest until he came to an American scientific magazine. A few minutes later he was propped up in bed reading an article on how clouds are formed. When the nurse returned, he asked:

"Why haven't you brought me any food today?"

After he had had a hearty meal and had reread the article on clouds, Navon asked him if he would see an American who was writing a book about him.

"Send him in."

When the American explained that he was a *goy* (a Hebrew word sometimes used for a non-Jew) the Prime Minister delivered a technical etymological explanation of the word.

" 'Goy' originally meant 'people,' so I am correct when I say that we in Israel want to grow to be a strong and independent goy."

The nurse brought in a jar of yogurt.

"I learned to eat this in Turkey. In that part of the world they claim it will make a man live to be a hundred."

His eyes were alive now. The wisps of white hair were standing on end. The whole room seemed to vibrate with the power of his personality.

He swung the spotlight of his mind from subject to subject. The visitor had just been to Ghana. The Prime Minister had sent one of his favorite diplomats to that country, and would have gone there himself for the independence celebration except for the Sinai crisis. Israel, although a poor country, had started a Point Four type program of aid to Ghana. He leaned forward in his bed.

"What is it like there? Tell me about it. Did you go to Kumasi, the Ashanti city? How is the climate, as hot as Israel? What about the humidity?"

Prime Minister Nkrumah had sent him a native costume made of brilliantly colored, hand-loomed Kente cloth. Wasn't this material too heavy for a tropical climate? How far from the equator was Accra?

Finally Navon signaled that it was time for the Prime Minister's lights to be turned out.

As the American left he said:

"If you ever get tired of being a Prime Minister, you should go back to being a reporter. I came to ask you a hundred questions, but you have done all the questioning yourself."

Exactly three weeks after the bombing and sixteen days after the suicide the Prime Minister, with one foot still in bandages, limped into the Knesset to make his first speech since the injury. He began with a modern David's lament:

"I am very sorry that for two days a grievous misfortune, the loss of Nehemiah, was concealed from me. I am sorry, but not angry . . .

"For about ten years Nehemiah and I worked together. I doubt if two men ever worked so closely together before. I cannot accurately estimate what share I have had in the achievement of these ten years. I know that it was the collective achievement of scores, hundreds, thousands of men; it included glorious deeds in no way inferior to the greatest in our annals, and even some to which there is no parallel in Jewish history.

"If I had some share in this achievement, it was the result of the partnership between myself and Nehemiah, a partnership without limited liability, without division and calculation, without any question of mine and thine.

"Nehemiah, like myself, was not perfect. There are no perfect men in the world. Even the Bible does not describe any perfect man, without fault or failing. Every man has good and bad qualities, and even the good are not generally perfect or complete.

"What was unique about Nehemiah . . . was that he had one quality to perfection . . . devotion and loyalty. . . . It may have seemed to be devotion to an individual, but essentially and morally it was devotion to a dual cause . . . the State and the

Army. Nehemiah was endowed with a rare and precious gift, the gift of great love. It was a divine fire that burned in him without pause, and by this fire he was consumed, in love and suffering.

"Permit me to stand here, alone, silent, for a brief moment, in respect to his memory."

CHAPTER TWENTY-NINE

ISRAEL reached her tenth anniversary with the extraordinary Ben-Gurion still guiding her firmly on her course.

His argument against celebrating birthdays had no application, so a twelve-month round of festivities began: parades, masked balls, music and dance festivals, sporting contests, carnivals, a ceremony honoring Dr. Weizmann, the official reopening of the great harbor of Elath after so many centuries, pageants portraying one short decade of modern Israel's history and four thousand torturous years of the Jewish struggle for existence.

There was mass jumping by the parachute troops who had landed in Sinai, air force displays, and naval maneuvers, but the greatest demonstration was the *Pageant of Peace*, which took its theme from the Book of Isaiah:

"Neither shall they learn war any more."

This in a country surrounded by powerful nations still avowedly bent on her destruction.

From the millions of words written during his long life by the man who was the undisputed leader, one short sentence was chosen to be emblazoned everywhere:

"A state is not created by a declaration; it is built day after day, by endless toil and the labor of years, even of generations."

In early April the visitors began to arrive for the celebration. They came from every part of the world. On one voyage of the *Queen Mary* nearly all the passengers were Israel-bound. Some nights there was hardly a bed, cot, or mattress from Dan to Beersheba not in use. Even the half-million-dollar hotel that had been built on the sands at distant Elath was full, night after night.

With the tourists came reporters, photographers, people who wanted to make films, radio and television crews, magazine writers looking for something exclusive from the Prime Minister. On some days public relations took all of his time.

He was more genial and co-operative than ever. He answered thousands of questions, posed for hundreds of photographs, did TV interviews without objecting. Several times he was asked if he would be willing to meet with Nasser.

"I will go to Cairo to see him," he replied, "any time he invites me. I would not hesitate to negotiate with him, man to man."

When Syria and Egypt formed the United Arab Republic and a Cairo broadcast reported that Israel was being invited to join, he said:

"If an invitation were seriously offered, I would seriously consider it. After all, we are Middle Eastern people, too."

Ben-Gurion told those who came to interview him the story of the first ten years partly in figures. Close to a million immigrants had been brought in. The population was now almost two million. What country, anywhere in the world, had doubled its size in a single decade? Only two out of a hundred immigrants had known anything about the soil before and only a few had worked in factories, but now a majority were farmers and industrial laborers. The reconversion was succeeding.

They had come from seventy countries, speaking almost every language known to man, even Japanese. But quickly they learned the mother tongue. Nearly five hundred villages and farm settlements had been established. A quarter of a million houses had been built.

Israel now grew three quarters of her food. Tel Aviv had become as large as Dallas. Elath had grown from one shack to a city of four thousand. There were steel mills at ancient Acre and a ceramics factory at Beersheba in the desert.

Even in science and the arts the results were impressive. Israel had become the second nation in the world, in proportion to population, in the publication of books. She had six orchestras and a hundred permanent choral societies, a scientific institute working on atomic research, theaters, art colonies, poets, singers.

When the state was created, less than a hundred thousand children had been in school; now there were nearly half a million.

Every department of the government flooded the Prime Minister's office with reports that gave proof of what the tourist could see: the miracle of the first ten years.

Never content to rest on the accomplishments of the past, the white-haired statesman talked more than ever during the anniversary year of the future. At this stage where everyone was boasting of accomplishments (with justice, of course), it was important to raise the sights, search out new targets, inspire the people to concentrate on them.

In another ten years he wanted a million more immigrants. The number living on farms should be doubled. A degree of self-sufficiency must be achieved. Israel would become an important maritime power. Maybe half a million pioneers would move to the desert.

Russia, America, and the Arab states might have something to say about how much of this dream would be realized, but as long as life held out, as long as Israel kept him as its leader, as long as he continued to have visions, he would always be urging his people on to new goals; always combining the material and the spiritual, his feet in two worlds; always discouraging either excess joy or self-defeating gloom.

The anniversary event that Ben-Gurion decided was "the most important of all" was an international Bible contest in which national winners from various parts of the world competed in Jerusalem.

The elimination finals to pick Israel's contender had been held one hot Monday in August in Tel Aviv's largest auditorium. Every one of the thousands of seats was taken. The Prime Minister sat for four hours in front of his radio listening to the questions and answers, as excited as a child at a circus. When he was told later that an estimated half a million other Israelis had done likewise, he rubbed his hands together in a gesture of approval and said:

"This shows a revival of Bible-mindedness in Israel. This is good."

The national winner was Amos Hacham, a thirty-year-old, partially paralyzed native of Jerusalem, who, as the result of a childhood accident, has a shriveled arm, a dragging leg, and a deformity of the mouth that makes it difficult for him to talk. But young Mr. Hacham knew the answers to almost all the questions and easily won the exhausting national finals.

The next day at the Jerusalem School for the Blind, where Hacham is a clerk, he received a telephone call:

"The Prime Minister would like to see you as soon as possible."

He borrowed a suit and a white shirt from a friend and hurried to the Prime Minister's office. There Ben-Gurion greeted him warmly, saying:

"I must tell you, Amos, that hearing the quiz over the radio was for me, as a Jew, a wonderful experience and I am sure the entire nation shares this feeling. You, Amos, have enhanced the glory of Israel, and we are all proud of you."

He told the young man that he must not be discouraged about his speech difficulty.

"I have been learning about speech control myself. There is something you can do about this."

Ben-Gurion then arranged for Feldenkrais to give Hacham lessons.

They talked a long time about their favorite subject, the Bible.

"The question I liked best last night," the Prime Minister said, "was the one that asked what is common to both King Jeroboam and Aaron the priest, aside from the fact that each made a golden calf?"

Hacham smiled. He knew the correct answer:

"Each had two sons with almost identical names. Aaron's were Nadav and Avihu, and Jeroboam's were Nadav and Aviya."

Then Ben-Gurion conducted a quiz of his own, trying to stump the champion. One question he asked was:

"Who was the Biblical character who wrote the biography of another man?"

"The prophet Isaiah," replied Hacham immediately. "He wrote the life of King Uzziah."

Ben-Gurion told Hacham of his admiration for the ancient king.

"You know, of course, Amos, that Uzziah was responsible for settling the Negev. Perhaps this is why he was privileged to have his life written by the greatest of the Hebrew prophets."

Then Ben-Gurion raised a technical Biblical question:

"Were heaven and earth created first, and then light, or was it the other way around?"

The conversation lasted for more than an hour. Before it was over, Ben-Gurion had discovered that this young man who had proved he knew the Bible better than anyone else in the Land of the Bible had never been awarded even an elementary school diploma, and in his elementary school Bible course had received a grade of only *kim'at tov* (almost good).

Several weeks later the fourteen other contestants arrived: a Baptist schoolteacher from the small town of Buford, Georgia; a forty-nine-year-old grandmother; a Seventh Day Adventist schoolteacher from Brazil; a young Roman Catholic from Malta who brought his parish priest with him; an Italian girl who came with the Pope's blessing; a Protestant convert from Mexico; others from South Africa, Argentina, Columbia, Finland, France, Luxembourg, Holland, Sweden, Uruguay.

The quizzing began one morning and was still going on at midnight. The last four hours were broadcast. Almost every radio in Israel was tuned in. The prize for which they were competing was modest by American television standards: a greenish, two-thousand-year-old vase found in a tomb in Beth Shearim, of little monetary value, but the excitement everywhere in Israel that night was great. Ben-Gurion himself was as tense as anyone.

The questions were not easy.

(Sample: The elders divided the watches of the night. How do we know that the number of night watches was an uneven number? Answer: In Judges 7:19 there is a reference to the "middle watch.")

Amos Hacham was easily the winner, with a French Baptist schoolteacher second and the Brazilian Seventh Day Adventist third.

Ben-Gurion the next day did nothing to hide his pride.

One of the pallbearers at the funeral of Nehemiah Argov had been his friend of many years, Colonel Chaim Ben-David, a native of Vienna, who had come to Palestine in his teens and worked his way up in Haganah until he became chief staff officer on the northern front during the Sinai campaign. At the start of 1958 he was in charge of officers' appointments, and in that capacity was asked to recommend a likely successor to the deceased military aide. He gave it considerable thought, and finally sent in three names. Days later, while he was wondering whether any of his candidates had been found acceptable, he received a message to report to the Prime Minister in Jerusalem.

Ben-Gurion greeted him warmly. They talked first of Argov. Then the Prime Minister abruptly asked:

"How would you like to be Nehemiah's successor?"

Ben-David mentioned that he had a wife and three children.

"I want a married man this time," Ben-Gurion replied.

Four days later the handsome, brown-eyed young officer began his new work. He was little more than half his superior's age; only a few inches taller; a keen-minded young man with an eagerness to serve. One of his first assignments was to arrange a corner in the office with all the books his predecessor had left behind. It was Ben-Gurion's idea to create a memorial to his friend in books rather than stone. They called it "Nehemiah's corner."

The only grave mistake the new military aide made was to order safe, desks, files, and other office equipment moved from Ben-Gurion's office to a new air-conditioned Ministry of Defense building that had been built in Tel Aviv.

The Prime Minister happened along in time to cut short this military operation. He had no use for air conditioning and he liked his old office. It had memories.

One day Ben-Gurion said to Ben-David:

"What languages do you speak?"

"Hebrew, German, Yiddish, Latin, and"—he hesitated before he added—"English."

The Prime Minister decided his aide should go to Oxford for several months of intensive work in improving his English. While there, he attended a series of lectures by a celebrated Lebanese professor on "Arab Nationalism" and "U.S. Policy in the Middle East."

There were other 1958 events. One of the most serious was a cabinet crisis. The government had been secretly negotiating with West Germany for the purchase of arms. The story leaked out, and Ben-Gurion, blaming the two ministers of a minor party in the coalition, submitted his resignation, saying that West Germany was the only place in the world where vitally needed equipment was available, and then adding:

"If you offer me a choice between all the ideals in the world,

glorious as they may be, and the security of Israel, I will un-
hesitatingly choose the latter."

This was putting it more bluntly than he or any of his critics
ever had. This was his own description of his obsession. This
explained Sinai, the break with Sharett, and almost everything
else about him.

Nothing was more important than the dream.

Yigal Allon helped re-cement the political coalition, and the
crisis ended.

Internal events were overshadowed by the mid-1958 Middle
Eastern crisis. The *coup d'état* in Iraq and the chain of developments it set off provided a critical moment for the West, but
for Israel, her very existence was once more at stake. Communist
encirclement would pose the threat of annihilation, but it would
be cold comfort if the United States poured additional arms into
neighboring Arab countries which still asserted that a state of
war existed with Israel and were determined that the Jewish
state must not be permitted to exist and prosper.

In this new critical period Ben-Gurion behaved more than ever
like an experienced statesman, preventing the independence of
his small country from being violated and quieting the fears of
his people.

Each year Hadassah gives an award in memory of its founder
to a man or woman of world distinction. Eleanor Roosevelt and
Justice William O. Douglas are among those already honored.
In 1958 the award for "distinguished humanitarian service" went
to David Ben-Gurion. Hadassah described him as well as anyone ever had:

"Man of action and man of thought, his life has been dedicated
to the survival of the Jews as a people, and the establishment of
Israel as a state, and to the rights of man everywhere.

"With insight derived of wisdom, with perseverance and courage inspired by prophetic vision, guided always by the spiritual
teachings of the Holy Bible, he has translated the moral concepts
of our ancient heritage into a humane and democratic leadership,
thus assuring for Israel and himself a unique and honorable place
in the history of man's struggle for freedom."

DATE DUE

MAR 19 1969			
GAYLORD			PRINTED IN U.S A.